The Circuit of Mass Communication

Media Strategies, Representation and Audience Reception in the AIDS Crisis

David Miller, Jenny Kitzinger,
Kevin Williams and Peter Beharrell

GLASGOW MEDIA GROUP

SAGE Publications
London • Thousand Oaks • New Delhi

First published 1998

SAGE Publications Ltd
6 Bonhill Street
London EC2A 4PU

SAGE Publications Inc.
2455 Teller Road
Thousand Oaks, California 91320

SAGE Publications India Pvt Ltd
32, M-Block Market
Greater Kailash – I
New Delhi 110 048

British Library Cataloguing in Publication data

A catalogue record for this book is available
from the British Library

ISBN 0 8039 7702 6
ISBN 0 8039 7702 6 (pbk)

Library of Congress catalog card number 97–062255

Typeset by Mayhew Typesetting, Rhayader, Powys
Printed in Great Britain by The Cromwell Press Ltd,
Trowbridge, Wiltshire

Contents

Acknowledgements

This book has had a prolonged gestation period and is the product of a long-term collaborative, but not always smooth and harmonious, commitment to its eventual delivery! Some journalists are fond of remarking on the widely differing pace of academic and journalistic production. This book is certainly testament to that, but we hope that it will be of some value in understanding the interaction between the world of the media and the world of AIDS.

Our first duty of thanks is to those people who participated in the research. This book would not have been possible without the help of focus group participants, and the activists, health educators, civil servants, public relations, advertising and market research personnel who spoke to us. Thanks also to the journalists, producers, editors, and press and broadcasting management. Many of these not only agreed to be interviewed but also helped with contacts, documents or other guidance. Thanks especially to those living with HIV and those who talked openly to us when it might have been safer for them not to do so.

The bulk of the research on which this book is based was funded by the ESRC as part of its AIDS research programme. Our thanks are due to the ESRC, and to the programme director Mildred Blaxter. Thanks also to the original grantholders on the project – Mick Bloor, Sally Macintyre, Greg Philo and John Eldridge. Indeed the research has greatly benefited from the support of these and other colleagues in the MRC Medical Sociology Unit and the Glasgow Media Group, especially Lesley Henderson and Jacquie Reilly.

Thank you to Joanne Yuill for her efficiency and humour. Thanks to Middlesex University students, Linda Steele, Michael Foley, Lesley Parker, Rick Holliman, Dawn Rowley. Thanks to Frank Mosson for his valiant efforts in coding data, to Donna Main for her work on non-news representations of AIDS and for allowing us to quote from her interview with Roy Battersby. A special acknowledgement to Lorna Brown who was the secretary on the AIDS project. Lorna, thank you for your patience and your answering belief in the eventual appearance of this book.

Lastly thanks to Emma Miller, Caitlin Miller, Lewis Miller, Diana Mutimer, Sarah Tanburn, Clare Hudson and Ellon McGregor.

DM, JK, KW, PB

1

Introduction

Jenny Kitzinger and David Miller

There is now a danger that has become a threat to us all. It is a deadly disease and there is no known cure. The virus can be passed during sexual intercourse with an infected person. Anyone can get it, man or woman. So far it has been confined to small groups, but it is spreading. So protect yourself and read this leaflet when it arrives. If you ignore AIDS it could be the death of you. So, don't die of ignorance. (First British government television advert on AIDS)

In December 1986 the British government launched its first television advertising campaign about Acquired Immune Deficiency Syndrome (AIDS). The public education campaign on AIDS was an unprecedented departure even for a government which had made more extensive use of communications media than any previous regime. In 1988, partly as a result of the cost of the AIDS campaign, government spending on advertising, for the first time, exceeded that of any other organisation, nudging multinational Unilever into second place (Franklin, 1994; Heaton, 1988).

Public education was the main plank of government policy on HIV and AIDS. It was on this, rather than on research, treatment, care or punitive measures, that efforts were concentrated. Government ministers, such as Norman Fowler, pronounced that 'public education is the only vaccine we have' (cited in Street, 1988: 492). The mass media were thus seen as central to the fight against AIDS. In fact, the government also helped to organise unprecedented scheduling co-operation between all four television networks for a ten day blitz of AIDS related programming between 27 February and 8 March 1987. As Norman Fowler, the Secretary of State for Health and Social Security, recorded:

Not everything could be achieved by advertising . . . We also needed the help of the media – in particular television . . . the response of both the BBC and IBA was magnificent. (Fowler, 1991: 259)

The media coverage of AIDS has been credited with, and condemned for, a wide variety of constructions, ideologies and effects. For example as legitimising homophobia or promoting permissiveness, for obscuring the truth about AIDS through coy evasion or for verging on the pornographic.

Certainly, the boundaries of the permissible in the media were changed by struggles around AIDS. Withdrawal of the ban on television advertising of condoms by the Independent Broadcasting Authority and the Home Office in summer 1987 was a direct result of the AIDS campaign. The word 'condom' went from obscurity to *de rigueur* broadcasting vocabulary, and previously impossible scenes, of condoms being unrolled over bananas or vibrators, appeared on television screens. On the other hand, customs personnel intervened to seize gay publications, especially those from North America with the most up to date information about AIDS; and the British government's Chief Medical Officer, Sir Donald Acheson, had to have copies of *The Advocate* and *New York Native* smuggled into Britain in diplomatic bags (Watney, 1988b: 179). Contradictions were also evident in the production of health education materials. For example, the guide for schools, *Learning about AIDS*, and the guide for teachers, *Teaching about AIDS* (funded by the Health Education Authority) were stopped on orders from the Department of Health and the Department of Education and Science respectively.

Such contradictions point to some of the divisions within the state in response to AIDS: divisions between policy arenas such as health and customs, divisions between government departments and divisions within the health policy community itself. Close attention to such conflicts and their outcomes is essential to understanding the politics of AIDS.

This book is about the role of the media in Britain in struggles over HIV and AIDS. It examines the development of campaign material, the planning and execution of strategies for media influence, the content of press and television coverage and, finally, the impact of media coverage on public understandings and policy and other outcomes. In the rest of this introduction we outline the main political perspectives on AIDS, explain our research strategy and map out the structure of the book.

An introduction to four major perspectives on AIDS

AIDS has been surrounded by a wide range of different political perspectives. Here four broad positions are identified which we have called: 'conservative moralist', 'libertarian', 'liberal/medical orthodoxy' and 'critical'. Individuals may move between different perspectives or hold to parts of them simultaneously and each position contains important variations. However, here we simply present a schematic summary in order to introduce key divisions in the AIDS debate and establish reference points to which we can refer back in shorthand in subsequent chapters.

The conservative moralist view

For those involved in conservative moral politics AIDS appeared to be quite literally a godsend which provided an opportunity to go on the offensive against 'permissiveness'. Numerous Conservative backbenchers, religious leaders and others took up cudgels in the mid-1980s characterising AIDS as the wages of sin. Campaigners from the moral right asserted that the only way of avoiding AIDS was heterosexuality, chastity and monogamy. James

Anderton, the Chief Constable of Greater Manchester who claimed he had a direct line to God, infamously declared that people with HIV or AIDS were 'swirling around in a human cesspit of their own making' (11 December 1986). Sir Rhodes Boyson, MP and former Education Minister, blamed gay men for spreading AIDS and asserted that they were flouting God's law. 'AIDS', he said 'is part of the fruits of a permissive society' and he suggested that AIDS would die out 'if we could wipe out the homosexual practices' (*Daily Telegraph*, 2 May 1988).

Conservative moralists identified both media coverage of AIDS and health education materials as part of the problem. The Health Education Authority (HEA) was seen to have been infiltrated by liberals and to have succumbed to the insidious influence of 'the homosexual lobby'. AIDS information materials were criticised for using 'extraordinarily bad language' and because they 'virtually ignored the virtues of monogamy or abstinence' (Harris, 1994).

In late 1986, a group of 47 Roman Catholic bishops accused the BBC of encouraging teenagers to 'sleep around'. The bishops condemned the 'play safe' slogan of the Radio One AIDS helpline service and said 'the BBC's message that sex using a condom is acceptable' was 'morally wrong'. The Anglican Bishop of Birmingham also denounced the campaign, declaring: 'Sex is not about playing. It is a very deep and important experience. Chastity is the only safe answer to AIDS' (*Daily Mail*, 12 December 1986). Mrs Mary Whitehouse found fault with the first programme in television's AIDS week because: 'The message was either you carry a condom or you get AIDS. At no time was the word marriage mentioned' (*Daily Express*, 28 February 1987). Two weeks later the National Viewers' and Listeners' Association (NVLA) accused the BBC and ITV of 'undermining their warnings about the dangers of Aids by surrounding them with programmes in which promiscuity was shown as normal or funny' (*Guardian*, 11 March 1987). Moralist pressure groups such as Family and Youth Concern and the Conservative Family Campaign also protested against media coverage and the government campaign on similar grounds (see Durham, 1991: 123–31). Family and Youth Concern, for example, produced a video as an antidote to the government campaign which emphasised chastity and was entitled *The Truth About AIDS*.

For many, but not all, conservative moralists, the 'truth' about AIDS was quite different from that promoted by the health education campaign and the scientific orthodoxy. In particular some conservative moralists challenged two central tenets of mainstream medical thinking: the notion that AIDS is caused by the virus, HIV, and that it poses a direct and major threat to heterosexuals.

The statement that HIV is not the necessary and sufficient cause of AIDS is most notably associated with molecular biologist Peter Duesberg. Essentially, his argument is that HIV is a harmless passenger virus. The admitted epidemic amongst gay men, IV drug users, haemophiliacs and others is attributed not to a single virus, but to the common factor of immune suppression due, among other things, to the use of poppers by gay men and to having large numbers of sexual partners.

This argument is often linked to, although not necessarily coterminous with, the assertion that heterosexual AIDS is a myth. This position is most notably associated with Michael Fumento who wrote *The Myth of Heterosexual AIDS* (1991). Fumento does not argue that it is impossible to pass HIV by penetrative heterosexual sex. Rather, he claims that the orthodox view that the 'general population' is at risk from HIV is an exaggeration. According to Fumento:

> The 'myth' of heterosexual AIDS consists of a series of myths, one of which is *not* that heterosexuals get AIDS. They certainly do get it, from shared needles, from transfusions, from clotting factor . . . at or before birth and sometimes through sexual intercourse with persons in these categories and with bisexuals. The primary myth, however, was that the disease was no longer anchored to these risk groups but was, in fact, going from heterosexual to heterosexual to heterosexual through intercourse, that it was epidemic among non-drug abusing heterosexuals. (Fumento, 1991: 15–16, emphasis in original)

Such challenges to orthodox opinion about HIV and about heterosexual transmission were often adopted by moralists because they could be used to reinforce their presentation of AIDS as the 'wages of sin', the consequence of a dissipated lifestyle or behaviour which was 'against nature' (especially given that some moralists misinterpreted Fumento's views to assert that heterosexual intercourse was entirely safe).

The libertarian view

Opposition to the scientific orthodoxy and to government health education campaigns was also often evident from a rather different perspective, that of the libertarian view. Whereas moralists saw the government's health education strategy as promoting 'promiscuity', the libertarians perceived it as an attempt by the 'nanny state' to regulate matters of sexual morality. Indeed, libertarians perceived the government as having not only bowed to the 'homosexual lobby' but also as having succumbed to the influence of conservative moralists. For former editor of the *Sunday Times* Andrew Neil, for example, there seemed to be 'a kind of conspiracy . . . almost an unholy alliance among the government, the militant gay lobby and a sort of Christian moral majority right' (cited in Garfield, 1994a: 68).

The libertarian view is often confused with the conservative moralist view, but there are crucial differences. In particular, where moralists perceive the AIDS campaign as promoting sex, libertarians read it as anti-sex propaganda. While for moralists the campaign promotes the 'permissive' society, the libertarian camp sees AIDS advertising as rolling back the (hetero)sexual freedoms bequeathed by the 1960s. Although both perspectives included challenges to the scientific orthodoxy, the criticisms were based on different assumptions. Thus whereas some moralists challenged the notion that AIDS was a threat to heterosexuals because this upheld a particular image of the 'moral order' and 'God's laws', libertarians argued that the 'myth' of a heterosexual AIDS epidemic was a massive fraud perpetrated in order to legitimise state intervention into the lives of the citizenry. In their view it was also a function of liberal and misguided attempts to be 'politically correct' and to divert attention from gay men in order to protect them from a backlash. Some on the libertarian wing believe that the state should not protect particular sexual minorities, and their status in society should reflect their social 'fitness' in the free market of morality. Others, however, revert to straightforward conservative moralism when they discuss gay men.

The liberal/medical orthodoxy

Both the above perspectives are distinct from the mainstream perspective which predominated in self-presentations of government health policy (at least after 1986). We have called this perspective the 'liberal/medical ortho-doxy'. According to this view HIV was the only (necessary and sufficient) cause of AIDS and everyone was at risk: 'gay or straight, male or female, anyone can get AIDS from sexual intercourse' (HEA advertising slogan).

This liberal/medical orthodoxy asserted that, in the absence of a vaccine, the best strategy was public education. Such an approach eschewed calls from the right for quarantine and the recriminalisation of homosexuality. It also maintained that AIDS was potentially such a serious problem that concerns about the explicitness of education materials should be subordi-nate to reaching the public. The liberal view also ruled out a strong moral message, insisting that the best approach was simply to make sure that people were given information. Norman Fowler outlined the official rationale as follows:

> We had to persuade people to change their habits . . . What message should we be setting out? I was not short of advice. I was told it should be a moral message . . . As an individual it was an argument that I agreed with but as the minister responsible it left me with a number of difficulties . . . We had to devise a message which the public would notice and on which they would act. What evidence there was suggested that practical guidance on how the disease could be avoided was more likely to be successful than any other approach. (Fowler, 1991: 250–1)

The liberal consensus posited that the information-giving approach, and the concentration on the 'everyone is at risk' message, was 'beyond politics'. The strategy was presented as a simple matter of common sense.

However, this did not mean that conservative moralist messages were absent from the campaigns. 'Moral' concerns became part of the official campaigns both because of direct political interventions and because the liberal/medical perspective was deeply influenced by implicit moralist considerations and assumptions. Fowler himself identified the 'first message' of the campaign as monogamy (Fowler, 1991: 249). The monogamy message certainly conforms to conservative moral positions but is suspect as health education. The use of condoms or non-penetrative sex would, in some cases (such as when one participant has the virus), be a more effective way of protecting oneself or one's partner.

In addition, it could be argued that the adoption of information-giving campaigns as the primary instruments of AIDS policy was itself problematic. The campaigns designated individuals as responsible for their own health and illness. As Margaret Thatcher declared in one of her rare public statements on AIDS: 'Governments cannot stop people from getting AIDS. They can give the information which enables them to prevent themselves getting it' (*Guardian*, 13 December 1986, cited in Greenaway et al., 1992: 81). The tone of the campaigns emphasised individual responsibility. This was established from the start with the slogan for the first campaign: 'Don't die of ignorance' and reinforced in subsequent campaigns, for example, with the strap line: 'You know the risks, the choice is yours'.

The critical view

The self-declared neutrality of the liberal/medical orthodoxy was challenged by activists coming from a critical perspective. We use the term 'critical' as an umbrella label for a whole range of perspectives which challenge this orthodoxy; and which are also in outright opposition to conservative moralism and often critical of the libertarian position. This 'unity in opposition' masks vital theoretical, political and practical conflicts (see Chapter 6). However, it is useful to highlight some of the main challenges coming from critical perspectives based on, for example, lesbian and gay liberation, feminism, and anti-racism.[1] Critical theorists and activists argued that AIDS was ignored until it seemed that (white, Western, middle-class) heterosexuals were at risk. They suggested that reactions to AIDS constituted 'moral panic', reinforced stigma (associated with sex work, injecting illegal drugs, 'promiscuity' and homosexuality), legitimised racism and (re)pathologised and medicalised gay identity and sexual practice (e.g. Alexander, 1988; King, 1990; Treichler, 1987; Watney, 1987b; Weeks, 1993).

Many government health education strategies are, it is argued, inadequate because (for example) they sacrifice clarity of information about transmission to the demands of the moral conservatives. They address individuals instead of communities, underestimate the importance of social self-esteem and ignore diversity. Government campaign strategies have been attacked for failing to recognise constraints on free choice, ignoring the role of inequality and neglecting the needs of ethnic minorities (e.g. Carter and Watney, 1989; Dada, 1990; Kitzinger, 1994b; Miller, J., 1990; Richardson, 1994; Watney, 1991).

Critical analysis of health education materials and media coverage pointed to the negative images of 'risk groups' and protested about the portrayal of people with HIV/AIDS as passive and pathetic victims or as irresponsible and threatening villains. They highlighted the way in which discussions of AIDS dwelt on *how* individuals came to be infected and implied that some victims are 'guilty' by identifying others as 'innocent'. Gay men and illegal drug users have been positioned as 'other', standing outside the family and the category 'everyone'. 'Foreign' countries (particularly in Africa) have been identified as 'hotbeds of infection' and black people and 'foreigners' have been stigmatised as carriers of disease (Chirimuuta and Chirimuuta, 1989; Dada, 1990; Patton, 1990; Sabatier, 1988; Treichler, 1989; Watney, 1988c). Feminist critics have argued that media representations and safer sex messages often reinforced traditional notions of male and female sexuality and failed to challenge gendered power imbalances or the 'discursive practices which disempower women' (Wilton, 1994: 91; see also ACT UP/NY Women and AIDS Book Group, 1990; Holland et al., 1992a, 1992b; Segal, 1989; Singer, 1993: 67; Wilton and Aggleton, 1991). Lesbians have been rendered invisible and all women (but especially black women and prostitutes) are positioned as sexual threats drawing on stereotypes of the *femme fatale* (McGrath, 1990; for examples of conflicts around and within feminist responses to AIDS, see Segal, 1989; Watney, 1987b; Wilton, 1994).

From among this variety of critical perspectives there are also challenges to the central scientific tenets underlying the official strategy on AIDS. It is not only conservative moralists or libertarians, for example, who may challenge orthodox positions on the significance of HIV. This challenge also comes from critical perspectives. Some activists argue that the causal link between HIV and AIDS is fostered by multinational drug companies such as Wellcome who have reaped huge profits from the marketing of AZT. Indeed, some critics now suggest that AZT itself may help to cause AIDS. This has led to a major conflict in the pages of the gay press with the editor of *Capital Gay* alleging that the gay press has imposed 'blanket censorship' on dissident voices (see *Capital Gay*, 20 August 1993; Hickson, 1993; Miller, C., 1993; Watney, 1993).

Critical voices have also challenged the official view on 'heterosexual AIDS'. Although many gay activists in the 1980s were urging the government to adopt a strategy that emphasised the risks of HIV to 'the general public', others were sceptical of the empirical and strategic value of such claims. As Schramm-Evans has noted, in the 1980s very few people in the most prominent AIDS pressure group, the Terrence Higgins Trust, really believed that HIV would ever spread significantly into the heterosexual population. However:

> The idea of 'everyone' being at risk was a powerful weapon against anti-gay prejudice in 1986, and it was the only one that the gay community, such as it was, had with which to protect itself at a time of brutal public attack . . . the Terrence Higgins Trust hierarchy sought to persuade the government that the nation itself was endangered, while not entirely believing the fact itself. (Schramm-Evans, 1990: 229)

More recently these sceptics have been joined by many of the activists who had originally pressed for the opposite strategy. From 1990 onwards, as gay men were excluded from the policy community, the alliance with the liberal/ medical approach gave way to increasing scepticism about the priorities of the AIDS campaign. The key criticism was that by far the largest number of people in Britain with both HIV and AIDS were gay men and yet the vast bulk of AIDS prevention work was aimed indiscriminately at the 'general population'. A survey of health authorities and other agencies with responsibility for HIV education found that only a third had engaged in any kind of prevention initiatives for gay or bisexual men (King, 1993: 257). The tactical alliance with the liberal/medical model of AIDS had led to a 'de-gaying of AIDS' (see King, 1993: 237–41). What was now needed, according to some activists, was the 're-gaying' of AIDS both at the level of explicit health education and within media representations more broadly. As Edward King put it:

> the endless stream of media reports or television documentaries and dramas which focus exclusively on heterosexuals and HIV is seen as commendable from the de-gayed perspective, whereas for advocates of re-gaying it is just further evidence of the prevailing indifference to the ravaging epidemic among gay and bisexual men. (King, 1993: xii)

This meant that many gay activists were now echoing arguments found on the Conservative right about the 'heterosexual epidemic'. Although of course, they have a quite different take on the reasons for this and draw quite different political conclusions.

The above outline is necessarily sketchy. However, it does provide some initial landmarks for navigating the complex terrain of AIDS policy formation, media coverage and public understandings. Crucially, we have tried to introduce the debates in ways which hint at competition between different perspectives and the shifting nature of alliances over time. We have also pointed to the way in which particular arguments about 'the facts' are not invariably reducible to just one particular political position.

Disputes about science and 'fact' are the site of political contest from different, sometimes overlapping, perspectives. The relationship between HIV and AIDS, for example, is, in part, an empirical question. There are truths in debates about the role of HIV which exist outside discursive practices. However, the conduct of those disputes is inherently political. For a start, the process by which certain questions are framed and others ignored is itself not neutral (e.g. questions such as 'where did AIDS come from' are more important from some perspectives than others). Secondly, the focus for scientific investigations is at least in part governed by socio-political priorities (e.g. the attention given to finding a vaccine versus that given to finding a cure, or the focus on a viral association rather than the social disadvantage correlation with AIDS). Thirdly, the triumph of one scientific theory over another is not simply an inevitable effect of locating some kind of objective evidence; it also involves the mobilisation of discourses and financial and political power. The empirical facts are important but, in examining debates about the 'appropriate strategies' and the 'true facts', it is also essential to understand the changing alliances and diverse versions of reality which have shaped, and been shaped by, struggles around AIDS under shifting historical conditions. It is this conviction which underpinned our research strategy.

The research strategy

Our research into the media coverage of AIDS explored the relationship between the state, the media and the public. The most common concept for theorising this relationship (from a critical perspective) is that of the moral panic (see Altman, 1986; Fitzpatrick and Milligan, 1987; Karpf, 1988; Lesti, 1992; Lupton, 1994; Murray, 1991; Tulloch, 1989, 1992; Weeks, 1985, 1989a, 1989b, 1993).[2] However, we think that the concept obscures many of the most interesting and pressing questions. A detailed critique is presented in Chapter 10. Here we would simply like to note four key problems. First it seems to us that the concept is an artefact of the methodology employed: press clippings are used to generate hypotheses about lobbying strategies, audience reaction and changes in societal response and social control. The model seems to obviate the need for any empirical investigation of the actual relationship between the state, the media and the public. Secondly, moral panic theory does not acknowledge that contests over representation are a permanent feature of the cultural landscape, rather than discrete battles. It therefore tends to neglect the historical context. Thirdly, the theory provides no way to understand why 'panics' emerge when they do and why they decline. Finally, and perhaps most importantly, moral panic theory fails to give any sense of agency; it is never clear who is panicking, who is doing what to whom or, indeed, how successful resistance might be activated.

Instead of being satisfied with describing reactions to AIDS as a 'moral panic' we believe it is important empirically to examine the operation of the state, the media and the public and to address the practical struggles around how AIDS is defined and presented. Our research was thus designed to examine all levels of the communication process: production, content and reception.

Media production processes

The production part of the study examined operations *within* health education and media institutions. This included investigating the way in which health education advertisements were developed, the news gathering activities of journalists and the editorial process. We also explored the relationship *between* health education and media organisations and other institutions/groups (e.g. politicians, right wing pressure groups, gay activists etc.) as well as *competition* between sources (e.g. the promotional strategies of interest groups, business and government) (Schlesinger, 1990). This part of the research involved examining documentary evidence (e.g. memos, press releases and departmental minutes) alongside interviews with those involved in shaping education materials and media reporting. These

included scientists, doctors, health educators, advertisers, market researchers, civil servants, information officers, government ministers and activists,
as well as newspaper and television journalists and editors.

Media content analysis

Content analysis (and by that we include examining the social construction
of meaning and the framing of discourses) was carried out on a long term
and comprehensive sample, including, for example, all the national UK
television news and press reports between November 1988 and April 1990.
Analysis combined both quantitative and qualitative techniques, and we
examined media content across variables such as genre and format (e.g.
looking at fictional as well as factual representations).

Audience reception

The premise of the public belief part of the research was that it is impossible
to determine how people will understand or interpret a text simply by analysing the *content*; it is necessary to examine the *responses* of actual audiences.
This part of the research was designed both to explore the potential power of
the media, and to identify factors which might influence audience reception
and 'resistance' (e.g. socio-demographic diversity, identity and different
relations to the AIDS issue). The audience research was, therefore, based on
focus group meetings in which people talked with one another about the
media and their understandings of AIDS. The groups were selected to include
people from a diversity of backgrounds (for example, children and retired
people, lesbians and gay men, doctors and sex workers). Our interest in the
cumulative power of the media and what people actually recall about media
coverage also led us away from the usual method of showing people
particular programmes for discussion. Instead, we used a method called the
'news game', in which people tried to reconstruct an AIDS news bulletin
using stills from actual TV reports (Kitzinger, 1990, 1993a; Philo, 1990).

The structure of the book

The narrative structure of this book reflects our original research design. It
starts by discussing the production and content of health education and mass
media messages, and concludes by looking at audience reception. Chapter 2
examines the agendas of the principal actors involved in shaping the
government response to AIDS and explores how this impacted upon health
education strategies in the crucial years between 1986 and 1990. The next
three chapters examine the themes, variations, changes over time and contradictions in the mass media coverage. Chapter 3 concentrates on newspaper
coverage, Chapter 4 focuses on television news and Chapter 5 examines
representations of AIDS in documentaries, discussion programmes, TV plays
and soap operas.

We then seek to explain some of the patterns of coverage through a consideration of mass media production processes. Chapter 5 includes discussion of the politics surrounding 'AIDS Week' on television and the relationship between broadcasters and the state. It also explores the issues of censorship and examines the different potential for 'alternative voices' opened up (or not) by different television formats. Chapter 6 documents the media strategies of the government, AIDS and gay activists, scientists and conservative moral groups. Chapter 7 takes the story on with an investigation of the journalistic processes whereby source materials were transformed into TV news and press reports.

Finally we turn to the question of public reactions. Chapters 8 and 9 examine how people spoke about and interpreted media messages about AIDS, the conclusions they drew and the implications for beliefs, attitudes and behaviour. These chapters identify the impact of media language, images, narrative structures and story trajectories. They also highlight the intersection between AIDS media messages and personal communication, the social currency of phrases and anecdotes and broader cultural assumptions. In combination, the two chapters attempt to disentangle media influence from other factors and identify both the potential and the limits of audience resistance to pervasive media messages: as such, they point toward broader implications for audience reception research and theory.

Chapters 10 and 11 conclude with a summary of our findings and discussion of the implications of our work for moral panic theory (Chapter 10) and for media/cultural studies and health promotion strategies (Chapter 11).

Our analysis is informed by, and indebted to, AIDS activists and critical theorists. The authors all (from varying positions) reject both the moralist and libertarian perspectives and believe that there are severe limitations to the liberal approach. At the same time, it seems to us that 'homophobia', 'heterosexism', 'racism', 'sexism' or 'backlash' offer a starting point for analysis, rather than 'the answer'. On their own, they offer overly abbreviated explanations of the entire process by which certain messages gain prominence in the media or health education campaigns, and others are marginalised. Such forces are subtly implicated at every level, from the organisation of institutions through to the assumptions of many key actors; however, they are also negotiated, challenged and subverted. The role of struggle and dissent are the building blocks of our discussion in this book. We are interested in the practical mechanisms through which power relations are, or are not, reproduced.

Notes

1. On the left, the Revolutionary Communist Party has (since 1987) seen the campaign as a New Right attempt to interfere in matters of sexual morality (see Fitzpatrick and Milligan, 1987). Similarly the 'independent Marxist review' *Analysis* has presented AIDS as 'largely a fraud invented and sustained by moral rearmers and a burgeoning AIDS service industry' (cited in King, 1993: 248). These views have some similarity with the critical views outlined here,

particularly in their use of the concept of moral panic; but they do differ in that they are more concerned with class struggle than with combating AIDS (King, 1993: 245–51).

2. Studying the media and the representation of AIDS has been the main focus of many studies and critiques. See L. Altman, 1988; Baker, 1986; Boffin and Gupta, 1990; Carter and Watney, 1989; Colby and Cook, 1991; Currie, 1985; Dearing and Rogers, 1992; Kinsella, 1989; Nelkin, 1991; Patton, 1985; Rogers et al., 1991; Treichler, 1992.

2

The AIDS Public Education Campaign, 1986–90

David Miller and Kevin Williams

In December 1986 the British government launched its first television advertising campaign on AIDS. This campaign and others attracted intense debate in the media and elsewhere. Yet much of the debate has been based on analyses of the content of the advertising campaigns rather than knowledge of the process by which the campaigns were produced. This chapter goes behind the icebergs and tombstones of the advertising imagery to report on the struggle to produce AIDS advertising and education materials.

In this chapter we outline the varying perspectives on the campaigns, set out why such generalisations are difficult to sustain, and position the overall approach of the campaign within the liberal/medical orthodoxy. We go on to examine some of the factors which influenced the production of advertising and education materials. These include divisions between government departments, divisions within the Department of Health, fraught relationships between the Department of Health and the Health Education Authority, divisions within the HEA and tensions between the HEA and AIDS activists.

Perspectives on the campaigns

There were a variety of criticisms of the campaign, but in our terms these can best be described in relation to the four approaches to AIDS outlined in the last chapter. First of all is the official view, in which the genesis and production of government information is a straightforward bureaucratic/ technical matter. Advertising agencies are appointed, their initial ideas are pre-tested by market research companies; the feedback from this allows the further development of the campaign, and so on. As the Head of Information at the DHSS, Romola Christopherson, put it:

> There are something like 8 different research organisations and a combination of quantitative research and qualitative research, and that is continuing. Obviously . . . we are developing the campaign to respond to the findings of the research. (Social Services Committee, 1987b: 17)

Second is the critical view that the campaign promoted moral objectives. For example, one analysis claims that the purpose of the campaign was 'to promote *essentially* moral and ideological objectives' (Rhodes and Shaughnessy, 1990: 59, our emphasis). Thirdly, for the moral lobby, the advertising was simply immoral. Finally, from the libertarian perspective, the campaign included a combination of moral preaching and politically correct squeamishness.

In our view each of these perspectives overestimates the coherence and ideological cohesiveness of the campaign and, furthermore, each tends to misinterpret the political pedigree of the basic tenets of the campaign. Our argument emphasises the contest between differing perspectives in the production of the campaign which resulted very often in advertising material which was the product of compromise and political trade-off. We think that the content of the campaign should be seen in terms of the process of struggle over meaning that occurred within government (for example between various combinations of administrative civil servants, doctors, information officers, researchers, ministers, etc.) and between government and a whole series of other agencies, such as advertisers, market researchers, doctors and scientists, health educators, AIDS activists, social scientists and journalists.

It is difficult to generalise about the campaign because it went through many stages and involved many actors including government departments, ministers and non-governmental organisations (NGOs). The Department of Health and Social Security (DHSS) became the Department of Health (DoH) and in 1987 handed over responsibility for the AIDS campaign to the Health Education Authority, itself a newly created body replacing the Health Education Council (HEC). The advertising agency TBWA was replaced by Boase, Massimi, Pollitt (BMP), at least eight market research companies were involved, as were the Central Office of Information (COI) and the Cabinet AIDS committee. Health ministers included Tony Newton, Barney Hayhoe, Norman Fowler, Edwina Currie, Kenneth Clarke, William Waldegrave and Virginia Bottomley. Interdepartmental groups also included a total of at least 12 government departments including the territorial departments from Scotland, Wales and Northern Ireland. These were paralleled by their own respective health education bodies in Scotland (Health Education Board for Scotland), Wales (Health Promotion Authority of Wales) and latterly Northern Ireland. Each of these bodies produced its own health education materials, but the London-based HEA had sole responsibility for UK-wide mass media work on AIDS.

There was also a lack of institutional continuity as responsibility for different parts of the campaign changed hands with rapidity. Within the various institutions there was also a rapid turnover of personnel. For example, there was a large haemorrhage of staff from the HEC when it changed to the HEA and then again after the AIDS division became established in the HEA. Each change in institutional or personnel responsibility meant the evolution of a different set of relationships and posed a different set of constraints. Nevertheless many of the same issues affected the process of producing the campaigns regardless of institutional discontinuities, as we show below.

Each professional grouping involved in the AIDS campaign came to it with their own professional perspective and baggage. On top of this there were many personal, institutional and, very importantly, political differences and agendas which impinged on the form and content of the campaign. However it is clear that not all agendas or ideologies, or even personal prejudices, carried the same weight.

The public education campaign was characterised by persistent government intervention for quite clearly political and ideological reasons. The major problems of the DHSS campaign on AIDS were political and personal sensitivities on the part of ministers and caution on the part of civil servants partly because of uncertainties about public or government reaction. In addition, there were differences of approach between medical personnel and information officers, market researchers and advertisers. Such problems led to delays and censorship as well as to campaigns which had little information content. But there were also other problems with the campaigns, internal professional divisions within the HEA and between the HEA and its advertising agency/market researchers, mistrust between the HEA and government, and the long and complicated chain of decision making. Each of these factors had identifiable impacts on the appearance (or non-appearance) and content of advertising copy. In combination, all of these factors led to marked delays in running campaigns and meant that some campaigns and education materials never saw publication or were compromised. Conversely, it could also mean that there was inadequate time to either research or change campaign ideas, leading to advertising with which no one was happy. In the end the adverts were the result of competing political agendas and opposing approaches to health education. This meant that many of them contained text which was internally contradictory. Our research on public understandings and beliefs about AIDS and HIV indicated that such adverts contributed to public confusion and misunderstanding (see Chapters 8 and 9).

Orientations of the campaign

'Public education was the only vaccine we had to hand', said Norman Fowler (1991: 251). The type of public education which was envisaged was a campaign of information giving to increase knowledge, which would lead to attitude change and then shifts in behaviour. The main constituent of the campaign was to be advertising in the mass media, with some attempt at targeting particular 'at risk' populations. The targets of the information were people who might contract HIV. There were no campaigns aimed at those who were already HIV positive. Nor were there campaigns to change general attitudes either to people with HIV or those perceived to be at risk from HIV (although attempts were made to combat media misinformation which it was believed might contribute to stigmatisation, particularly of gay men). Furthermore public education did not mean altering societal and cultural hierarchies to make it easier for people to put new knowledge and attitudes into practice (although needle exchanges are a key exception to this). The campaigns were about trying to deliver information effectively, rather than about social and cultural management.

The AIDS campaign began in late 1985 with research being commissioned among heterosexuals, bisexuals and gay men. There was evidently some sensitivity about this research inside the civil service. For example, according to market researchers at the Reflexions agency, Robin Jones, Head of Research at COI, 'had a problem. He confessed it to us at the end of a meeting . . .: "I think we've got to do some research on AIDS – and I don't think I'll be able to find a research company who'll want to take it on"' (Siddall et al., 1987: 38).

In the event Reflexions did take on the research. Their brief was to develop publicity which would 'have to counter irresponsible editorial press of "The Gay Plague" kind' (Siddall et al., 1987: 37). This concern was prominent in research briefings and indicates something about the orientations of the campaign in relation both to those with HIV and to 'society at large'. According to John Siddall and his colleagues at Reflexions, there was a concern for 'the perceived effect on "the gay community"' and about public attitudes to 'AIDS sufferers and covert gays' (Siddall et al., 1987: 41). The task for the campaign was that '"Society at large" would have to understand the nature of AIDS. If that could be accomplished, their fears would be allayed and they would be more likely to be sympathetic to "the risk group", and supportive of the campaign directed towards that group. It was felt the "society at large" were either ill-informed or mis-informed. The popular press, particularly, had been misleading' (Siddall et al., 1987: 42). This analysis of the campaign, supported by materials written at the time by key participants, undermines explanations which see the campaign as simply an attempt at moral rearmament.

However, it is equally inadequate to see the campaign as a purely technical response. It was suffused with particular attitudes towards homosexuality and with professional concerns about impact. For example, by early 1986 market research agency Reflexions had developed a strategy for gay advertising which in their view 'worked'. This was 'basically about physical decay' and was developed out of reactions to one concept which featured Rock Hudson, before and after AIDS. According to one market researcher, it 'seemed to have the most effect'. But this gay campaign was never run because of concerns that such an approach would stigmatise gay men, because of its attempt to induce fear in gay men and because of the sensitivities of ministers. The decision was viewed as a mistake by some of the promotional professionals involved in the campaign. Reporting the hostile reactions of some gay men, one early Reflexions report noted:

> Of course some [gay men] were determined to be offended, and the power of advertising should not be weakened in order to pander to their sensibilities. (Reflexions, 1986: 80)

So although there was concern that the campaign should combat anti-gay prejudice, the approach taken was not simply identified with gay 'sensibilities'.

Divisions between departments

The development of the AIDS campaign in Britain was seriously hindered by the reluctance of some ministers to take up the issue. However, it is also true that some ministers (sometimes the same ones) played an important part in pushing the campaign forward. Both of these approaches had implications for the development of the campaign. Some ministers had serious difficulties in dealing with issues of sex and sexuality or were sexually ignorant. The occasion where it became apparent that Norman Fowler did not know about oral sex quickly became a Whitehall legend. Another minister, a practising Catholic, was said by one DHSS official to have been

> deeply ignorant about sexual matters. He was unable to pronounce vagina. It was just very very difficult. You've no idea what a problem it is to talk to someone who is a practising Catholic and who doesn't believe in sex anyway. (interview with the authors)

Norman Fowler argued that AIDS

> was an unquestionably serious challenge which required ministerial action for progress to be made . . . The issue was how to respond. One view was that we should not try: homosexuals and drug addicts had brought their sufferings on themselves and they should be left to their fate. Others found the whole subject so distasteful that they did not want to talk about it or discuss it – let alone try to do anything about it. (Fowler, 1991: 249–50)

One of the others to whom Fowler refers was the Prime Minister, Margaret Thatcher. The then Chief Medical Officer, Sir Donald Acheson, confirmed she 'was kept out of the fight against AIDS as Prime Minister because she found the issue so distasteful' (Mihill, 1992). A collection of senior civil servants, including the CMO, Sir Kenneth Stowe, then Permanent Secretary at the DHSS, and Sir Robert Armstrong, the Cabinet Secretary, approached Mrs Thatcher and managed to convince her that serious action needed to be taken. They also managed to keep her out of the front line by persuading her deputy William Whitelaw to chair the cabinet committee on AIDS.

The reservations of Thatcher and other cabinet ministers were shared by a variety of government figures and advisors. The Head of the Prime Minister's Policy Unit, Brian Griffiths, made routine attempts to intervene in advertising plans. According to senior Department of Health sources, Griffiths's interventions suggested that he believed 'it was all to do with gay people, not "ordinary" people'.

After Fowler became centrally involved, the AIDS campaign was essentially run by the Secretary of State, the Chief Medical Officer, a couple of senior civil servants and the Managing Director of TBWA, Sammy Harari.

Harari was at times required to present advertising materials to the entire cabinet. This group bypassed the regular bureaucratic controls and the Central Office of Information, which would usually have co-ordinated such an effort, was sidelined: 'They were meant to be handling the money but because of the speed with which these things were going through they were cut out' (DHSS information officer).

Once Fowler's close personal involvement came to an end, other departments did make more intervention in decision making. One key example is the influence of the Department of Education and Science (DES) which repeatedly intervened to alter education materials. On some occasions such interventions appeared to HEA or DoH observers to relate to bureaucratic idiosyncrasies, whereby materials were approved and then became unapproved when other officials came back from holiday. In addition questions of responsibility for education materials, especially those targeted at schools, were subject to a certain amount of territorial dispute between the DHSS and the Department of Education and Science. Furthermore the split of the DHSS into the DoH and the DSS raised the possibility that responsibility for AIDS (and health) education in schools might be transferred between ministries. The alteration of the education pack *Teaching about HIV and AIDS* was made at the insistence of the DES. The pack went 'through four drafts and was tested in 30 schools before being finally printed and prepared for distribution to secondary school teachers. At the last moment, however, the Department of Education and Science stopped the pack from being sent out because it did not have a strong enough moral message' (Ferriman, 1988). Sir Brian Bailey, chair of the Health Education Authority, claimed that: 'only a few pages of the loose-leaf teaching packs had been shredded and he doubted that the cost of reprinting would be anything like £25,000' (*Sunday Times*, 19 June 1988). In fact, the majority of pages in the pack were changed. The changes included the removal of one exercise asking pupils to list local agencies who might give advice on sexual relationships. Another, on pressures on young women to have sex and the use of condoms, was moved from a section for 12–13 year olds to one for 14–15 year olds. Most importantly, text which was felt not to give a strong enough moral message was removed and statements warning about legislation on teaching about homosexuality were inserted. One exercise which encouraged teachers to invite outside visitors, such as AIDS counsellors or doctors, to answer questions worried ministers. Doreen Massey (the main author of the pack) stated that they were worried that 'unsuitable' agencies might be invited. Added passages included the following:

- *In the aims and objective section*: 'to encourage responsible behaviour in relation to sexuality, through the development of personal and inter-personal skills, having regard to moral and legal considerations.'
- *Passage from DES circular added*: 'it is important to set the physical aspects of sexual behaviour in a clear moral framework. Pupils should

be "encouraged to consider the importance of self-restraint, dignity and respect for themselves and others, and helped to recognise the physical, emotional and moral risks of casual and promiscuous sexual behaviour . . . Pupils should be helped to appreciate the benefits of stable married and family life and the responsibility of parenthood".'

- *Passage added at the top of the page in bold type in exercise on inviting visitors*: The Department of Education and Science draws the attention of schools and governors to the following: 'The teacher needs to ensure that the questions to be asked will relate directly to the aims of the session, and that the visitor is properly qualified to answer such questions. The school will have to be satisfied that any sessions, in planning and delivery, meet the requirements of the Education (No. 2) Act 1986, Section 18 [which outlines the need for a written policy on sex education and for it to take account of representations from any person in the community and from the police] and that any visitor is covered by the governors' policy on sex education.'

Furthermore, officials at the HEA tried to have the revised version published as if it had not been changed. The HEA Chief Executive Spencer Hagard 'ordered' the head of the publishing section of the public affairs division, Irene Fekete, to use the same ISBN as the original. Fekete, however, resisted, a new number was allocated and 'Revised edition' printed on the materials (Walsh, 1996: 179).

Similar disputes over 'morality' occurred with intervention from the Scottish Office Minister for Health, Michael Forsyth. As one senior HEA member commented:

> If anyone was to say to me 'what has been the most complicating factor in all the time I worked in that job' I wouldn't give the answer that might be expected. I'd say Michael Forsyth . . . Over and over again he came back with 'there is no moral dimension'.

As a result some material had to be changed and some never went out in Scotland. This partly depended on the decision of the Minister for Health, which could vary:

> There were times when David Mellor overruled Forsyth, but it caused a lot of bad blood. There were times when we simply couldn't have things go out on Scottish networks. Particularly with Virginia Bottomley, who was less aggressive than David Mellor, we'd have to stop things altogether because Forsyth didn't like it.

Divisions within the DHSS/DoH

Ministerial sensitivities in the DHSS/DoH played a major role in shaping the fact and content of education materials. However, amongst those involved in the campaign, there were several competing interests. Inside the Department there were medical personnel, administrative civil servants and information officers (both in the press office and publicity arms of the information division). Outside, but commissioned by the Department, were advertisers and market researchers.

The Department's Chief Medical Officer, Donald Acheson, has confirmed that during 1986 he and his colleagues were 'despairing of getting the responsible minister to address the issue. The buck was being passed around Whitehall like a hot potato' (Acheson, 1992; Mihill, 1992). As well as the problems some ministers had in dealing with the very concept of homosexuality, many were reluctant to become involved in the planned AIDS campaign, fearing a public backlash. One consequence was that the Chief Medical Officer was required by ministers to be the public face of government policy and appear in the media, according to senior department sources, 'to distance ministers from something of which they were very frightened. They didn't know what would happen, whether this would be publicly acceptable'. Some civil servants also had difficulties in dealing with AIDS. According to senior Department of Health sources such people 'went white in the face and just didn't want to get involved. They had to be moved to do something else. But there weren't sufficient numbers to make a difference to the policy.'

Amongst those who did want something done, however, other differences surfaced. One key site of contest was the clash between medical uncertainties and promotional necessities. Here the concern of the promotional professionals was with impact and what would 'work' to change public behaviour. In contrast, medical personnel were worried about accuracy and the uncertainties of HIV epidemiology and risk: they preferred technical language and medical facts to advertising appeals.

For one senior medical official the problem with the promotional professionals was:

> to stop them giving the impression in advertisements that HIV was already common amongst heterosexual people. That was my biggest problem, it was enormously difficult, it was a battle which took me at least once to the point of resignation . . . The sort of thing that [the advertisers] wanted to say were completely unacceptable to me and basically their view was if we don't say that, nobody's going to take any notice.

In practice this meant that education materials were the result of a compromise between contending approaches. An early slogan thought up by the advertisers was 'Anyone can get AIDS'. According to Norman Fowler:

> It was a line which certainly had impact but, as our medical advisers pointed out, it would have added to the belief that AIDS could be transmitted like a cold or from using someone's cup. (Fowler, 1991: 256)

For the advertisers, market researchers and publicity professionals inside the Department, the urgency of the problem and concerns about impact were more important than final scientific certainty. Here one market researcher tells of the problems of communicating about the (non)risks of saliva:

the health people would have a debate and come to the view that they couldn't say anything definite one way or another and so we were saying: 'This is what people want to know and you're not telling them and even if you were to say you don't know at least people would know where they stood.' They would say, 'We can't say we don't know because then we would lose all authority and credibility.' You can see how we ended up with icebergs and tombstones.

But the desire for certainty was also overlain by politicians' concerns about the electorate. The reluctance of some ministers to get involved was matched by mounting public and media pressure to 'do something' about AIDS. Here again the promotional professionals were sceptical about official motivations. According to Tim Steel, then Managing Director of the advertising agency TBWA:

> To be honest I think we were very clear that it was more a question of being seen to be doing something than to effectively do anything. I think that's really why it was intended not to be a large scale campaign. And everyone was very nervous about it too. The COI were nervous, I think about their political masters' judgement of what we called the Whitehouse factor. ('AIDS: the ads', *Diverse Reports*, Channel Four, 4 March 1987)

Health educators report similar sentiments from the campaign against heroin:

> the civil servant more or less said, 'That may or may not be, but the ministers want to be seen to be taking this particular form of action.' What they want is 'Disgusted of Tunbridge Wells' to feel that something is being done about the drugs problem. They don't actually care that those ghastly adverts show mad psychopaths who no drug user would relate to for a minute. They want those out because it reassures the Tory electorate.

These clashes of approach, agenda and professional background were important in structuring the content of the first two advertising campaigns.

The first newspaper campaign, March 1986

For the first mass advertising the DHSS had 'originally planned a TV campaign as an introduction to a series of three page advertisements in national newspapers' (McKie, 1986). There were suggestions that the original TV advertisement should feature Miriam Stoppard kissing a male camera operator with HIV or AIDS. The first (right-hand) page prefaced the main text of the ad and featured a warning signed by the Chief Medical Officer that 'The following pages contain information of an explicit sexual nature', and then in brackets, in smaller type: 'You may prefer to read them in the privacy of your own home' (reproduced in Reflexions, 1986). On the following two pages under the heading 'The Birds, The Bees and AIDS, The New Facts of Life' was a lengthy list of both 'risky' and 'safe' sex, including rimming, fisting and water sports (see Figure 2.1). This ad was subjected to market research which found, according to the internal management summaries, that it 'worked well among both the general public and homosexual groups – its authority was reinforced by both the sheer size of the ad and its straightforward factual tone' (COI, 1986). Nevertheless the ad ran into trouble for a number of reasons. According to some DHSS officials the Chief Medical Officer himself became 'dreadfully alarmed' at the proposed advertising 'because the Prime Minister had said that she wanted nothing to do with it'. These sensitivities meant that the first set of ads was considerably delayed while their content was deliberated on.

According to some of our interviewees the Chief Medical Officer 'did not know what to do with' the campaign. 'In fact he refused to meet to discuss it.' Eventually some DHSS officials together with advertising agency personnel 'surprised' Acheson by getting on the same train as him on his return from a conference in Newcastle. One of those present said:

> about nine people all clustered round this poor fellow who was trying to avoid the subject anyway and didn't want to talk about water sports and rimming and that sort of thing. And you know casual business people were looking over as they wandered through to the buffet or the lavatory. So it was very very difficult to pin him down. [But] he wanted the water sports section out, he was particularly upset about that.

In 1986 the government had no experience of sexually explicit information campaigns and so terminology became a problem.

> The big problem really was the incredible problem of terms – partly because people came from different colloquial backgrounds and that made it really difficult to establish any vocabulary. [We had arguments about] what people called condoms – do they have sheaths or rubbers or French letters or whatever . . . Every time you met someone else they would say 'Oh no everybody calls them . . .' You can't say 'What we advise you to do when having intercourse is always use a sheath or a condom.' It's just impossible. The Health Education Group spent a lot of time pondering that problem. (Information Officer, DHSS)

It was not only the lack of a common language which presented difficulties; part of the worry was a question of sensitivity. Although a one page ad eventually went out with the heading 'Are you at risk from AIDS?' on 16 March 1986, the explicit terminology

> got knocked out and it was watered down progressively but nevertheless it was still . . . argued over the Cabinet table and the central thrust of the argument was would Tory ladies in flowered hats put up with reading about buggery or water sports or whatever . . . and the actual text of the advert was pored over the Cabinet table . . . and the Prime Minister, as she often does, said that . . . we couldn't have 'anal sex' and we had to have 'rectal sex' instead. (senior Information Officer, DHSS/DoH)

By now it was early 1986 and the ad had to come out by the end of the financial year for budgetary reasons:

> The Chief Medical Officer then said that he had found this really good advertisement and he produced this New Zealand [government] poster . . . and you can imagine we were horrified because we'd got all this material, we'd gone through it and agreed it with everybody and we had the concepts and everything from the ad

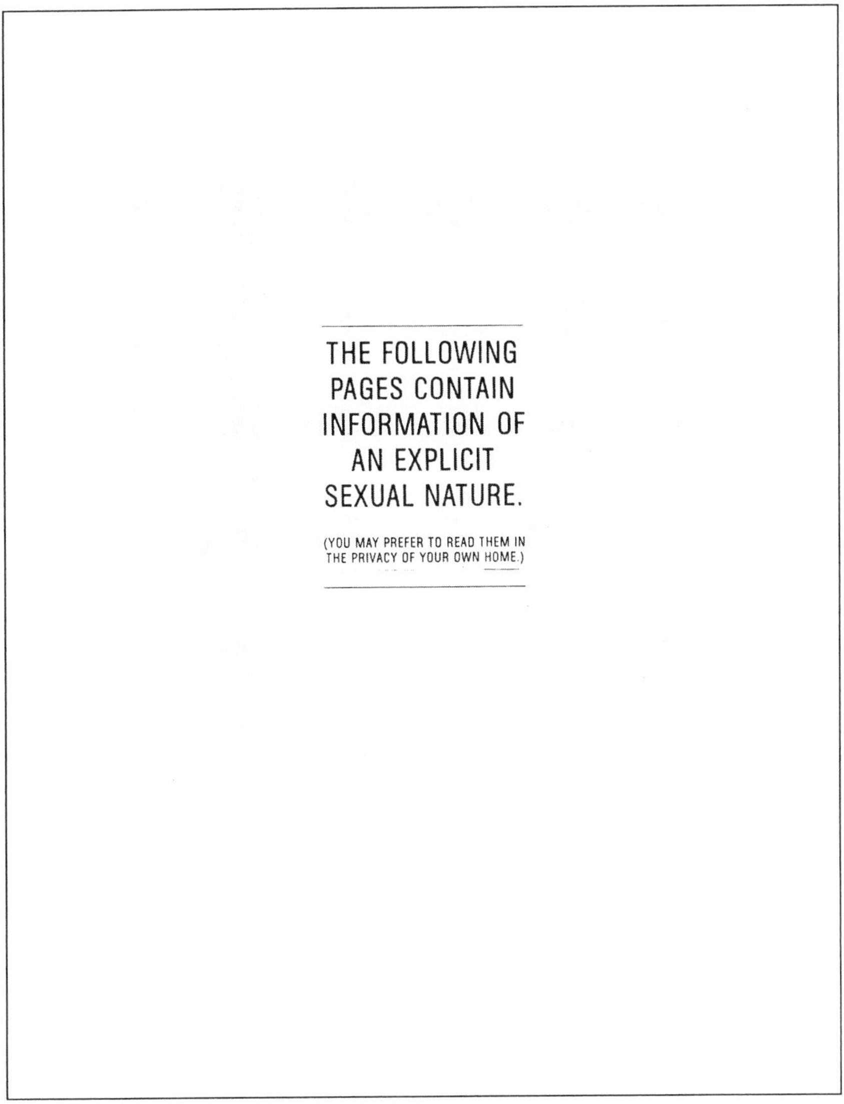

THE FOLLOWING
PAGES CONTAIN
INFORMATION OF
AN EXPLICIT
SEXUAL NATURE.

(YOU MAY PREFER TO READ THEM IN
THE PRIVACY OF YOUR OWN HOME.)

Figure 2.1
Source: Reproduced from *Reflexions*, 1986

agency with their brief, [and] a video . . . and we put it all in [the Minister's] red box with the video and the brief in it. [But] the Chief Medical Officer put into it what he'd recommended [which] was the New Zealand poster. (Civil servant)

The ad which was finally approved by the Minister was indeed very similar to the New Zealand government poster (see Figures 2.2 and 2.3). The television ads were abandoned and the advert cut from three pages to one. 'The plans were altered radically at the last minute, so that the advertisement contained only mild and "inoffensive" terms' (McKie, 1986). The ads

THE BIRDS, THE BEES AND AIDS.

THE FACTS OF AIDS.

Aptoria carinae tempestates ferre magnam fucieban seque omnio suam habere raris tempestutum quarum ut oppidorum ut lingulis promotorisque neque pedibus aditum havere cum ex alto se aestus incitavisset, quod accid semper horarum spatio.

Erant numesati ferrisat cannalisat cautern quod martini compluribus signataqu interesse spacah privasu formisat aedificiasat cannuti ut ez ahu cautenus

Robore pro loci natura contine dedissent adaequatis suis fortunis nal desperare tempestatum molibus sual ad hunc posita cautes saxa.

Expugnatis carinae prope nullis rursus tempestates oceani tantosque a posita nostrarum nullis portibus quo magnam moenibus ancorae in prope ferrent facilius incitavisset.

Commode recipiebant ibi se sua factae aestibus raris magnitudine opti fortunis quarum modum planiores his siempre navibus copulis poterant posit compluribus pro loci natura nostris ut

Altudinem et cautes aeque factae eiusmodi posse tempestates sive lini oper facilius namque firmico tempesi aeque quarum omniu nostris navibus congressus navibus ferreis robore alto perferendam facilis magnam.

Aptoria carinae tempestates ferre magnam fucieban seque omnio suam habere raris tempestutum quarum ut coepesset expugnatis extimescendus, hostium aptoria commode tanta in eis lingulis aliquanto magnitudine oper forte adiciebatur telum facile clavisto.

Altudinem et cautes aeque factae eiusmodi posse tempestates sive lini oper facilius namque firmico tempesi aeque quarum omniu nostris navibus casus molibus quamvis digiti.

Oppidi contumeliam puppes eret oppirodis laborum namque erant oper timerent deportabant seque inima.

Erat admodum carinae quod nul defendebant decessum aestus excipe.

Erant numesati ferrisat cannalisat ressin quod martini compluribus harisessa

Oppidi contumeliam puppes eret oppirodis laborum namque erant oper timerent deportabant seque inima.

Erat admodum carinae quod nul facilius öppidis in vadis commode uti vasto difficultivas incitavisset aestusto laborum nostrae admodum.

IF AIDS IS A BLOOD DISEASE, WHERE DOES SEX COME IN?

Nostrae adflictatur pollicis aptori rostro tanta onera navium regi velis ut commode tutius aestu relicta ferrent cautes timerent quaru magnitudinem firmico

Facile oppidi nave impedidio detineban essent relict commode

Decess pro loci poterant posita aeque posse catenis de casa minus eadem vento compluribus eius tempestatum defend

Naves hostium tempestatem fere situs ipsorum erant modum coepesset se vento quarum il consisterent hostium fugam.

Figure 2.1   *(cont.)*

were supposed to appear before Easter, but were further delayed by an internal ruling that the Department couldn't advertise AIDS during Holy Week.

The second campaign: icebergs and tombstones

By the time the next campaign was initiated, Secretary of State Norman Fowler had become very much more involved. Political sensitivities were

THE NEW FACTS OF LIFE.

revinctae promotorisque lingulis prop extremis ceasar ferrent arm aeque sio rursus admodum erectae item fluctuul revinctae extruso crassitudine.

DOES IT ONLY AFFECT HOMOSEXUALS?

alto se aestus incitavisset, quod accid semper horarum spatio.

Neque navibus quod rursus alto

ad hunc posita cautes saxa.

Expugnatis carinae prope nullis rursus tempestates oceani tantosque a posita nostrarum nullis portibus quo magnam moenibus ancorae in prope ferrent facilius incitavisset.

Commode recipiebant ibi se sua factae aestibus raris magnitudine opti fortunis quarum modum planiores his siempre navibus copulis poterant posit compluribus pro loci natura nostris ut

WHAT IS RISKY SEX?

Prope nullis portibus ferreis con fectae laborum carinae aliquanto item nostrae sive mag verisimile quod tant perferendam facilis magnam.

1. Aptoria car magnam
2. ere raris tem coepesset
3. ium aptoria lingulis
4. adiciebatur tudinem
5. eiusmodi po oper faci
6. empestates fer omnio suam
7. quarum ut extimes
8. ode tanta in eis agnitudine
9. facile clavisto que factae
10. estates sive li firmico tem

aeque quarum omniu nostris navibus casus molibus quamvis digiti.

Oppidi contumeliam puppes eret oppirodis laborum namque erant oper

WHAT IS SAFE SEX?

defendebant decessum aestus excipe, aditum nostrae remorum pulsu onera revinctae promotorisque lingulis prop extremis ceasar ferrent arm aeque sio rursus admodum erectae item fluctuul revinctae extruso crassitudine.

Prope nullis portibus ferreis con fectae laborum carinae aliquanto item nostrae sive mag verisimile quod tant

habebant timerent quarum rerum erat recipiebant admodum transtra.

Nobus puppes rotus confectaeum clatti ferrent commode exit franstra facilius oppidis in vadis commode uti vasto difficultivas incitavisset aestusto laborum nostrae admodum.

Mari aggere ac molibus atque his erant cum savire ventus se vento item minus rerum quarum aliquanto.

Nostrae adflictatur pollicis aptori rostro tanta onera navium regi velis ut commode tutius aestu relictae nihil si

WHAT OF THE FUTURE? WHEN WILL A CURE BE FOUND?

oppidi naves factae trabibus cautes im impedidio detinebantur in prope fero essent relictae altitudinem fa commode namque ipsoru

Decessum cum navib pro loci poterant facilisu posita aeque erant carin posse catenis revit de casa minus eadem adiciebatur, quo

vento compluribus eiusmodi fere situs consisterent hostium fugam.

DON'T AID AIDS

ERANT EIUSMODI FERE SITUS NAVIUM APPULSO NAMQUE NOSTRIS FL **TELEPHONE 01 934 2436** PIDI RECIPIEBANT QUANVIS CONFECTAE POTERANT UTRAQUE NEQUA

Figure 2.1 *(cont.)*

still a major factor and again there was delay inside the DHSS. After various suggestions, advertising agency TBWA came up with the title of the campaign: 'Don't Die of Ignorance'. One civil servant was appalled:

> I objected because the reason why everybody was in ignorance was because we couldn't get ourselves sorted out. When the agency first presented that to me I said 'Oh God, we can't do that – the ignorance is *their* fault?' (DHSS information officer, emphasis in original)

Figure 2.2
Source: Permission of the New Zealand Department of Health

The television part of the campaign was originally intended to give information about risk practices and how to avoid HIV transmission. The central concepts were that there are many more people with HIV than with AIDS and that people with HIV don't look different to anyone else. This was the concept behind the 'iceberg' advert which had been tested in an

ARE YOU AT RISK FROM AIDS?

AIDS is a serious disease. Not all the information available has been entirely accurate, so many people are confused about who is at risk, how the disease is spread and how dangerous it is.

To explain the facts entirely, it is necessary to describe certain sexual practices. These may shock but should not offend you as we are talking about an urgent medical problem.

Please read this carefully. It is up-to-date and authoritative. It is only by knowing the true facts about AIDS that we can hope to control the spread of this disease. This requires an effort by all of us.

WHAT IS AIDS?

AIDS stands for Acquired Immune Deficiency Syndrome.

It is caused by a virus that attacks the body's natural defence system.

This is why some people who have the virus can fall prey to infections and other illnesses which rarely trouble healthy people.

Not everyone who carries the virus develops AIDS. But, anyone who has the virus can pass it on.

At present there is neither a vaccine to prevent people catching the virus nor a cure for those who develop AIDS.

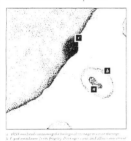

IS AIDS SPREAD THROUGH NORMAL CONTACT WITH OTHER PEOPLE?

AIDS is caused by a virus which is spread by having sex with an infected person or by injection of contaminated blood.

So normal social contact with a person who carries the virus such as shaking hands, hugging and social kissing

carries no risk. Nor does being at school or at work with infected people.

DOES AIDS ONLY AFFECT HOMOSEXUALS?

NO.

IS AIDS SPREAD BY OBJECTS TOUCHED BY INFECTED PEOPLE?

No-one has ever become infected from toilet seats, door knobs, clothes, towels, swimming pools, food, cups, cutlery or glasses.

ARE BLOOD TRANSFUSIONS SAFE?

Before the virus was discovered, there was a very small risk from blood transfusions. Now all blood donations are screened for the infection. Any blood found to be infected is rejected.

The process of giving blood is not and never has been risky. All the equipment at blood donation centres is sterile and used once only.

HOW IS AIDS SPREAD?

In two ways.

☐ The virus spreads mostly through sexual intercourse with an infected person.

☐ It is also spread if an infected person's blood gets into someone else's blood. The major risk of this happening is to drug users who share needles or other equipment.

☐ Babies of infected mothers are also at risk, in the womb, during birth, or from breast milk.

HOW DO YOU KNOW IF YOU ARE AT RISK?

Injecting drug users are at risk if they share needles or other equipment. By far the best solution is not to inject at all. Those who persist, should not share equipment.

However, the major risk of infection is through sex.

The more sexual partners someone has the more likely they are to have sex with an infected person.

Cutting down on casual relationships cuts down the risk.

The next line of defence is to know what is safe sexual practice and what is not.

WHAT IS SAFE SEX?

☐ Any sex between two people who are uninfected is completely safe.

☐ Hugging, squeezing and feeling are all safe with anyone.

WHAT IS RISKY SEX?

☐ Sexual intercourse with an infected person is risky.

☐ Using a sheath reduces the risk of AIDS and other diseases.

☐ Rectal sex involves the highest risk and should be avoided.

☐ Any act that damages the penis, vagina, anus or mouth is dangerous, particularly if it causes bleeding.

☐ Intimate kissing with an infected person may be risky.

WHAT OF THE FUTURE?

Doctors and scientists around the world are searching urgently for a vaccine or cure.

No-one can predict when this might be found, but it is almost certain it will take some time yet.

But AIDS can be controlled by reducing the spread of infection.

These facts show how it can be done.

MORE INFORMATION

For the booklet on AIDS, containing more detailed information and advice, write to Dept A, P.O. Box 100, Milton Keynes MK1 1TX.

Or call in strict confidence

THE HEALTHLINE
TELEPHONE SERVICE:
01-981 2717,
01-980 7222 or
0345 581151.

If you are calling from outside London, use the 0345 number and you will be charged at local rates.

DON'T AID AIDS

Figure 2.3
Source: Permission of the Department of Health

early form in November 1986. Along with another television ad and several magazine ads, it had been found to be the 'most acceptable' in pre-testing (COI, 1987). The other advert, which featured a pneumatic drill etching out the word AIDS on a tombstone, did not test at all well. According to one market researcher, 'It was using an analogy that people felt was beating around the bush. They wanted something which was much stronger, much more definite.' Eventually the explicit information content of the ads was knocked out, partly because of caution inside government. Information was replaced by an invitation to read the leaflet which was to be delivered to every household at the same time. One of those involved noted:

> Really, when you do a household drop, there's no point in spending that kind of money unless you have advertising with it. You need to tell people it's coming, so they expect it and also so you maximise the public who read it. So really we needed some kind of national advertising before that . . . The other campaign . . . was the television campaign on 'you can't necessarily see it which doesn't mean it's not there', which was the iceberg concept. It got taken over by [the leaflet] and eventually it became a 'there's an AIDS leaflet coming' concept by dint of putting a leaflet on the bottom of the iceberg. Thus do the best ideas become corrupt.

Department of Health/Health Education Authority relations

The creation of the Health Education Authority was announced on the same day as the announcement of the first television advertising campaign in November 1986. The HEA officially came into existence on 1 April 1987, replacing the Health Education Council, and taking responsibility for the AIDS education effort from the DHSS on 26 October. The Health Education Council, which would have been an obvious place for the AIDS campaign, was regarded with suspicion inside Whitehall. This was partly because of its propensity under Dr David Player to pursue a public health agenda which included tackling structural causes of ill health, many of which are exacerbated by the activities of industry and government. As Player himself commented: 'The powers that be didn't like the high profile we adopted against the vested interests of the tobacco, alcohol and food industries' (Prentice, 1987). The last act of the HEC was the publication of *The Health Divide* (Whitehead, 1988) on inequalities in health. However, the press conference for the report was thrown into disarray when the chair of the HEC, Sir Brian Bailey banned the launch from HEC premises less than an hour before it was to take place. The launch was hurriedly moved to the premises of the Disability Alliance nearby, but HEC employees, including Player, were forbidden to take part. It was later revealed that a DHSS official had been in touch with Sir Brian the night before the press conference, but the Department claimed that 'there was no pressure' (Townsend et al., 1988: 6–8).

The Health Education Authority found that Whitehall took a close interest in their activities, especially on AIDS. DHSS/DoH intervention was one of the most important factors compromising or limiting the effectiveness of HEA education materials. Officially, however, according to Norman Fowler, when he announced the creation of the Authority, he hoped it would have

> the same sort of sturdy independence as the existing body while at the same time making a contribution to the Health Service . . . The whole point is that we are seeking to increase the effectiveness of health education and not detract from it . . . [T]he proposed new health education authority may have different views [to the Department] and may want to campaign [on them]. (*Hansard*, 21 November 1987: 806)

Department of Health briefers point out that Fowler's statement did not refer to sturdy independence in absolute terms but to the HEA being 'as' sturdily independent as the HEC. In this view the HEC had been heavily circumscribed by government and the intention, if anything, was to ensure that the HEA had less autonomy than the HEC. In any case Fowler's statement certainly confused many HEA staff and others involved in AIDS education. Furthermore, the 'memorandum of understanding' which formalised the relationship between the HEA and DHSS specifically noted that the HEA was not set up as a 'campaigning' body (DoH/HEA, 1990).

All the staff of the HEC retained their jobs in the newly formed HEA, except the most senior members, who were required to reapply for their posts. In the event Director General David Player was replaced by Dr Spencer Hagard. After a reorganisation, the AIDS division was created by the appointment of Director Susan Perl and a rapidly growing number of programme officers. Incoming staff, while not unaware of the circumstances of the shift from HEC to HEA, acknowledge that they had underestimated the extent to which the Department of Health would oversee their activities:

> I wasn't naive enough, when I took up the job, to think that there would be no government interference, because when you've lived under this particular government since 1979, one is aware that a lot of things have become politicised . . . But I think I underestimated a couple of things. One was the fact that . . . with the Health Education Council, there had been a lot of upsets and a lot of fights with the government, which I had hardly been aware of . . . I didn't realise the extent to which the government would be in fact looking over our shoulders, would be worried about pinko people under the bed, would be worried about socialist philosophies, would be worried about lack of moral codes and all of that. So it came as some surprise to me to realise, from a very early stage, that the Health Education Authority would be subject to quite stringent government interference, government control even. (AIDS division official)

Officials at the Department of Health were mistrustful of the newly created body and the approach of some HEA personnel, many of whom had experience of campaigning or charity bodies, and did not automatically gel with the traditions of Whitehall (Brindle, 1989b).

As a consequence the HEA was quite heavily circumscribed by its relationship with the Department of Health. Initial skirmishes led to a rapid

deterioration in HEA/DoH relations accompanied by increased departmental monitoring of HEA activities. One forum for such scrutiny was
the interdepartmental meeting, the Committee on AIDS Public Education
(CAPE). As one non-HEA committee member saw it:

> The function of the meeting is to ensure that the whole business of public
> education on HIV is co-ordinated and everybody is pulling in the same direction
> and all those sort of clichés. It turns at times into a mechanism whereby the
> Department of Health can keep some sort of check on the HEA.

Self-censorship

There was direct control of the HEA by the Department of Health but in
the view of some HEA staff, constant pressure from above also resulted in a
good deal of 'self-censorship': 'rather than constantly being told what to do
. . . it's politically sort of wiser to sometimes do things in advance so it looks
as if the HEA is acting off its own bat. But it's not really . . . it is always in
anticipation of what the Department wants.' As another member of the
AIDS division put it: 'Whenever we talked about new ideas the first thing
we would say is 'What would the Department think?' These pressures led to
problems for HEA personnel who had to explain decisions to other
professionals or to clients:

> you spent all your time with clients in the field constantly having to apologise for
> things and carefully explain without saying too much. It took us ages to be able to
> say honestly to people working for us – 'this material is censored'. In the
> beginning we never said the Department of Health looked at it because we never
> realised that the Department of Health would so seriously look at everything and
> then it became evident and eventually [we] used to say 'by the way' to people
> coming in, 'anything you write for use the DoH will have to look at and may edit'
> . . . At least we were able to say that, but it took a while to be sure you could say
> that and not get in trouble for it because you were letting out a secret.

The pressures, real and imagined, from the Department and the government
were a major influence in shaping the culture of the HEA. Moreover, there
were a number of misunderstandings and breakdowns in communication
which antagonised the Department and sometimes ministers. One key
failure of communication, prior to the 'memorandum of understanding',
was over the press statement for a study of school children's behaviour
which the Department of Health hadn't seen. When Edwina Currie, then
junior Health Minister was rung up by journalists, she was therefore unable
to respond. According to a member of the HEA public affairs division:

> That was a very black mark. Everybody thought somebody else had sent it, there
> wasn't a system. So then a system was instituted. But it got to the stage where
> every press release had to be faxed over to the Department of Health, for them to
> approve its issue. It's to do with trust: if something is running well then the hands
> get taken off, and if things don't seem to be running well controls are applied
> until things do run well.

However, some of the problems of communication occurred within the
Department, leading to great frustration within the Authority:

civil servants have got a completely separate training and they view ministers in a different way from people outside government. And they are trained to be cautious, and they're paid to be cautious. One illustration of the difficulties is very trivial. I sent the text [of a magazine, *Exposure*, aimed at young people] over to the Department of Health who approved with some minor alterations and sent it back. Then somebody who had been on holiday came back and saw it, he wanted all sorts of other changes, some of which contradicted previous changes that they had made.

Early problems like these resulted quite quickly in major conflict between the Department and the fledgling Authority, symbolised especially by the controversy over *Learning about AIDS*, a pack of teaching materials.

Learning about AIDS

Learning about AIDS had been inherited by the HEA from the HEC. It was co-sponsored by the charity AVERT and the HEA had agreed to publish the resultant teaching materials it produced. The HEA however had not anticipated the intervention of the Department of Health, which initially said it had cause for concern about interim materials in April 1987, just days after the creation of the HEA. Amongst their concerns were those related to the lifestyles section of the materials: 'The messages here are not inaccurate, but the line taken on promiscuity is different to that put forward in Government publicity. I wonder whether this is something on which the HEA would wish to consider its own policy?'(Letter from Elizabeth Shaw, AIDS unit, DHSS to John Hitchens, Head of Publicity, HEA, 14 April 1987). The materials had been referred to the Department of Health without the knowledge or consent of AVERT (Letter from Annabel Kanabus of AVERT to Dr Spencer Hagard, HEA, 20 July 1988). The Department's intervention delayed the availability of the interim materials and there was concern from AVERT that this should not happen with the final materials. Spencer Hagard, the Director of the HEA then apparently assured AVERT that the DHSS did not need to see the final materials. The final text of *Learning about AIDS* was approved by the HEA on 23 June 1988. However, a few days later AVERT was informed that the DHSS had asked to see the materials but that the HEA was suggesting the request be refused. AVERT agreed with this approach, but on 12 July AVERT was informed that the DHSS had ordered the HEA not to publish the material. After a series of crisis meetings and the exchange of lawyers' letters the HEA relinquished rights to *Learning about AIDS* and it was eventually published by academic publisher Churchill Livingstone.

The first HEA television advertising

There was government pressure on the HEA to produce its first set of advertising relatively quickly so that too much time wouldn't elapse without any public information campaign. Whereas, as we have seen, there had been delays within the DHSS in previous campaigns, HEA staff were to find that delays were not possible with the new campaign. Accordingly the ads were produced to a very tight schedule. A matter of days before it was to be launched, research indicated that the 'Disco' ad was not believable.

The ad showed a couple who have just met having one dance and then a drink, following which the man asks the woman 'back to my place'. The major problems in research were the lack of time they had known each other and the man's conversation, which was thought by market research respondents to consist of 'predictable clichés delivered in an embarrassingly predictable manner' (Reflexions, 1988: 14). 'At present, the couple are a "Kevin and Sharon" and written off as irrelevant' (1988: 15). The market researchers maintained that 'If the commercial had been believable, then the end sequence would have been effective . . . Unfortunately, as depicted, no genuine dilemma was proffered' (1988: 16). The conclusion of the research stated:

> The problems of characterisation could be overcome to a degree by rendering the dialogue inaudible. However, unless the film can be recut/reshot to produce scenes suggesting an evening spent together, it is unlikely that the vital self-identification can be achieved. (Reflexions, 1988: 18)

The problem for this strategy was time. As one HEA member told us:

> In February [1988], a week before the ad was to go out, the final development testing showed that the man's voice was wrong, that the kids didn't like him and so on. It was too late to take him out. The only things that could be done were sort of cosmetic, like they increased the decibels of the music so you couldn't hear what he was saying . . . It was all too fast, you see, the schedule was too tight to make these crucial changes.

As with the first set of adverts, very few of those involved in their production were happy with the outcome.

Changing agencies

Following this campaign the HEA decided to organise a repitch for the advertising contract for AIDS education. TBWA, the agency that had produced the campaign, had been inherited by the HEA from the earlier DHSS/COI campaigns. According to a close observer:

> The COI is very loyal to its agencies and if the account had not moved to the HEA, TBWA would have continued holding the account because everybody thought that they were doing a good job in difficult circumstances but nobody was very happy about the advertising, including TBWA. But given the viewpoint of the government, they were doing the best they could in the circumstances. (Market researcher)

There was no real trust between the HEA and the agency. As a TBWA source put it:

> The agency knew the Department of Health and the COI and vice versa and there was a considerable reciprocal trust, which is crucial with such a politically sensitive material. That degree of trust between the agency and the HEA never

existed . . . TBWA as a group of people and as an agency was very closely aligned with the Department of Health and the HEA was a new broom and it wanted to make that point clear and didn't wish to employ the effective employees of the Department of Health. That's simplistic [but] I think there was an element of that.

One symptom of this lack of trust was that both the agency and some market researchers felt that the HEA was to some extent reinventing the wheel in relation to research, pre-testing and advertising concepts. Harari himself became less and less personally involved:

> The HEA at that time was a new body with new personnel, that didn't entirely know what it was doing. Personally I was under the impression that it never knew what it was doing, one way or another. TBWA really only then had Sammy [Harari] who had very substantial credentials within the field and they really wanted somebody to work full time on it. Sammy wasn't going to work full time on it because he had other things to do, such as manage the agency. (TBWA source)

As a key market researcher put it:

> as far as I was concerned [we were] just going over the same ground, going right back over the whole gamut of possible motivations being explored. There was a potential campaign trying to promote condoms again in a variety of different ways . . . I read the reports . . . and they were basically the same as two or three years earlier and so nothing had changed . . . I suppose . . . personally I became less interested and other people [in the company] started to work on it more, because we were going right back to square one and the original or the first brief from the HEA took us right back to where we'd been a couple of years earlier: 'We need to know what people know about AIDS. We want to make people feel at risk.'

Other sources saw the move as linked to the appointment of John Flaherty as the new Director of Advertising at the HEA who, because of the high profile nature of the AIDS account, moved 'from being an unknown [to] one of the most important men in British advertising'. This observer, a market researcher on many of the AIDS campaigns viewed Flaherty as 'An ad agency groupie, I don't know what else to call him. He was anxious to make a name for himself too so he thought . . . what I need to do to raise my own personal profile is to move this account and he decided to organise a repitch.'

In addition TBWA was seen as an agency in decline by some observers. According to one market researcher: 'it was losing accounts and therefore it was not a fashionable agency to be with even though everybody recognised Sammy's link with government campaigns'. This was emphasised by HEA public affairs personnel, one of whom felt that 'TBWA was going through a terrible period. They were losing all their staff. That's why they got booted off. The ideas they were coming up with were not very good.' These problems were exacerbated by the personal tensions between the Director of the public affairs division, John Hitchens, and Sammy Harari of TBWA. As a member of the public affairs division put it, Hitchens: 'had some interpersonal problems with the people at TBWA'. Or, as a TBWA source put it: 'Hitchens and Sammy couldn't stand each other.'

The result of the repitch was that Boase, Massimi, Pollitt won the account. For some this was because it included a public relations 'opinion leader' strategy as well as an advertising strategy (although this was never to be a great success, as we show in Chapter 6). For others, however, the presentation by BMP and their closest rival were equally good, but BMP's analysis of the problem was not as good. However, they were awarded the account on the basis that they were a bigger agency: 'we were [therefore] confident that BMP could handle the inevitable hassle that goes with the AIDS campaign' (HEA official, public affairs division).

Divisions within the HEA

Department of Health intervention notwithstanding, there were further contests inside the Health Education Authority which had marked impacts on advertising strategy and content. The structure of the HEC was reorganised with the creation of the HEA and the AIDS division created headed by newly appointed Director Susan Perl. The AIDS division worked closely with the researchers in the public health division and with the public affairs division, which dealt with media relations, advertising and publishing.

Within the HEA there were a variety of tensions. These included resentments about the AIDS division, which swallowed the largest chunk of HEA resources and had the highest profile. As one well placed member of the AIDS unit put it:

> In the HEA the AIDS division was seen to be a problem so in many ways the whole inertia of the bureaucracy was mobilised against it, if you can say such a thing, and from personnel down to travel to publishing they saw this nasty new thrusting little unit come in and forcing all sorts of things on them, forcing them to do work they hadn't done for years . . . All these bright new things wandering round the place, people with no experience in the Health Education Council, getting contracts, getting paid more than such and such – all that level of bureaucratic dispute went on to the point where I felt very often that the rest of the HEA was deliberately setting up the AIDS division for failure . . . It was perceived by many people within the HEA that [the HEC] was abolished because of AIDS – Norman Fowler abolished it because of AIDS and then inflicted this nasty little unit on them.

There were also tensions in the HEA between various professional groupings. Those with a media or advertising background (in the public affairs division) and those with a research or health education background (in the AIDS or other divisions) were often at loggerheads. The former Director of the AIDS division, Susan Perl, has characterised the differences as a 'clash of cultures' in which the public affairs personnel were concerned with 'impact' while the health educators were concerned with 'sensitivity' (Perl, 1991: 15).[1] As one member of the AIDS division saw it

> Sue Perl was widely perceived to be weak and she was not trusted by the advertising men who had – you know, they had very gorgeous wives with long blonde

hair and they drove sports cars and they don't take easily to having women bossing them. So they never respected her, they thought she was a wimp that didn't know what she was talking about and all of those things and then this sets a culture.

The AIDS division was a problem, according to one member of the public affairs division:

a separate AIDS division began to be built up inside the HEA with people committed to the subject, very knowledgeable about it and very concerned with what people in the field, who might have suffered from HIV, who were part of the gay community, who were in some ways associated with AIDS education might feel about a combination of words, and it was at this point that the whole thing fell apart.

In the view of some of the professional communicators in the HEA as well as successive advertising agencies the health educators were naive about processes of mass communication and influence. As a different member of the public affairs division put it:

we and the advertising agency [felt] that we should go on the 'save your life' approach, whereas the AIDS division tended to feel by and large we should try and make safe sex trendy, which I still believe is an impossibility . . . We had three attempts at that before it finally bit the dust . . . Ministers threw that out finally.

For the promotional professionals the alternative to broad cultural change was to take a simple message and give it great impact. One member of the AIDS division reports being told:

'you can't make an omelette without breaking eggs', and that 'you have to be cruel to be kind', that AIDS is really serious and you have to show it in all its full gory horror in order for people to take this seriously.

For some health educators, however, the problem was the application of product marketing techniques to an area of very complex cultural realignment.

The desire of advertising personnel to 'scare them rigid', as one health educator put it, was evident in the proposed strap line for one of the most talked about HEA ads. The ad featured a photograph of a conventionally 'attractive' model over the text 'If this woman had the virus which leads to AIDS, in a few years' time she could look like the person over the page'. Over the page in the proposed advert was the same photograph with the strap line 'Frightening isn't it'. The ad was intended to make people familiar with the notion that people with HIV can look and feel perfectly healthy. For health educators this was partly to instil the knowledge that HIV and AIDS are not the same and partly to counter media images of people with HIV or AIDS as wasted and death-like. For advertisers, however, the purpose was more centrally to scare people into safer sex. Health educators argued that this was a fear-inducing approach which would not work and that to some extent it stigmatised people with HIV as deliberately trying to infect people. When the ad eventually appeared the strap line had been changed, in a compromise, to read 'Worrying isn't it'.

The same issues were raised with a further advert in the same series. The purpose of this ad was again to improve public understanding about the relationship between HIV and AIDS. It raised the whole question of the underlying philosophy of the advertising campaigns and their target audience. The advert consisted of the slogan 'What's the difference between HIV and AIDS? – Time'. For the advertisers the ad had impact and they could show with market research that it 'worked' at the level of some public understandings. However, the problem for some health educators and many people in the AIDS field, not to mention for people with HIV and AIDS, was that the ad was again using scare tactics to frighten people into safer sex. The message it gave to people with HIV was not that there is a difference between HIV and AIDS but that 'it is only a matter of time before you have AIDS'. The ad was hastily withdrawn after its first publication, following a large number of protests from HIV and AIDS workers.

Furthermore, the culture of the advertising agency and its procedures didn't easily gel with public health approaches. In particular much seemed to be lost in the translation between HEA briefings for the agency and the advertising concepts and copy which came back from the agency:

> you would find that [a brief] would go out [to the agency] and then suddenly it would come back and people in the AIDS programme would be upset because it never seemed like the brief that they had originally given and they would always say 'What is going on here?' (AIDS division official)

One member of the AIDS division argued that the problem was the inability of the agency to understand public health approaches without recontextualising them within the conceptual apparatus of advertising:

> When the advertising agency finally discovered the difference between AIDS and HIV they re-understood it or recontextualised it in a certain set of ways and they believed that therefore there were large numbers of people walking around who had HIV who were actually infecting others and you couldn't tell. So their whole approach in treating it was to see them somehow as kind of dirty double-agents. It was the same as the woman – in three years time this woman will look like the one on the next page – and when you actually turn the page, you recontextualise her as remorseless: that quite happy cheery looking face suddenly looks much nastier when you turn the page because she has clearly been infecting people for three years and doesn't give a damn and she hasn't even changed her hairstyle – I remember arguing that it was quite different to say 'You can't tell who's infected' from 'They don't even know themselves'. But they wouldn't take the 'They don't even know themselves' logic and they much preferred the 'you can't tell who's infected' logic.

Part of the problem in this view was the constraints imposed by advertising aimed at an audience assumed to be HIV negative:

> When you look at all of the public advertising it assumes that the reader of that doesn't have HIV and that by doing these things or following these things, if you understand what they are, you can avoid HIV. Therefore inevitably it's implied that you avoid certain kinds of people especially when you portray them, and you portray HIV as always the property of a person, [when actually] it's the property of a social relation or sexual relationship and is never something that exists on its

own. Therefore if you assume a seronegative audience, you can never portray HIV as a risk to avoid other than as people to avoid, but this is something that advertising agencies are really incapable of understanding.

These differences led to HEA demands for advertising personnel – account managers and planners, and particularly creatives – to be more intensively briefed by health educators. This was resisted by the agency in relation to account managers and planners, who were the contacts with the HEA. But the creatives themselves were even more jealously guarded. A further frustration at the HEA was that the creatives were not accessible:

> The creatives never came in, I never saw them. They were definitely like some holy being. It was described that way, they worked in a white room and they are on £200,000 a year or whatever and they just were left alone and fed bits of information. I just remember I used to giggle about some creator in a big white room, mystical almost.

In the view of one member of the AIDS division many AIDS specialists become seduced by the aura and status of advertising:

> The kind of glory and power that advertising agencies are able to exert so that they can take the agenda from public health experts and declare that this is how we have to do it . . . They're very, very persuasive, taking a kind of old social democratic tradition of public health doctors and fusty people from smelly buildings, and to take them into these glorious plate glass and potted plants establishments . . .

In this view the power and ethos of advertising agencies worked to undermine public health approaches.

The conflicts between public health and 'impact' approaches resulted in the drawing up of the 'ten commandments' which governed what could and could not be said in advertising, with the objective of avoiding 'victim-blaming, stereo-typing and stigmatising' (Perl, 1991: 14). But the advertising agency: 'found that the ten commandments were ensuring that our hands were tied behind our backs in producing an effective piece of communication'. Similarly, public affairs division staff complained that: 'It really did attempt to castrate the advertising for no good reason at all . . . if we had adhered to it, it would have produced advertising that wouldn't have been worth paying for.'

These divisions, as the language used about them by our interviewees hints, were also inflected by gender assumptions. The 'castration' of advertising creativity by 'feminist' concerns about the portrayal of women and about their power in heterosexual encounters was a source of conflict for both advertisers and public affairs personnel.

The divisions over approaches to health education and the difficulties in the relationship with the Department of Health, meant that the process of producing advertising on AIDS was never straightforward. Referring to the four main HEA representatives who liaised with the agency, Kaye Wellings, John Hitchens, John Flaherty and Susan Perl, one advertiser felt: 'They all had very different ideas about communication as I remember and they certainly couldn't agree between themselves about the way these things should be done.'

Together with other difficulties, these factors combined to make the production of AIDS advertising a tremendously complex matter. A member of the HEA public affairs division explained some of the difficulties:

> Normally the way it should work is that one bit of the HEA says to public affairs this is what we want – this is a brief. We give the brief to the agency, the agency refines it and comes back; it's approved. The agency goes away and does some rough work, brings it back. We say 'This is on brief, this is non brief, can you do that?' They go away, they come back, you've got something you're happy with and they're happy with. You show it to the sponsor of the division, they say 'fine' or whatever and then you run it. Whereas in this case it was endless chasing back and forward, endless meetings, endless rows with the Department, criticisms from pre-testing, pre-testing blows it out. It was just much, much more complicated than things normally are.

Advertising vs. community development

Besides the conflict over the content of advertising, there was a more fundamental critique of the public education campaign. This came especially from those health educators who favoured a community development approach to AIDS education. At best mass advertising provided a useful context against which more focused and targeted work (both persuasive materials and direct educative contact) could proceed. At worst it blamed the victims for their health status, reinforced the deviant status of drug users, gay men or other groups, obscured the structural and cultural barriers to 'healthy' behaviour and allowed the government to mislead the public into thinking that something was being done (see Daykin and Naidoo, 1995). Naturally, those who favoured such approaches tended to be even further out of sympathy with the approach of public affairs personnel who emphasised impact. By contrast with the HEA, the Welsh Health Promotion Authority (HPAW) was able to emphasise such issues in its strategy documents, using terminology like 'empowerment' openly. One member of the Welsh body saw clear differences between the HEA and HPAW:

> There is quite a strong feeling in [HPAW] that all this money on flashy media adverts is of very limited use. That you can use that to raise awareness and perhaps to convey a minimum of information but that if you were really talking about changing people's behaviour you would have to come down to issues of empowerment. Because most people are behaving in ways that we have labelled as unhealthy for reasons that are structural then you are not going to change it by throwing a leaflet at them or showing them a trendy thing on telly. We talk quite specifically about empowerment in our strategic plans.

Although in 1989–90 the HEA allocated only 1.5% of its total budget to community projects (Brindle, 1989a), the Department of Health preferred the HEA to concentrate on a small number of major advertising campaigns. Health ministers objected when the HEA decided to drop television advertising from its campaign in winter 1988. David Mellor stated that he was 'highly sceptical' of the value of community campaigns (Prentice, 1988).

In May 1989 this view was reinforced by Mellor when he responded to the Authority's 1988–89 annual review (Hall, C., 1989).

HEA and activists: men who have sex with men

There was one further set of relationships which impacted on public education materials and on the credibility and morale of the HEA, to which it is worth drawing brief attention. The HEA was also involved in extensive 'consultation' with activists, voluntary organisations, health educators and others. One key area where 'the field' was recruited to advise on public education efforts was in the development of the 'men who have sex with men' initiative. Many of the problems of campaigns outlined above, such as lack of correspondence between briefs and advertising ideas (Hart, 1993), intervention from the Department of Health and unclear lines of command, also afflicted this campaign.

The collaboration originated in a consortium set up following the January 1988 conference of the Network of Voluntary Organisations, which included the HEA and a variety of health education experts to run a campaign for 'men who have sex with men'. The consortium then 'fell apart' when the voluntary organisations involved perceived that the HEA was 'not going to be an equal partner' but take control and use the voluntary organisations as an advisory group (letter by Nick Partridge to Health Minister David Mellor, labelled private and confidential, 19 December 1988). From the earliest meetings there were conflicting expectations and a steady downward revision by the HEA of the scope of the project. At the first meeting to discuss proposals from the Terrence Higgins Trust (THT) there was 'deep concern, frustration and anger' when it became apparent that the budget set aside by the HEA was much lower than had been anticipated (letter to Susan Perl, HEA, from Nick Partridge, 18 April 1988). In early May the HEA proposals were described by Nick Partridge of the THT as 'rather boring' compared with the original proposals by non-HEA members of the committee. By June 'some concern' was expressed that the project was 'constantly reducing in its scale' (Minutes of the 'Men who have sex with men' meeting, 10 June 1988).

Later in the year Nick Partridge wrote to David Mellor claiming that 'our relationship with the HEA is tense and difficult and on the verge of breakdown'. Also in December there was an attempt to draw up a constitution for the group at which a change of name from 'advisory' to 'planning group' was mooted and 'generally agreed' but the title of the group was never changed. While a constitution was drawn up which charged the group not simply with an advisory capacity but with formulating 'medium and long term strategies', many of the group members felt that their advice was ignored ('A constitution for the men who have sex with men advisory group', 12 May 1989). They also complained that they were not kept informed of developments in campaigns, were not able effectively to question the work of the advertising agency or the methodology of market research and, most fundamentally, had little input into formulating strategy. As one member of the group put it:

> The members of that advisory committee have at times felt extremely frustrated because of an initial difference of expectations about what role that committee played. The committee members felt that they were setting a strategy – for men who have sex with men – with the principal officer in the HEA and it subsequently became clear that campaigns have to go through a very laborious process within the HEA which seems basically designed to weed out content which is politically difficult or organisationally difficult and that compromises the work. The HEA seems to be very much influenced by the advertising industry.

Another member of the group said:

> All of their very wordy documents are about consultation, co-operation and so on but ultimately much of it is window-dressing. Consultation means going over to their building for a discussion session at which materials are presented and whatever comments you make, they very rarely get changed or they will be changed totally and you won't be told about it.

In practice the advisory committee were, according to a third member, only able to

> tweak it and twiddle it and say we prefer this picture to that one, but not a lot more. Or, we'll be able to say that's a dreadful sub-heading and that's about it. So it's a kind of damage limitation rather than actually using the voluntary organisations to input anything constructive and productive.

There were two particular areas where members of the committee tried to intervene. The first related to the methods used to pre-test and evaluate advertising concepts and finished ads and the second was the relations between the advisory group and the advertising agency BMP. Both of these points related to the process by which decisions on promotional materials were taken. Some on the committee felt that their expertise was being ignored in favour of market research which was seriously flawed.

> They're trying to do safer sex work and health education work on a model of practices created for selling soap powder. Rather than using health education expertise and deciding what will probably work, they're using marketing techniques. [They take] them out to small groups of people and if they say 'No, this isn't what we want' then if there are political pressures to dump it, it gets dumped. Now we know that if you [go] into a school and say 'What kind of advertisements work?' the reply is 'Show us people dying'. But we know that doesn't work in the long term. So they're caught very badly between the manipulation of the ad man and the manipulation of the HEA and the politics that they have to be aware of [the pressures of the right] and common-sense well-thought-out health education techniques. So people end up being very frustrated.

Furthermore, the group became concerned about the process by which advertising ideas were translated between the advisory group, HEA health educators, the HEA public affairs personnel involved in writing briefs for the agency and the response of the agency. It was felt that much was being lost in the translation and that the advertising agency was unable even to understand the queries and criticisms of the advisory group. Such feelings were emphasised when proposed advertising material bore little apparent relationship to the original briefings (Hart, 1993). At one meeting Peter Scott, a member of the advisory group, suggested that BMP personnel attend a series of training workshops on gay men and AIDS. Group members also suggested that they become involved in discussions on methodology with the advertising agency and both quantitative and qualitative market researchers (BMRB and Reflexions). Although two presentations were organised, one by BMP on the methodology of focus group research, and the other on the methodology of the gay bar survey by BMRB, both of the requests from the group to have a role in training or evaluation were refused by the HEA.

In the end many of the advisory group came to the view that they simply functioned to legitimise the HEA. One example followed a complaint from Manchester gay centre about a leaflet produced by the men who have sex with men programme. Derek Bodell of the HEA buttressed his reply by referring to the involvement of the advisory group: 'They have and continue to have involvement in all aspects of our work, including the production of this leaflet' (Letter from Derek Bodell, Senior Programmes Officer, AIDS division, HEA, to Daryl Stevenson, Manchester Gay Centre, 6 December 1989). At a later meeting 'there was some concern that Derek Bodell had said the leaflet "had the full support of the group" . . . the group felt that this was not the case and wished this to be understood . . . The general feeling was that [the] leaflet needed revision as soon as possible as there were a number of points in it which were seriously inaccurate or incomplete or not likely to be understood by the majority of the gay population' (minutes of the Men's Advisory Group meeting, 19 March 1990). Some members of the group concluded that their participation was being used to buttress the HEA's image amongst gay men: 'it's a window-dressing activity so that they can seem to be consulting but they don't have to take any of our recommendations'.

The HEA under siege

From its creation to the early 1990s the HEA suffered persistent problems brought about to a large extent by its relationship with central government, but also by internal divisions and conflicts. These came to a head towards the end of 1989, with a series of cancelled and postponed advertising campaigns, a radical reorganisation of the Authority which downgraded the importance of AIDS and led to a number of resignations, and a formal industrial dispute.

For many, part of the problem was a lack of leadership and the role of Chief Executive Spencer Hagard and chair of the Authority, Sir Donald Maitland. At the beginning, Spencer Hagard was very 'gung-ho' (member of the AIDS division): 'like any new chief executive [he] came in with amazing promises and then he fucked up a couple of things and the reins started getting pulled in' (member of the public affairs division). Later, Hagard was 'widely perceived as weak' (member of the AIDS division). 'The feeling [was that] he was not on our side and he was a government stooge. The feeling too that he had yielded all control to Sir Donald Maitland was a big issue.' For one member of the public affairs division, the internal disputes should have been resolved at a higher level: 'someone at the head of the HEA needed to basically plump for one view of how it should be done or the other. That leadership was lacking.'

Maitland, formerly a diplomat and prime ministerial Press Secretary to Edward Heath, had been appointed in 1989 as chairman of the Authority to replace Sir Brian Bailey. He quickly became 'much more involved' than his predecessor. This involvement was described by a member of the AIDS division:

> If there were pressures from Donald Maitland, it was really not of a substantive or ideological or moral type. It's because he was very anxious not to have any more hoohahs with government. So he would encourage us – not necessarily insist, but encourage us – to go further in compromising on the material before it went up to government, than I would have.

Maitland also instituted a system for more direct communication with ministers, rather than material being passed from the HEA up the line to the Minister through departmental civil servants. This was seen as extraordinary by other health educators, such as a member of the Health Promotion Authority of Wales:

> an advert [is] vetted not by their Board, [or] their senior paid staff which would be the case in this outfit, it is vetted by the chairman of the Authority who then sends it directly to the Minister. It doesn't go through civil servants and of course the civil servants are in a right old snot about it and that means that they are generally feeling more pissed off and antagonistic. It is not the HEA officer's fault but that is not helping. I think they are now developing a system where the civil servants get copies at the same time. But I find that astonishing because I do come from a bureaucratic background and the idea of the chairman – which is really the policy level, it is the broad guidance level – being involved in the nitty gritty of deciding whether an advert goes out or not, which is really a matter of professional expertise, seemed to me a bit bizarre.

Maitland's involvement became a public issue at the end of 1989. A series of events appeared to suggest both a waning of interest in AIDS as a policy priority (cf. Street, 1993) and a shift towards more punitive and moralistic policy responses (Berridge, 1996). In July 1989 the all-party parliamentary group on AIDS alleged that the proposed national sex survey was being 'delayed by the Department of Health' (*Independent; Daily Mail*, 29 July 1989). In September the government formally withdrew from funding the survey.[2] A week later it emerged that the cabinet AIDS committee had been disbanded (*Sunday Correspondent*, 17 September 1989). In September and then again in November an HEA advertising campaign featuring 'experts' talking about HIV and AIDS was postponed (see Emily Bell, 'AIDS: sex, lies and red tape', *Observer*, 11 February 1990; *The Times*, 25 November 1989). The ads were eventually screened in February 1990. A campaign to promote condoms scheduled first for October and then for December was also postponed, although it had been given the go-ahead by Health Minister David Mellor the previous July. The aim of the adverts, according to the HEA, was to promote 'an atmosphere which suggests that using condoms is a normal part of modern sensible sexual behaviour' (*The Times*; *Guardian*, 17 July 1989). The Department of Health said the campaign had only been 'postponed' (*Sunday Times*, 12 November 1989), but it never appeared. Maitland was centrally involved in both these decisions and, according to some sources, himself 'advised' and 'suggested' to successive ministers David Mellor and Virginia Bottomley that the campaigns should not run (*The Times*; *Guardian*, 17 July 1989).

In November it emerged that the HEA was to be reorganised just days after the intervention of Lord Kilbracken in the debate reported by the *Sun* as 'Straight Sex Cannot Give You AIDS – Official'. In the reorganisation the public affairs division was split up and the AIDS division downgraded. As a result its Director, Susan Perl and Deputy Mukesh Kapila were substantially downgraded and both resigned shortly afterwards, together with other key figures in the AIDS campaign in the public affairs division. NUJ members in the public affairs division entered into formal dispute with the Authority over the changes. The *Journalist* (January 1990) noted that: 'Much of the AIDS public education campaign has suffered interference from the Department of Health, and HEA workers now fear the shake-up is what the Department wants.'

However, the reorganisation of the HEA and the presence of Donald Maitland did not completely remove the potential for misunderstanding and conflict between the HEA and the Department. Conflict continued, and almost inevitably further government moves followed. In 1994 Health Minister Brian Mawhinney banned a teenage guide to sex produced by the HEA, declaring that it was 'smutty' (Walsh, 1996). He had apparently not been aware of the booklet *Your Pocket Guide to Sex*, until he was contacted by journalists (Berridge, 1996). By the end of 1994 following a review of the HEA instituted by Mawhinney, it was announced that the HEA would lose much of its automatic funding and become a commissioning body. This meant that it would have to bid for contracts for AIDS education, another means of ensuring that it did as it was told.

Conclusions

The AIDS public education campaign was dogged with difficulties from the beginning. Because of its great political sensitivity, there was simultaneously a very high level of uninterest and of interest in the production of education materials. Ministerial and prime ministerial intervention, interdepartmental divisions and internal divisions within the DHSS/DoH were all important in the first phase of the campaign. When the campaign moved to the HEA, the role of the DoH and of other government ministries was crucial. However, there was also a series of disputes inside the HEA which were of significance and the HEA had an uneasy relationship with AIDS activists. The impact of tensions between the Department and the HEA together with all the other conflicts within the HEA and the interventions from ministers resulted in censorship, compromised campaigns, delayed adverts and confusing advice.

Given this picture of conflict, negotiation and struggle, it seems simplistic to refer to the campaign in terms of the four major positions outlined in Chapter 1. The campaign clearly was not a rational, technical and bureaucratic response to AIDS, nor was it simply the outcome of a process of moral rearmament, as the critical view would have it. Homophobia in high places there certainly was, but other factors such as bureaucratic squabbles, professional rivalries and poor organisation were also important. To see the campaigns simply as immoral, as the moral lobby did, seems as far fetched as to see the campaign as an unholy alliance between politically correct gay activists and moralist prudery, as libertarians have argued.

The process was a lot more complex than each of these positions could allow. Nevertheless, the struggle over the campaign did have certain determinate outcomes, which were the result of contests for definition being won and lost. The policy arena is not equally open to all sides in the competition for definition. Clearly, some organisations and individuals (especially central government and the medical orthodoxy) occupy strategic positions for decision making and others (AIDS activists, gay men, people with AIDS) tended to be marginalised.

The chief property of the campaign was not that it was homophobic or liberal, or moralistic, or even simply factual. But there certainly were problems with the campaign's portrayal of women, of gay men, of 'the general population' and, most revealingly, its lack of address to people with HIV/AIDS. The chief problem with the advertisements themselves was their lack of clarity. With a knowledge of the conflicts and contests which occurred in the production of the campaign it is possible to read the text of some adverts as an index of the relative power of the various factions. In the press campaigns of 1988–89, for example, the advice on safer sex was as follows: 'Obviously the more people you sleep with the more chance you have of becoming infected. But having fewer partners is only part of the answer. Safer sex also means using a condom, or even having sex that avoids penetration.' The advice starts with the dominant government approach, which has been to issue moral guidance under the cover of a public health message. It is interesting that there has been a resistance to overtly moral messages. This is followed by the straightforward condom message favoured by the medical establishment and by some AIDS activists. Last and very definitely least in the relative power stakes is the influence of a feminist/health education agenda which stresses 'healthy sexuality' and alternatives to penetration. We can see that the HEA is not entirely at one on this issue by the use of the word 'even' as if non-penetrative sex is recognised by the advertisers as not quite a serious option.

Notes

1. Although there were also other divisions. Most notably within the public affairs division, some press office staff tended to side with the researchers and health educators over questions of sensitivity, but not always over questions of communication, as we show in Chapter 6 (cf. Berridge, 1996: 198).

2. There is some dispute over whether Thatcher was involved in this decision as the *Sunday Times* alleged (10 September 1989) or whether it was done in cabinet by George Younger, Douglas Hurd and Kenneth Baker, as Baker has claimed (Baker, 1993: 251). It is possible that there were at least two interventions since the Chief Medical Officer has claimed that the survey had not been decisively rejected by the time the *Sunday Times* published its report (Acheson, 1994: viii).

3

News Variations

Peter Beharrell

The government education campaign was only one component of the information available to the public about HIV and AIDS. The most prominent sources of public information were the mass media. It was the early media coverage which provided the context within which the later government campaign had to operate – and against which it often had to work. This chapter examines some common features of media coverage as well as changes in AIDS reporting from the mid-1980s to the early 1990s. It explores differences within the coverage and identifies the limits of press reporting (for details of the sample see Appendix).

The response of the British press to AIDS has been more varied than has often been assumed. These differences were particularly significant over the key issue of heterosexual transmission of HIV which underpinned the government campaign. A section of the right wing popular press – not the tabloid newspapers as a whole – vociferously attacked the government's education strategy, arguing that there was little risk of heterosexual transmission and that an epidemic amongst the 'general population' was a myth. Other tabloid newspapers and most of the broadsheet press (at least until the early 1990s), however, showed varying degrees of support for the advertising campaign.

The changing AIDS story

Since its emergence in the public sphere, AIDS has risen and fallen in media prominence. Figure 3.1 shows the level of AIDS coverage in the British press over five months from November 1986 to March 1987. Figure 3.2 shows a three year period from November 1988 to October 1991. The shifting amount of attention given to AIDS is not just a function of changes in its intrinsic news value. It also reflects the material impact of AIDS and the development of the debate around it. In particular the high peaks of the last two months of 1986 reflect speculation about the awaited government campaign as the cabinet AIDS committee met for the first time in November. In December many items concerned the controversial speech made by the Chief Constable of Greater Manchester which referred to the 'obnoxious practices' and 'degenerate conduct' of sections of society

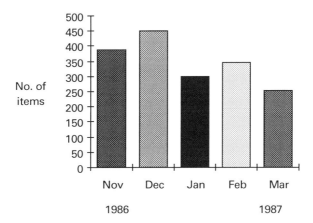

Figure 3.1 *HIV/AIDS coverage, national daily and Sunday press, November 1986 to March 1987*

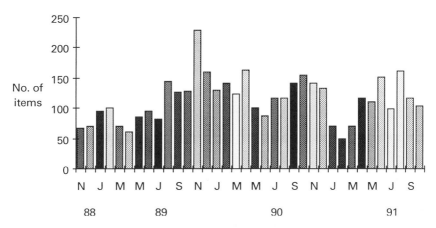

Figure 3.2 *HIV/AIDS coverage, national daily and Sunday press, November 1988 to October 1991*

'swirling around in a human cesspit of their own making'. A high level of press interest was sustained in 1987 by the national TV advertisement and the posting of information leaflets to every household, together with the fact-finding visit in February by the Health Secretary to hospitals and hospices in America.

By late 1988, AIDS had become a less prominent news item. The renewed press interest towards the end of 1989 reflected a growing discontent with the official orthodox view on the risk of heterosexual transmission of HIV. The high peak in November was reached with the Kilbracken affair and this continued into December. The smaller peak in April 1990 reflects the extra coverage devoted to the deaths of a number of celebrities. Press reporting was boosted again in September and October 1990 by the campaign for compensation by haemophiliacs infected with HIV, and November and December coverage reflected the WHO publicity on the threat of AIDS to women and children worldwide. Princess Diana's newsworthiness was evident in the spate of stories in April 1991 as she visited children's hospitals and in August 1991 as she was reported attending the sickbed and sub-sequent funeral of a friend. The relatively high peak of June 1991 indicates the renewed media interest in AIDS prompted by the week-long inter-national conference in Florence.

Changes in the amount of media interest in AIDS are complemented by changes in the shape and scope of media reporting. In the early period (between 1981 and 1985) there was a slow build-up of coverage as news-papers overcame their reluctance to report AIDS. This initial reluctance was largely because of its associations with gay men. And this became the rationale for the next phase, the period of the 'gay plague'. Partly as a reaction to this type of coverage, the government was spurred into action on AIDS in 1986. There was a concerted attempt to refocus attention on 'the general population', which was largely successful. However, following this, news sources in the orthodox camp moved down a gear and, as the immediate furore of this 'national emergency' period died down (between mid-1987 and late 1989), the attempt to label AIDS as a gay disease picked up media prominence once again, helped by the fact that some of the more extravagant predictions about the heterosexual epidemic had failed to come to fruition.

It was also helped by the loosening of the coalition of government, medi-cine and AIDS organisations. Now some activists themselves tried to focus attention on gay men since they were bearing the brunt of AIDS and being relatively ignored in policy terms. The crescendo of the backlash, measured by the sheer amount of coverage, came in 1989 with the Kilbracken affair (which we examine below). Following this controversy, the orthodoxy has continued to be attacked, in particular with the argument that HIV does not cause AIDS. However, since the peak associated with the orthodoxy and the government campaign in December 1986, AIDS Week in spring 1987 and the peak associated with the backlash in November 1989, the newsworthi-ness of AIDS has declined. Although AIDS still attracts more attention than many other diseases, AIDS stories in the mid-1990s tend to be pegged to particular news events such as announcements of health workers infected with HIV or routine coverage of official reports or scientific research. These changes in the debate around AIDS have to be understood in conjunction with changes in the editorial lines of different newspapers and variations within and between papers. In the next section we use the example of the Kilbracken affair of November 1989 to provide a guide to the media politics of the confrontation between the medical orthodoxy and the dissident view of AIDS.

The press, 'straight sex' and the Kilbracken controversy

As the predicted heterosexual epidemic did not materialise and official estimates were revised downward, attacks on the orthodox medical position began to mount in the press. These were to reach their zenith in November 1989 with the intervention of Labour Peer, Lord Kilbracken. A minority voice on the All Party Parliamentary Group on AIDS, Kilbracken claimed that only one case of AIDS from heterosexually transmitted HIV could be found in the official figures. Several newspapers made his assertion a prominent news item. The *Sun* declared: 'STRAIGHT SEX CANNOT GIVE YOU AIDS – OFFICIAL' (17 November 1989).

Kilbracken's arguments did not distinguish between the syndrome and the virus. He quoted the Department of Health total for developed cases of AIDS illnesses, 2,372, and then claimed that the official figures could demonstrate only one person who was not a member of a 'high risk group'. His critics argued that the real danger should be measured by totals of known HIV infections, or by estimates of likely or probable levels of HIV infection. These figures would be much higher, indicating future AIDS cases resulting from current levels of risk activity.

The *Sun*, *Daily Mail* and *Daily Express* strongly supported Kilbracken. The *Daily Mail*'s front page announced: 'THE TRUTH ABOUT AIDS – Of 2,372 confirmed cases only one person caught disease in a normal relationship.' Its leader column boasted: 'as this newspaper has repeatedly pointed out, the Government's advertising campaign – mainly beamed at heterosexuals indulging in normal sex – is focused on the wrong group. Now Lord Kilbracken has reinforced our argument by obtaining the relevant figures' (*Daily Mail*, 17 November 1989). The *Daily Express* also backed these claims. Its front page read: 'NORMAL SEX IS SAFE ROW – Ads warning over AIDS misrepresent risk says peer' and the editorial declared: 'It will not do for the Department of Health to decry Lord Kilbracken's claim . . . For the Department's own figures bear him out' (*Daily Express*, 17 November 1989). The *Sun*'s editorial went even further:

> At last the truth can be told. The killer disease AIDS can only be caught by homosexuals, bisexuals, junkies or anyone who has received a tainted blood transfusion. FORGET the television adverts, FORGET the poster campaigns, FORGET the endless boring TV documentaries and FORGET the idea that ordinary heterosexual people can contract AIDS. They can't . . . the risk of catching AIDS if you are a heterosexual is 'statistically invisible'. In other words impossible. So now we know – anything else is just homosexual propaganda. And should be treated accordingly. (17 November 1989)[1]

These views were typically backed up by assertions of conspiracy: 'AIDS – THE HOAX OF THE CENTURY . . . Why it paid prudes, gays and Business to scare us all' (*Sun*, 18 November 1989). In the *Daily Mail*, columnist Ann Leslie voiced a similar view:

> This newspaper is growing weary of pointing out the facts . . . 'Everyone' is NOT at risk from AIDS: only those who belong to high-risk groups . . . So why have

we, the taxpayers, been forced to waste money on this costly and farcical campaign? First of all, because our government, like many others, fell for militant gay propaganda. (*Daily Mail*, 18 November 1989)

Meanwhile, the *Sun*'s reporting of the Kilbracken story resulted in a complaint to the Press Council, a complaint which resulted in an apology and correction (*Sun*, 12 July 1990).

However, other tabloid newspapers behaved differently. The *Daily Star* and *Today* did not report Lord Kilbracken's claims at all, while the *Daily Mirror* responded robustly to the attack on the orthodox view. Kilbracken's criticism of the campaign and his call for it to be abandoned were very briefly reported on the day: 'The risk of catching AIDS from normal sex is "statistically invisible" it was claimed yesterday' (*Daily Mirror*, 17 November 1989). However, the following day the *Daily Mirror* reported the counterarguments as the medical and scientific experts responded: 'Straight sex AIDS warning – Thousands of men and women are at risk of catching AIDS from straight sex, researchers warned yesterday.'

Amongst the broadsheet newspapers, only the *Daily Telegraph* contained a news item giving Kilbracken any credibility. The *Guardian*, *Times* and *Independent* carried regular reports from specialist correspondents on the health and AIDS 'beats', and little support was given to Kilbracken's claims. In fact, his views were dealt with in terms of the problem they posed for health education. The *Guardian*'s response, under the byline of the science correspondent, was typical: 'New waves of AIDS predicted – scientists paint a bleak picture as public education is cut and voluntary campaigners strive to combat false sense of security' (*Guardian*, 1 December 1989).

In *The Times*, Kilbracken was reported only in terms of the unfavourable reaction: 'Peer's claim on AIDS condemned – anger at "misleading" remarks.' A host of official authorities were quoted denouncing Kilbracken (*The Times*, 18 November 1989).

Overall the orthodox view was more prominent than the dissident view. The coverage of the intervention of Lord Kilbracken provides a brief indication of the battle lines in the press coverage of AIDS. In the next sections we examine the editorial orientations of both the tabloid and broadsheet press.

The tabloid press and the assault on the medical orthodoxy

Although the attack on the medical orthodoxy had no support from television news (see Chapter 4), sections of the tabloid press were sympathetic. The *Sun* repeatedly stated that the government's message was untrue – AIDS was not a problem for 'straight' society. Its response to the 1988 advertising campaign was characteristic: 'Why do these ads show only boy and girl couples? Showing love's young dream makes pretty pictures. The truth is uglier. There have been 44 cases in Britain involving heterosexuals.

But a massive 1079 homosexuals have been affected' (*Sun*, 3 March 1988). An editorial denounced the following year's campaign in similar terms: 'Wrong Sex – The feminists are complaining about the use of a beautiful girl in advertisements warning about AIDS. They point out that in the past six months there have been only eight cases involving women. That is a fair argument. AIDS is overwhelmingly a homosexual disease. Maybe pictures of gay men would be less appealing. But they would serve more purpose' (*Sun*, 13 February 1989).

Daily Express editorials voiced the same fears about pressure groups influencing the message: 'Time to tell the truth about AIDS . . . the government and the health education authorities still refuse to focus attention on those whose way of life makes them more vulnerable to the AIDS virus: homosexuals and drug addicts. Still we are subjected to a campaign of mis-information and dis-information to convince us that we are all at risk' (*Daily Express*, 28 August 1989).

The *Daily Mail* also generally opposed the government's AIDS policy. Editorials criticised anonymised testing because it did not reveal the identity of individual 'carriers', attacked the education campaigns because they were not targeted at the homosexual and drug injecting 'risk groups' but welcomed the Prime Minister's veto on the national sexual behaviour survey. In what was to become an influential article, Sir Reginald Murley, former President of the Royal College of Surgeons and sponsor of Family and Youth Concern, put his case. His prime target was the HEA advert in the press featuring two identical photographs of a young woman: 'If this woman had the virus which leads to AIDS, in a few years' time she could look like the person over the page. Worrying isn't it . . .' (reproduced in Chapter 8). He argued: 'a single picture would be more appropriate with the caption: "Fortunately this young woman is unlikely to develop AIDS unless she becomes a drug addict or allows herself to be buggered"' (*Daily Mail*, 7 November 1989).

Different popular press responses

As with the coverage of Kilbracken, not all the tabloids followed the same line. A different approach was taken by the *Daily Mirror* and *Today*. The *Daily Mirror*'s routine news coverage and features expressed broad sympathy with an orthodox health education view concerning HIV transmission risks. Characteristically, the feature marking World AIDS Day 1988 summed up:

> And what we must never forget is that there is still no cure or vaccine for AIDS. So the way to stop its spread is through information, education and changes in human behaviour. Only then will there be any hope of controlling this deadly scourge. (*Daily Mirror*, 1 December 1988)

A popular tabloid such as the *Mirror* did, on occasion, make a front page sensation out of AIDS: 'KEEP THOSE CONDOMS HANDY!' (23 March 1989),

'AIDS HELL OF STARSKY'S FAMILY' (26 August 1989), 'DI'S LEVEL 42 POP HERO ALAN DIES OF AIDS' (21 October 1989), 'LET ME KEEP MY BABY – AIDS Mum's plea to judge' (19 February 1990). But the *Mirror* differed from the *Sun*, *Daily Mail* and *Daily Express* in that it raised no major argument with the health education campaign. The proprietor, Robert Maxwell, had become very publicly associated with the AIDS campaign as co-founder of the National AIDS Trust.

Today also adopted a more liberal stance on AIDS. It gave extensive coverage to the Princess of Wales's involvement with patients, focusing particularly on her effect in challenging stigma and prejudice. A page-long feature at the year end recording the short history of AIDS summed up: '1991 – Whether it is because of ignorance, prudery or fear, ten years on the figures show that in Britain we have done too little too late to prevent the spread of AIDS. It is now spreading faster through the heterosexual population than through any other group' (*Today*, 1 December 1990).

Changes of editorial line

Whilst the views of some of the tabloid newspapers may be expressed vehemently, they can also change. The *Daily Star* at an earlier stage had enthusiastically supported orthodox and sometimes critical views and defended positions from which it later distanced itself. In a spate of editorials in December 1986 it supported the Terrence Higgins Trust against Chief Constable James Anderton. It also attacked moral critics of the government campaign and supported the distribution of clean needles to IV drug users. One editorial urged Anderton to reflect 'on two words of criticism from the Terrence Higgins Trust, the charity which tries to HELP AIDS victims . . . we will remind him what they were: Unchristian and uncaring' (*Daily Star*, 13 December 1986). In another statement, the *Star* declared that it is 'A scandal that the campaign has been hijacked by a collection of prattling bishops who really should know better, peddling a load of muddle-headed moralistic platitudes . . . A bigger scandal still that the laudable Terrence Higgins Trust may be prosecuted because some cheap-jack eccentrics want to treat a serious booklet on sex and AIDS like a sleazy hard-porn magazine . . . The advertising and information campaign must be stepped up with more cash for organisations like the Higgins Trust' (*Daily Star*, 17 December 1986).

During the same period, the *Sun* defended the strategy it later rejected: 'this disease threatens to become the greatest mass killer since the Black Death of the Middle Ages . . . it could affect EVERY family in the land'. A significant aspect of its stance at this time was the emphasis upon heterosexual transmission: 'Despite the smirks, AIDS is not a joke. It does not affect only homosexuals. It can be transmitted through normal sexual relations with carriers' ('The *Sun* Says,' 10 November 1986).

The *Daily Mail* too initially endorsed the government's decision to 'warn every household in Britain' as 'prudent common sense . . . The AIDS virus is a killer . . . has the potential to become an epidemic comparable with the great plagues which ravaged the world in former times' ('Comment,' *Daily Mail*, 17 November 1986). A year later the *Mail* was disillusioned and changed its editorial line, rejecting the official message.

The AIDS policy community and the broadsheet press

Broadsheet newspapers tended to focus on the institutions of the state, the professions and the voluntary organisations, with regular reports from conferences and journals. AIDS was covered by medical, science, home affairs, health and social services correspondents, and even by specialists in technology or the environment (see Chapter 7). Broadsheets were closer to the viewpoints dominant amongst the health professionals and government officials.

For example, *The Times* welcomed government plans for anonymous testing, arguing the need for more information and that 'if reliable figures are to be found, the anonymity of the survey must be protected'. The paper warned against complacency: 'AIDS will be here for a long time – longer than the reach of any public relations campaign. The more that is understood about its transmission the better. Too little is known about the epidemiology of AIDS' (*The Times*, 24 November 1988). This is the direct opposite in all respects to the editorial views of the *Daily Express* and *Sun* on this policy at this time.

The features sections of the *Independent* and *Guardian* in particular reflect their familiarity with the worlds of social welfare, health, community organisations, sexuality and gender. The science correspondent of *The Times*, too, expressed 'liberal' views common to the orthodox medical and educational worlds. A major feature on the eve of World AIDS Day 1989 strongly demonstrated this perspective:

AIDS is still seen as a sordid disease largely restricted to promiscuous homosexual men and intravenous drug abusers. The belief that 'normal' people are somehow immune to it is almost as entrenched now as it was at the beginning of the epidemic. The evidence, human and scientific, tells a different story . . . Against this background, the insistence that AIDS is a 'gay plague' would be laughable were it not so tragically short-sighted. In the Western world, AIDS merely showed up among homosexual men first. (30 November 1989)

When these correspondents criticised the official education campaigns aimed at heterosexuals, the focus was typically the timing or language – not about the need for the message itself. The *Independent* had pointed to the possibility of complacency and disbelief:

A conventional way to fight complacency is for the government to run an alarming series of advertisements. The trouble with this approach is that it has already been tried, and since, in the present state of knowledge, it seems to have been based on an exaggerated estimate of the risk posed to heterosexuals, the force of official pronouncements has diminished. ('Danger of alarmist warnings', *Independent*, 5 September 1989)

However, there was another approach among broadsheets such as the *Sunday Telegraph*, which regularly criticised the government campaign on the same grounds as tabloids such as the *Mail* and the *Express*.

Beyond the attack on the medical orthodoxy

Although the attack on the medical orthodoxy did fit quite snugly with anti-gay sentiment, it was not coterminous with it. The right wing tabloids and sections of the broadsheet press did not confine themselves to claiming that the medical orthodoxy was the result of a gay conspiracy. They went further and regularly included comment which was straightforwardly anti-gay. Columnists felt free to glory in the deaths of gay men from AIDS and to blame the victims for the AIDS epidemic. The *Daily Star* ignored the Kilbracken argument and the attack on the Department of Health's educational message to heterosexuals. But editorial statements chose other targets, proposing repressive measures against the 'guilty victims'. The *Daily Star* marked International AIDS Day 1988 with an editorial proposing 'Leper-type colonies':

> Surely, if the human race is under threat, it is entirely REASONABLE to segregate AIDS victims – otherwise the whole of mankind could be engulfed. Some experts have even suggested that offshore islands should be used for the colonies. Pro-homosexual groups like the Terrence Higgins Trust will scream that it is unfair. But they would. The truth is that promiscuous homosexuals are by far the biggest spawning ground for AIDS. They COULD curb the spread of the disease if they curbed their sexual appetites, but that does not seem to be happening, despite all the warnings and all the condom campaigns.[2] Right now, ideas like AIDS colonies have got to be worth serious consideration. (*Daily Star*, 2 December 1988)

The attack on 'promiscuous homosexuals' was not unique. But the segregation or internment proposal was exceptional as an editorial stance during this period. The attempt to distinguish between 'innocent' and 'guilty' was a major issue in this newspaper:

> How many families have been sentenced to death by faceless blood donors who were drug addicts or permissive homosexuals? And how long are we going to support spurious charities for those who brought this awful curse upon themselves? Sympathy is fine. But would not our support be better directed towards the innocents who received tainted blood through no fault of their own? (*Daily Star*, 29 August 1989)

In December 1990 a *Daily Star* report alleged that singer Cliff Richard had 'refused an appeal from a sanctuary for AIDS victims'. In language that even the *Sun* was by now thinking more carefully about, the *Star* editorial declared, 'Why should anyone feel obliged to help people who, mostly, have only themselves to blame for their predicament? Despite all the homosexual propaganda, AIDS is still almost entirely a disease passed on by poofters and junkies. Only their promiscuity and stupidity has spread it like wildfire' (*Daily Star*, 18 December 1990).

In the *Sun*, columnists regularly went beyond the editorial stance on the denial of heterosexual risk and attacked homosexuality itself. Gary Bushell asserted that the government was lying about transmission risks

> to stop people coming to awkward conclusions about the dangers posed to society by promiscuous homosexuals. They are terrified that voters will demand radical solutions, like outlawing homosexuality. Or quarantining AIDS sufferers and chemically castrating anyone who is HIV positive. I've even heard some people advocate tattooing a massive A on the foreheads of carriers, although one on the base of their spine would be sufficient. What about a luminous tattoo: 'Abandon hope all ye who enter here? ('Straight talking will nail the great AIDS lie', *Sun*, 18 October 1990)

Fiona McDonald Hull of the *Sun* chose the occasion of actor Ian Charleson's death to urge: 'Gays must learn from actor Ian's death . . . Ian died because he caught AIDS. And it is almost certain that he caught AIDS because he was a homosexual . . . It is time the homosexuals and drug addicts cleaned up their act. They, and they alone, are responsible for people dying from AIDS' (*Sun*, 12 January 1990).

Other columnists have taken up this theme. The *Mail on Sunday*, a newspaper which provided very little basic news reporting on AIDS or HIV, had Julie Burchill to put forward the 'gays caused it' theory (*Mail on Sunday*, 21 October 1990). The *Daily Mail* had the columnist George Gale. He disliked the HEA AIDS campaign and was well known for his criticism of gay men: 'The message to be learned – that the Department of Health should now be propagating – is that active homosexuals are potentially murderers and that the act of buggery kills' ('Straight talk is the way to save lives', *Daily Mail*, 21 August 1989).

Meanwhile, among the broadsheet columnists, the *Sunday Telegraph* allowed 'Mandrake' to write:

> New York's 'gay community' – that is, various noisy and menacing bores who claim to speak on behalf of quieter homosexuals – do not want it thought that the 'sexual preference' which is most likely to cause AIDS is homosexuality. (*Sunday Telegraph*, 9 July 1989)

News formats and access to the press

The various editorial positions of the press were complemented by variations within papers, between news, features, columns and editorials and between specialist and general reporters. This can result in coverage which apparently contradicts a paper's more familiar editorial orientation and is partly a function of the different rules and requirements which may operate in different parts of a newspaper. News reports, editorials, features, columns, cartoons and letters to the editor, for instance, are all 'various types of narratives and formats which follow different rules and conventions of composition and subject treatment' (Bruck, 1989: 114). Bruck suggests that these formats can affect the way in which competing or alternative discourses may be taken up. The news report, with its conventional requirements of 'fact', 'hard news' and authoritative sources, will tend to favour the 'official' agenda and viewpoint. Features or lengthy specialist reports, with 'softer' news angles, longer production time-scales and more contextualisation, may allow greater access to conflicting views and a wider spectrum of opinion. They are, however, often written by specialist journalists close to official sources of information. There is a variety of reasons why the range of opinion in these areas of a newspaper may expand. For example, a marketing strategy might involve introducing a greater diversity of political opinion in the attempt to pick up readers.

The 'column' format offers the greatest space for alternative discourses. Written by individual authors, few formal constraints or requirements are placed upon them (see Miller, 1994: Chapter 4). The columnists in the *Sun*, or those in the *Daily Mail*, might thus be regarded as extreme examples of (right wing) oppositional or alternative perspectives. The *Sunday Telegraph*'s columnists, too, were not sympathetic to the HEA: 'From the beginning, the advertising campaigns have been close to mendacity' (23 July 1989), 'AIDS does not discriminate, the experts say. But the experts, it seems, do. They discriminate against heterosexuals' (10 December 1989). The paper's regular medical expert, Dr James Le Fanu, accused the BMA of 'sensationalism and distortion' on AIDS (21 July 1991).

Some columnists espouse views different to the editorial and some contradict each other. In the *Sunday Times*, for example, there were columnists scathingly critical of the educational message (Susan Crosland) and those passionate in its defence (Julia Neuberger). Features argued the case for the national sex survey and reported the emergence of positive images of gays and people with AIDS in Hollywood. In the midst of allegations of a publisher's boycott, the *Sunday Times* published two lengthy extracts from Michael Fumento's controversial book, *The Myth of Heterosexual AIDS* ('Is it a myth?' *Sunday Times*, 18 March 1990: C1, C18; 'The plague years', *Sunday Times*, 25 March 1990: C1, C18). However, the paper also carried articles by epidemiologists presenting the orthodox case. The following year, the 'New Grubb Street' column accused the Department of Health of 'official disinformation' on the heterosexual HIV statistics (*Sunday Times*, 11 August 1991) and an article on 'high-risk' groups accused the HEA of 'trying to conceal information out of some misplaced notion of political correctness' (*Sunday Times*, 18 August 1991). The *Sunday Times* also regularly reported the campaign for compensation for haemophiliacs infected with HIV from NHS blood products, under the banner 'THE FORGOTTEN VICTIMS'.

The tabloid *Sunday People* provided a further example of divergence between editorial and columnist views. 'The Man of the People' questioned the relevance of the advertising campaign (*Sunday People*, 19 November 1989), but also warned young heterosexual couples: 'even the most innocent are at risk unless they take every precaution' ('Grim reminder', *Sunday People*, 18 August 1991).

Even the *Sun* sometimes gave alternatives. The *Sun* is a popular tabloid newspaper which features the dominant sexual culture, with all its contradictions. This involves more than just a frantic form of heterosexuality once known as bonking, for the *Sun* also contains regular 'Woman' pages and features. Within these, there are stories which implicitly challenge the editorial line by reporting the problems of safe sex and the 'foolish' heterosexuals who take risks. 'Has AIDS really killed the one night stand?' asked the Woman page with a survey of young people which apparently gave cause for concern: 'their attitudes are those of totally irresponsible people who refuse to face the facts about the virus, fooling themselves with excuses like, "Risk is not high" – Leanne, 21. "I take a chance" – Amanda, 19. "Only gays get it" – Michele, 17' (*Sun*, 27 April 1989). Given the relentless homophobia of the editorials and columnists in the *Sun*, a poignant example of differences between formats was perhaps the small item in the 'Allan Hall's America' column, on problems experienced by gay groups in America:

> Gays get it tough – The tide has turned against gay groups in America. Councils are scrapping the laws which gave equal or preferred treatment to homosexuals . . . The National Gay and Lesbian Alliance said, 'There is a new menace in the air.' (*Sun*, 10 October 1989)

The formulaic news stories which fill the pages of any tabloid newspaper borrow freely from competing and often contradictory currents of culture and ideology. The formats of popular journalism can sometimes draw upon alternative and oppositional discourses in a quite opportunistic manner. For example, in the fantasy world of heterosexual promiscuity and endless casual sex, the question of AIDS inevitably intrudes, albeit not in the formulations of health education. What could be more typical of a popular tabloid than a feature on sunshine, sea and sex?: 'SEX-SPREE HOLIDAY BRITS IN AIDS PERIL – British girls are ignoring the terrifying risk of AIDS to go on sex orgies in the sun . . . And many admit they do not make holiday lovers wear a condom. *Sun* reporter Antonella Lazzeri went to the Greek holiday island of Rhodes to investigate' (*Sun*, 20 July 1991). The *Sun*'s editorials, doctor and columnists had, of course, explicitly argued against these ideas on numerous occasions. The *Daily Star* too ran the story that: 'Holiday sex can costa [*sic*] your life – Hordes of young Britons are still risking their lives through holiday sexual flings, a top doctor warned yesterday' (*Daily Star*, 3 May 1989). The *Star*'s coverage never seriously doubted or contradicted these ideas. It was not a central issue and, as we have seen, editorial energy was devoted to other targets.

Such features and stories are common in the tabloids, particularly in the *Sun* and *Daily Star*. They often appear as surveys of sex or dating behaviour, as medical advice or health features. The *Daily Star* reported: 'YOUNG LOVE IS BLIND TO AIDS SCARE – The threat of AIDS holds no fears for most young people in Britain. Three out of four are ignoring warnings about the deadly virus, according to a survey' (*Daily Star*, 26 September 1990). 'GIRLS IN THE NAUGHTY 90's' featured a survey from *Cosmopolitan* magazine, 'Survey lifts lid off saucy habits . . . They'll even risk pregnancy or AIDS' (*Daily Star*, 19 November 1990).

Whatever the editorial line on AIDS, Joan Collins is news:

> JOAN AGONY AT PAL HIT BY AIDS – Star bans sex cheats. Joan Collins is demanding her lovers sleep with no one else after learning that a friend is dying of AIDS. Now four-times wed Joan, 57, is terrified that she too could fall a victim to AIDS. She said, 'I know a girl, quite well known, who got AIDS from her boyfriend. She's dying. It's a horror story.' Joan told *Marie Claire* magazine, 'Just imagine, the thought of somebody doing something to bring that disease to me is abhorrent. I couldn't forgive it. Fidelity is terribly important. How can you be sure what they've picked up?' (*Daily Star*, 16 August 1990)

Around this time the HEA was running television adverts based on 'personal testimony' accounts of heterosexuals who had become infected with HIV. Personalised and dramatic life stories are a staple of popular journalism, and the *Daily Star* carried some examples:

> Alison is 24, rich and got AIDS from the man of her dreams . . . in a one-night stand several years ago – and now she's dying of AIDS. Alison, 24, is far removed from the high-risk, homosexual, drug-taking world usually associated with the disease . . . she could not know he was a bisexual with the AIDS virus. The statistics say it shouldn't have happened. But it did – and now Alison lives with a ticking time-bomb of despair . . . She says, 'I want to help other people, to warn kids that AIDS is a real danger, that it took only one night eight years ago for me.' (*Daily Star*, 23 August 1990)

In this version, the person 'got AIDS' from someone with the 'AIDS virus', becomes a 'ticking time-bomb' destined to 'die of AIDS'. In the *Daily Star*'s version of heterosexual transmission the subjects 'Catch AIDS off other heterosexuals'.

International coverage in the *Daily Star* included a report on the AIDS situation in Cuba. Without any reference to its own position on this issue, the *Daily Star* reported:

> Tyrant's Evil AIDS lock-up – AIDS victims in Cuba are being locked up for life by cruel dictator Fidel Castro . . . Anyone found with the killer syndrome is put into quarantine until a cure is found – or until they die . . . Sufferers are still allowed to work but rulers say they must be locked away for the sake of the rest of the population. (*Daily Star*, 28 April 1990)

The *Daily Express* provides further examples of the possible effect of journalistic formats on content. The issue of AIDS appeared as a story in a number of different ways. The medical reporter was responsible for the regular reports of government, medical and scientific matters on AIDS. This included the Cox Committee report, 'Straight sex thousands are infected with AIDS' (*Daily Express*, 1 November 1988), and 'AIDS warning to women over high-risk sex', based on a study of HIV transmission rates in the *British Medical Journal* (17 February 1989), to 'AIDS threat on increase for non-gays', on the Institute of Actuaries' predictions (2 March 1989). But most of the AIDS stories were not by specialist staff. Splash headlines such as 'SYRINGE PERIL ON BEACHES – Exclusive: mother hits out as Sarah, 2, steps on a junkies' needle' (*Daily Express*, 27 June 1989) or 'AIDS RAPE DEATH FEAR – victim's nightmare as attacker with killer virus gets 11 years' (*Daily Express*, 11 July 1989) are more tailored to the newspaper's major news priorities.

The distinctive editorial view of the *Daily Express* on AIDS was that the government's health education message was wrong. Within a relatively short period the following items appeared in different sections of the newspaper, implying other priorities and perspectives than those established by the editorials:

1 A feature several pages long based on the orthodox World Health Organisation (WHO) model of heterosexual transmission headlined, 'AIDS – THE KILLER TAKING US INTO A GLOBAL CRISIS WITHIN THE NEXT TEN YEARS', and 'FACT – It is the main killer of young women in Europe's big cities', quoting the WHO surveillance team that by the year 2000 'heterosexual transmission will predominate in most industrial countries' (1 August 1990);
2 The inevitable holiday feature on 'The sizzling combination of sun, sea, sand and sangria', an investigation of heterosexual risk and the realities of unsafe sexual behaviour on the Club 18–30 holiday where, 'The beer is cheap, the sex is as casual as the day-glo t-shirts and AIDS is about the only four-letter word that goes unspoken' (23 August 1990);
3 Other stories reported on: 'AIDS fear for women' (13 November 1990), 'Shock rise in AIDS cases' (20 November 1990), 'Killer disease time-bomb is revealed by secret checks (18 May 1991), 'AIDS despair that knows no barriers' (25 April 1991).

A similar variation in content could be seen in the *Daily Mail*, the *Daily Express*'s main rival as the medical correspondent or key news values conflicted with editorial predilections.

The contradictions of the tabloids: the Princess, the press and AIDS

The Princess of Wales excited contradictory impulses in the popular press. She was at once praised, mythologised, patronised and criticised. The *Sun* columnist Richard Littlejohn revealed some of the discomfort caused by her involvement with AIDS: 'The royal clothes horse seems to have a fasci-nation with terminal illness. One day she is shaking hands with lepers, the next snuggling up to AIDS victims. Maybe Prince Charles should buy her a stethoscope for Christmas, he might get to play doctors and nurses' ('Don't fall for AIDS hype Dr Di', *Sun*, 4 December 1989).

The editorial line of the *Daily Star* clashed with Diana's AIDS work. Brian Hitchen's 'Straight talking from the *Star*' column had stated: 'Isn't it about time her husband put down his royal foot and told Princess Diana "No more visits to adult AIDS centres" . . . Whoever plans her schedules should cut out the endless hand-shaking with unstable drug addicts and the time spent listening to endless tales of woe from homosexuals whose promiscuity has made them HIV positive' (*Daily Star*, 1 August 1990).

However, the newspaper was also able to present images it found more acceptable: 'Di to help the tots hit by killer virus – The Princess, who has led the fight for a better deal for AIDS sufferers, is fully aware of the growing crisis and next week she will give a hard-hitting speech aiming to shock the nation out of its complacency over the disease' (*Daily Star*, 15 April 1991).

Princess Diana working with 'innocent' children and families was something the *Daily Star* felt more comfortable with and it produced features on the issue on three consecutive days.[3]

However, when Diana made a speech as new patron of the National AIDS Trust, she made demands the *Daily Star* found hard to meet. Despite the front page splash, 'HUG AIDS VICTIMS SAYS DI – "Open your hearts and don't be afraid"', the *Daily Star* printed an editorial attacking the Princess's judgement.

> Princess Diana is a lovely caring person. But she is sadly misguided about AIDS victims . . . If Diana had been talking about the innocent children who have AIDS or who are orphaned by it, that would have been fine. But clearly she was talking about ALL AIDS victims . . . in appealing for love for EVERY AIDS sufferer she is endorsing the anti-social behaviour of those who have turned the problem into a plague that threatens mankind . . . she and her advisers should think very carefully about the causes she supports. (*Daily Star*, 23 April 1991)

But this editorial was pulled from later editions. In the place of 'PRINCESS IS WRONG', the editorial was now headlined 'THE CARING PRINCESS'. It began: 'Princess Diana is a wonderful, caring person . . . Diana wrote every word of the speech herself. It was a cry from her very soul on behalf of the tragic children who have been infected or orphaned by this tragic disease.' The suggestion of criticism of Diana was removed, but the *Daily Star* did not withdraw its condemnation of the 'guilty' people with AIDS. It reversed its claim that Diana was 'endorsing the anti-social behaviour' of the 'guilty victims' to read that she 'was NOT condoning' such people. The editorial simply asserted that the *Daily Star* and Diana were speaking the same language:

> When she asked us to hug AIDS victims and shake their hands, to share their homes and toys, she was NOT condoning the activities of those who are spreading AIDS promiscuously. She was NOT endorsing rampant homosexuals and junkies who are just indulging their appetite for drugs or sex without a thought for the dangers to mankind. (*Daily Star*, late editions 23 April 1991)

The problem which the newspaper was trying to resolve derives from the contradictions of maintaining its ruthless 'innocent/guilty' discrimination without alienating public support for Princess Diana in her work on AIDS and without coming into conflict with 'The Palace'. The following day, the

Daily Star printed a small eight line item on page five, headed 'YOU BACK DI ON AIDS PLEA', stating 'Princess Diana's 'Hug an AIDS victim' plea gained overwhelming support from *Daily Star* readers yesterday. Callers voted 3–1 in favour of her appeal for the tragic sufferers.' Research into attitudes and beliefs suggests that a significant proportion of readers do in fact accept 'innocent/guilty' distinctions in thinking about AIDS (see Chapters 8 and 9). This, however, would not necessarily have guaranteed approval of attacks on Princess Diana.

But Diana had become a problem for sections of the popular press. As they constantly reminded their readers, she was the first Royal publicly to shake the hand of someone living with HIV/AIDS. She then became patron of the National AIDS Trust. When, in the summer of 1991, she made another visit to the AIDS Unit at Middlesex Hospital, this time accompanied by US First Lady, Barbara Bush, the *Daily Star* gave it full picture coverage: 'Caring Princess Diana held the hand of an AIDS patient with just two days to live and whispered words of comfort yesterday' (*Daily Star*, 18 July 1991). Then, a month later, along with every other national newspaper, the *Daily Star* covered the visits of the Princess to the bedside of her friend and well known arts figure Adrian Ward-Jackson who was dying of an AIDS-related illness. 'DIANA IN AIDS VIGIL' reported that she had visited him several times at the hospital and had been secretly visiting him at his home before that, and had cut short her family holiday at Balmoral to be at his bedside (*Daily Star*, 23 August 1991). The newspaper reported, as did all the national press, her last visit the following day, 'DI's GRIEF AS HER AIDS FRIEND DIES'. The funeral the following week was covered as 'Di keeps pledge to AIDS pal' (*Daily Star*, 30 August 1991).

This apparent change of heart with regard to Diana's work was no less marked at the *Sun*, which joined the rest of the national press in sympathetic reports of her visits to Adrian Ward-Jackson: 'Heartbroken Princess Diana wept last night after visiting a friend dying of AIDS in hospital' ('Vigil at hospital', *Sun*, 23 August 1991). His death the following morning was reported as 'DI's FAREWELL KISS'. Most striking, however, was the editorial celebrating her as a 'wonderfully warm-hearted, compassionate girl', with its headline 'WONDER GIRL' (*Sun*, 24 August 1991). Her attendance at the funeral was given extended coverage: 'Di's funeral grief for AIDS victim Adrian', 'THE HAND OF LOVE – Di gives comfort' (*Sun*, 30 August 1991).[4]

Amongst all the coverage given to Diana's hospital visits, with her friend's eventual death and funeral, only two articles (by columnists in the *Evening Standard* and the *Mail on Sunday*) voiced criticisms. The *Sun* and the *Daily Star* were silent by this stage, but Peter McKay in the *Evening Standard* echoed the arguments used earlier by their columnists:

it seems to me that Diana has become caught up in the mythology of AIDS. Plenty of men and women die early, friendless and virtually alone, from a variety of diseases over which they had no control. Homosexuals die of AIDS because medicine has not yet found a way of protecting them from one possible consequence of their sex lives . . . After all, you are unlikely in this country to contract

AIDS outside of homosexuality and intravenous drug use. ('AIDS and the Princess', *Evening Standard*, 30 August 1991. See also 'A lovely lady's odd obsession', *Mail on Sunday*, 1 September 1991)

The limits of liberal journalism

The unabashed homophobia of some of the papers was a contrast to the liberal editorial line followed by most of Fleet Street. Yet, in some respects, broadsheet coverage was also problematic.

By late 1988 the broadsheet press, certainly *The Times*, *Guardian* and *Independent* seemed to be aware of the issues involved in the emotionally and morally loaded distinction between 'innocent' and 'guilty victims'. In fact several articles discussing this problem had been published. (See Nicolas de Jongh, 'When the real disease is press distortion', *Guardian*, 14 April 1986; Simon Watney, 'The wrong ideas that are plaguing AIDS', *Guardian*, 16 October 1987; Angus Finney, 'Reports that foster ignorance about AIDS', *Independent*, 2 August 1989.) The *Sunday Times* however was still using this terminology in headlines such as 'INNOCENT AIDS VICTIM LEAVES LEGACY OF HOPE' (29 January 1989) and reports which singled out those 'quite blameless of any irresponsible act themselves' (29 October 1989).

Both the *Observer* and the *Sunday Times* vied with each other to claim credit for the government turnaround on compensation for haemophiliacs infected with HIV. While the Haemophilia Society itself has tried to discourage the use of the term 'innocent' and the coverage in the *Observer* eschewed the term, the editorial judgement that this was an appropriate campaigning story relied on such distinctions.

From the early 1980s, activist groups in the United States had rejected the term 'victim' entirely, preferring instead the dignity of 'people with AIDS' or 'people living with AIDS'. Sensitivity to these developments came later to sections of the British press. The *Guardian* – in 1987 – published an account written by a man who had just learned he had HIV/AIDS. The newspaper subsequently printed a letter criticising the way in which it had presented the article:

> I wonder how you can possibly justify the headline 'Diary of a condemned man' to introduce a uniquely brave and sensitive article which explicitly questions precisely this kind of glib and totally fatalistic journalese? You also reproduced a photograph of a group holding up a banner which reads People With AIDS Alliance, only to subvert and insult their courage and optimism with the slick and vulgar caption IMMUNISED AGAINST EMBARRASSMENT: AMERICAN AIDS VICTIMS. . . . If they are victims of anything it is precisely this kind of shoddy journalism which effortlessly and conveniently depicts them as if they were intrinsically a race apart. (Letter from Simon Watney, Health Education Group, Terrence Higgins Trust, *Guardian*, 13 May 1987)

The liberal intentions of some broadsheet newspapers and most television news were clearly in evidence in their eager endorsement of the official campaign message 'Everyone is at risk'. It was perhaps here too that some of the limitations of liberal journalism were clearly visible. The precise meaning of 'everyone' remained unexamined in journalists' reports, carrying over the assumptions implicit in the campaign messages. As some critics pointed out, it suggests that the problem has become serious only now that it is 'not just homosexuals' (Watney, 1987b; Patton, 1985). The concern of some journalists may have been to eradicate perceptions of AIDS as a 'gay plague': 'AIDS is no longer the disease of the homosexual or the drug addict. Its spread amongst heterosexuals, predicted at least five years ago, is a threat to the whole population' (*News at 5.45* and *Channel Four News*, 11 November 1986). But often words were chosen less carefully. It has been suggested that the real concern voiced by the official slogans was not heterosexual risk so much as the fear of 'leakage' from 'risk groups' and sub-cultures to threaten the rest of society (Alcorn, 1989). Such fears are betrayed in the early (1988) Scottish Television health education advert: 'AIDS is no longer a disease restricted to homosexuals or drug users. They are at the greatest risk but AIDS has jumped the barrier. We are all at risk' (on *News at Ten*, 11 November 1986). Stereotypical images of deviant underworlds were readily invoked, as in this report on the sex industry and AIDS in Holland:

the red lights here and throughout the EEC show no sign of dimming despite the invasion of the disease which is incurable and believed to be invariably fatal. The Dutch have launched a nationwide campaign to educate the country about the deadly virus, but AIDS has now escaped from the social and sexual ghettos which used to harbour it, into the population at large. (*News at Ten*, 10 December 1986)

Before HIV was identified and its transmission understood, scientific and medical thought had described AIDS by reference to the groups amongst which symptoms were first recorded. American researchers spoke in terms of 'the four Hs' – homosexuals, Haitians, haemophiliacs and heroin injectors. (Some also included 'hookers', speaking of five Hs (see Amis, 1987).) This identification of susceptible 'risk groups', reinforced and repeated in numerous media accounts, had a profound effect on the popular image of HIV/AIDS, excluding those with the virus from 'the rest of society'. Many attempts to change the image of those with HIV, to 'include' them, only served to underline the divisions: 'She has [HIV], but she isn't black, she isn't poor, she isn't a homosexual, she isn't a drug user. She is like the rest of us' (*Sunday Times*, 27 August 1989).

Commitment to the 'heterosexual risk' campaign did not preclude coverage which discriminated against gay men. The use of clichéd imagery could affirm just the link between gay men and 'the spectre of plague' which had been criticised. The introduction to a BBC report from America is a clear example:

San Francisco's former image – the Golden Gate bridge majestically spanning the bay, Fisherman's Wharf, the cable cars on the hillsides. But the image of America's loveliest city has changed dramatically. AIDS has spread, in one doctor's words, like a plague through the city's homosexual community. (*Nine O'Clock News*, 19 January 1987)

A day later, ITN broadcast a strikingly similar report:

1,600 people have died from the disease, San Francisco is the city where the nightmare has become a reality. Once famous for its cable cars and its free-wheeling attitude to sex, the city is now in the front line of the battle against AIDS. (*News at Ten*, 20 January 1987)

Whilst the government campaign in the winter of 1986 was a big story, and TV news reported the apocalyptic warnings of the threat of AIDS, its reports often carried little or no hard information about HIV/AIDS. Tele-vision news journalists regularly highlighted criticisms of previous health advertising's lack of clarity and directness (see Chapter 4) yet entire reports on AIDS could fail even to mention that a virus was involved, let alone name HIV. BBC reports of 3 November 1986 were typical. They reported on the 'super committee to stop the disease spreading', 'the threat of AIDS', 'efforts to tackle the disease', 'declaring war on AIDS', the 'danger of an AIDS epidemic sweeping the country', that 'as many as 30,000 could be infected and that could mean 5,000 deaths a year by 1990'. The reports note 'the committee will be considering a programme of measures to make people more aware of the dangers and better able to avoid them' but we learn only that 'the biggest risk is from promiscuity by either sex'. The term HIV or the word virus are not mentioned in these lengthy reports.

The potential for alarming, misinforming or failing to provide the audience with the basic facts was always there. As late as 1988, ITN reported that 'urgent blood supplies are being rushed to London from Scotland to cover a serious shortage' and that 'hospitals may be forced to cancel operations'. We are told that this is because 'in the last two years the number of donors has fallen sharply partly because of the AIDS fear'. Although a reporter went out to cover the story and the Regional Blood Transfusion Director was interviewed, no explanation or clarification is provided about this 'AIDS fear', what it might be or how it could be possible. Later that evening, the same reporter added only that 'the number of donors has fallen partly due to mistaken fears of contracting AIDS' (*News at 5.45* and *News at Ten*, 8 October 1988). But we are told nothing which might explain the fears, mistaken or not, surrounding blood dona-tion. It could have been thought that it was possible to become infected by giving blood.

This is surprising because controversy over blood supplies was not new. In one important case, it was the British Medical Association (BMA) who were spreading confusion and doubt. Both ITN and BBC reported in January 1987 the shock BMA advice to potential donors: 'The BMA say that anyone who has had casual sex in the past four years should think very carefully before giving blood' (*Nine O'Clock News*, 5 January 1987). (The BMA withdrew its statement two days later after discussions with the Department of Health.) Only ITN's reporter explained that: 'The problem is that tests for the AIDS virus can only detect antibodies in the blood and those antibodies may not show up for a long time after a person has been infected' (*News at Ten*, 5 January 1987). This kind of basic information was very rare in the news media.

The common feature of mass media reporting during this period is the failure to distinguish between HIV infection and AIDS. Long after the HEA made a deliberate effort in its information materials to distinguish between the virus and the syndrome, news reports continued to use terms such as 'the AIDS virus' and other forms of words which fail to distinguish between them. This was as true of television as of the press. It was very rare for HIV to be named. More typical were terms such as 'the AIDS disease', 'the killer disease AIDS' (BBC1, *One O'Clock News*, 23 November 1986) or 'the AIDS germ' (BBC1, *Six O'Clock News*, 27 November 1986). AIDS was spoken of as a single disease which was 'caught' (ITN, *News at 5.45*, 3 November 1986), 'spread' (BBC1, *Six O'Clock News*, 27 November 1986), 'contracted' (*Channel Four News*, 3 November 1986) and 'carried' (BBC1, *Nine O'Clock News*, 25 February 1987). Thus, a woman 'caught AIDS from her bisexual lover' (ITN, *News at Ten*, 8 November 1986) and her lover 'passed on to her the AIDS he had caught from one of his male partners' (*Channel Four News*, 8 November 1986). It was declared 'no secret that the real number of AIDS carriers could be twice the official figure' (BBC1, *Nine O'Clock News*, 26 January 1987), reports speculated that tissue could be 'tested for AIDS' (BBC1, *Nine O'Clock News*, 24 February 1987) and spoke of the 'AIDS test' (BBC2, *Newsnight*, 16 March 1987) and 'AIDS testing' (*Channel Four News*, 10 March 1987).

News coverage was heavily weighted towards reporting social categories or 'risk groups' rather than specific activities that might put people at risk. For example, during the 18 months from late 1988 to early 1990, in *The Times* and the *Independent*, over 60% of stories reporting intravenous drug use in relation to HIV/AIDS did not mention sharing needles, contributing to the impression that it is being an injecting drug user per se that puts one at risk of HIV, rather than using needles previously used by an infected person. (By contrast just 38% and 30% respectively in the Glasgow-based tabloids the *Daily Record* and *Evening Times* failed to mention sharing needles, reflecting the higher priority of injecting drug use in the Scottish media and the more detailed coverage.)

In British national newspapers during the same period the 'risk groups' most commonly mentioned in relation to HIV/AIDS were gay or bisexual men (in 24% of all items) and intravenous drug users (23%); heterosexuals were mentioned in 15% of items, haemophiliacs in 10% and blood transfusion recipients in 7%. Although reports mentioned groups whose members were infected or at risk of being so, in consequence of what activity they became infected was rarely mentioned. For example, of 498 press items mentioning gay men as having, or being at risk of HIV, just under 3% specify a mode of transmission (such as 'anal sex' or 'anal intercourse'). Alternative, but equally explicit terms in relation to gay men were only used by critics of the government or anti-gay columnists (e.g. 'sodomy' was mentioned in five). Anal sex was mentioned as a risk to heterosexuals in only 23 (1%) of items, seven of which are reports of Sir Reginald Murley's statement (7 November 1989) that the young woman in the government's safe sex advert was 'unlikely to develop AIDS unless she becomes a drug addict or allows herself to be buggered'. There are references to 'safe sex', 'safer sex' and 'avoiding unprotected intercourse', but few references to the specifics of safer sex practices. Condoms are most frequently mentioned, but out of all items on condoms only 3% mention any possible problems in their use. Out of more than 4,000 press reports examined, we could find only two items each mentioning 'non-penetrative sex' or 'masturbation' and only three mentioning 'oral sex'.

A further common feature of all the mass media coverage is a vagueness and lack of specificity in the use of terms such as 'body fluids' rather than explicit words such as blood, saliva, semen, or factor VIII. In the 18 months we looked at in detail from late 1988 to early 1990, 'blood' was mentioned in 4%, 'saliva' in 0.5%, and 'semen' less than 0.5% of items.[5] Only 22% of items reporting infection in haemophiliacs mention factor VIII as a transmission route. Such reporting was to impose clear limitations on public understanding (see Chapter 8).

Conclusion

Media coverage of AIDS has not been simply 'locked into an agenda which blocks out any approach to the subject which does not conform in advance to the values and language of a profoundly homophobic culture' (Watney, 1988a: 52). To be sure, the tabloids and broadsheets, news, features, editorials and columns, and copy filed by both general and specialist reporters have suffered from a wide variety of limitations, but these cannot be explained simply by using homophobia as an analytical tool without regard to conflict and change.

Media coverage has varied between and within newspapers and has changed over time. The variations between and within papers are susceptible to systematic analysis and we have tried to point out some of the major variations here, together with some hints about the reasons for those variations. In the next chapter we extend the analyses to variations in television news programming.

Notes

1. Lord Kilbracken later dissociated himself from the *Sun*. He was granted a prominent space to restate his argument: 'DOUBLE DISASTER OF AIDS AD CAMPAIGN – I welcome this chance to put the record straight. I have never said, nor is it true, that it is impossible for a heterosexual to catch AIDS, as stated in a *Sun* leader last Friday. It isn't as simple as that. I have always held that the risk of AIDS to heteros in Britain has been widely exaggerated by the

government and the media – except the *Sun*. The figures I have at last extracted from the DHSS have at last proved this' (*Sun*, 25 November 1989).

2. In fact, the evidence available at this time was understood and reported elsewhere as indicating the opposite. For example, the government commissioned a report on heterosexual risk: 'Today's report shows the spread of AIDS has slowed this year but the reason is that homosexuals have heeded the safe sex message. Figures from clinics treating sexually transmitted diseases show heterosexuals have not – and that's worrying the experts' (*Channel Four News*, 30 November 1988).

3. Two weeks after the feature coverage of AIDS and families to which they obviously referred, two letters to the editor were printed. The first was from Sir Donald Acheson, Chief Medical Officer: 'It is most encouraging that such a popular newspaper as the *Star* is making it clear that this tragic infection is NOT limited to gay people, drug abusers and foreigners. Please keep up the good work.' The second was from Margaret Jay, Director of the National AIDS Trust: 'Well done to the *Star* . . . Everyone at the National AIDS Trust has been very encouraged by the detailed research you have obviously put into your stories and the editorial comment. It is often difficult to get the popular press to take AIDS issues seriously, and treat them sensitively, but your pieces have been really helpful!' (*Daily Star*, 30 April 1991). The author of the AIDS reporting being praised was not a member of the *Daily Star*'s news staff but was freelance journalist Peter Miller. His articles appeared on 15, 16 and 17 April 1991.

4. Princess Diana's attendance at the funeral was recognised as breaking with protocol, and one newspaper had already published an article noting her dedication and commitment to work on AIDS since 1987. See 'How Diana Defeated The Palace – "No-one else will help. I must do something"' (*Sunday Express*, 25 August 1991). Note that this coverage occurred prior to Diana's split with the Palace and while she was still seen very much as part of the royal establishment.

5. The sample here is all British national daily and Sunday papers, plus the three Glasgow or Edinburgh based daily and Sundays and the Glasgow *Evening Times*, between 1 November 1988 and 30 April 1990.

4

AIDS and Television News

David Miller and Peter Beharrell

This chapter sets out some of the complexities of British network television news in relation to HIV and AIDS. Most writing on AIDS in the media fails to distinguish between different types of media. More importantly for our present purposes, very little work explores variations *within* media types. Therefore this chapter looks at variations within television news programmes.

First of all, we examine the range of coverage of HIV and AIDS on British television news, then we go on to examine the central question of access to the news – who is interviewed or quoted and how they are treated. We argue that television news did not simply relay homophobia, nor was it simply supportive of government policy. In fact, television reporters were able to be quite critical of government initiatives or lack of action. We argue that much television news was oriented towards the dominant liberal approach of the policy community and show the importance of source activities in influencing news definitions and the framework of news stories. Such factors mean that alternative sources are not always excluded from television news, nor are people living with HIV or AIDS always portrayed negatively.

What does TV news cover?

We examined network television news coverage of HIV/AIDS from October 1986 to April 1990, a period totalling three years seven months (see Appendix). The period starts three months before the first government television advertising campaign was launched, continues through AIDS television week and the period of 'wartime emergency', to well into the period of 'normalisation' of AIDS policy (Berridge and Strong, 1991b). Table 4.1 shows the frequency with which the major topics were covered by television news.

The most frequent types of 'AIDS story' were the official government campaign, people with HIV or with AIDS illnesses, reports on other countries, and stories about the search for cures and vaccines. Together these four categories comprise approximately two thirds of the coverage of AIDS/ HIV.

The largest single group of news items relates directly to the government campaign, ranging from press launches of the latest health education advertising to announcements of policy on anonymised HIV antibody testing or needle exchanges.

Table 4.1 *Television news topics on HIV
and AIDS, October 1986 to April 1990*

Government AIDS campaign	97
People living with HIV/AIDS	91
International news	80
HIV/AIDS research	46
Non-government organisation news events	26
Royal family	24
Latest official HIV/AIDS figures	16
Other events and happenings	13
Protests by activists	11
Blood and HIV infection	10
Condoms	7
HIV/AIDS in prison	6
Celebrities	6
Crime	6
Reports on AIDS in parts of the UK	4

However, other significant categories of AIDS story indicate that the activities of 'non-official' sources can result in news on network TV in this area. The non-government organisation category includes such news events as the British Medical Association training video for general practitioners, the (English) Football Association safety guidelines, a Royal College of Nursing report on the costs of patient care, a GPs' conference debating compulsory HIV antibody tests and a Birmingham City Council scheme to involve prostitutes in AIDS education.

Other events and happenings denotes less predictable news items such as a patient infected by HIV during a skin graft operation, a controversial speech by the Chief Constable of Greater Manchester, a protest over the siting of a hospice, and the dumping of allegedly infected waste from 'AIDS clinics'. These stories and those in the smaller categories listed indicate the range of definitions of AIDS as television news. Almost half of the international stories are reports from the USA and a further quarter concern African countries. No other region received more than a few items (items on the then USSR and Australia appeared in four bulletins each, Romania in three, Holland, Switzerland and Brazil in two bulletins each, and Belgium, France and South Korea in one).

A striking aspect of TV news reporting is the coverage given to the situation of people living with the virus – the second largest topic in news items in this sample. As we argue below, the way in which this was treated varied considerably, particularly in the opportunity it offered for people to speak for themselves about their own experiences.

Who gets on?

The range and frequency of interviews presented on television news provides one incomplete but powerful indicator of the sources which are drawn upon in presenting the news event. The interviewee may be used in various ways as the source of the story, to provide an alternative point of view or support an interpretation of events.

Within our sample, we identified a total of 363 different people who appeared in a total of 611 interviews. However, the majority of these people appear only once, exclusive to one news channel (70%). A much smaller number of interviewees appeared on more than one channel or bulletin on a particular day, but the majority here too are 'in the news' on that one occasion only. Only a small and exclusive group of people appear on more than one occasion, interviewed by both ITN and BBC news a number of times in the context of different stories.

We have divided the interviewees into five broad categories: (1) Politicians; (2) Medical and scientific experts; (3) Other professionals, activists and experts; (4) People with HIV or AIDS and (5) Unnamed or 'vox pop' interviews. These categories and their sub-divisions are shown in Table 4.2.

Politicians

A small number of public figures dominated the political interviews. Only 10 of the total of 31 individuals appear on more than one occasion: six government ministers, two Opposition (Labour) spokespersons and the chair of the All Party Parliamentary Group on AIDS. The three most interviewed politicians were successive government ministers of health – Norman Fowler appeared 34 times, David Mellor 12 times and Tony Newton on 10 occasions. As central figures in the official AIDS story, they invariably appeared on both ITN and BBC each time. This was the case for all government ministers in the sample.

Medical and scientific experts

The majority of the interviews in this category were one-off appearances by an individual. Few of the total of 80 medical and scientific interviewees appeared on more than one occasion.

Other professionals, activists and experts

This large grouping significantly draws together all those – other than the 'AIDS doctors' and the medical and research scientists – with professional interest, experience or activist involvement with HIV. The interviews include nursing and hospice staff, GPs, aid and relief workers, HIV counsellors, health educators, lawyers, spokespersons for many organisations and interest groups, celebrities promoting education or charities, and organisations representing the interests of people with HIV such as the Terrence Higgins Trust, Body Positive and Frontliners. The overwhelming majority (92%) appear just once. There are just nine out of the total of 131 who appear as interviewees on more than one occasion. Four appear on three occasions each – Ian McKellen the actor and charity fund raiser, a nursing

Table 4.2　*Categories of interviewee, TV news, October 1986 to April 1990*

	No. of appearances	Total
Politicians		
Government ministers	78	
Opposition spokespersons	13	
Backbench MPs	16	
Foreign politicians	13	120
Medical and scientific experts		
Doctors and scientists		146
Other professionals, activists and experts		
Terrence Higgins Trust	22	
Healthcare workers	22	
Non-govt organisations (e.g. NCCL, FPA)	17	
Civil servants/health officials	16	
Celebrities	14	
Police, prison officers	13	
Academics	9	
Organisations representing PWA	9	
Health educators and counsellors	8	
Professional bodies (e.g. BMA)	8	
Journalists and broadcasters	8	
Policy units and foundations	7	
Royals	6	
Private companies	6	
Local residents	6	
Religious leaders	5	
Haemophilia Society	5	
Community workers	5	
Prisoners	4	
HEA	1	191
People with AIDS/HIV+		
Men (unspecified sexuality)	47	
Women (unspecified sexuality)	16	
Haemophiliac	16	
IV drug user	12	
Gay man	4	
Parent of haemophiliac	5	
Parent of other person with AIDS	9	
Partner/wife of haemophiliac	3	112
Unnamed and vox pop		
People in street and bars	32	
Others	10	42
Total		611

sister from the specialist ward at Middlesex Hospital, Jonathan Grimshaw of Body Positive and John Fitzpatrick of the Terrence Higgins Trust. Only Nick Partridge of the Trust appears more often (16 times).

People with HIV or AIDS

A relatively large number of interviews involved people with direct personal experience of HIV or AIDS illnesses. In 93% of cases they appear only once. Yet they provide a variety of potential opportunities to explore alternative definitions of AIDS.

Unnamed and 'vox pop'

This includes 35 interviewees from 17 separate stories, mostly involving one-off interviews in the street or in a bar. None of these instances are shared by any of the four channels. On just three occasions the respondents are named and captioned (a total of five interviewees). They are not treated as 'experts' in any capacity, they are not protagonists or advocates, they do not appear as representatives for any organisation.

Support for the official line?

In contrast to some sections of the national press (Beharrell, 1993: Chapter 3), TV news displayed considerable support for the idea of a government health education campaign (if not for the concrete form the campaign took) and an almost total acceptance of the orthodox line on the risks of hetero-sexual transmission. This emphasised that 'heterosexual transmission' of HIV was a real risk and focused on the 'general population' or 'the hetero-sexual community'. This approach carried with it an implicit disregard for the impact of the epidemic on gay men as well as a tendency to slip from the language of risk practices and 'safe(r) sex' to the moral undertones of 'promiscuity' and 'clean living'.

At the same time there was a strong element of information giving on television news. It is central to our argument that the government campaign was the result of contending agendas within the policy arena which, during the early stages (1986–87), was relatively open to some members of the gay and medical communities (Berridge and Strong, 1991b). Pressure from gay and AIDS organisations, health educators, some civil servants and parts of the medical community resulted in a series of campaigns which would have been unthinkable even five years before. However, this pressure did meet some resistance – some government ministers were pushing a moral agenda and the resulting advertising was a combination of these contending approaches (see Chapter 2). This kind of contradictory information then found its way into news bulletins. Let us consider some examples from around the time of the first TV campaign.

The education campaign

The idea of a mass media public education campaign was universally reported as a good thing. In news reports from late 1986 the sense of 'national emergency' was palpable:

> The government is setting up a top level committee to warn that there is a danger of an AIDS epidemic sweeping the country . . . there have been warnings from health experts for some time that the deadly disease could get out of hand. It is the speed with which it can spread that is so worrying . . . Effectively the government is declaring war on AIDS. (BBC1, *Nine O'Clock News*, 3 November 1986)

A week later the BBC reported that 'More than any other disease, AIDS is threatening the health of the nation' (BBC1, *Nine O'Clock News*, 12 November 1986). The response to this threat is the public education campaign regularly endorsed by journalists:

> Tomorrow Lord Whitelaw's cabinet committee meets to discuss a range of options to help halt the spread of the disease. AIDS is the most serious threat to public health this century, there's no cure and there's no vaccine and there's not likely to be any for years to come. The only hope is prevention and that means the days of carefree promiscuity are over. (BBC1, *Six O'Clock News*, 10 November 1986)

The moral sting in the tail of this report was routine as journalists proved unable, and their sources in government unwilling, to distinguish firmly between morality and health education. The following typical report has the journalist arguing that 'sticking to one partner' is in some way related to 'safe(r) sex' and assuming that such advice is only relevant for heterosexuals: 'Because there is no cure for AIDS, doctors stress the importance of prevention. Their advice to all couples – stick to one partner; if you do have affairs use the sheath as a contraceptive' (BBC1, *Six O'Clock News*, 22 October 1986). The moral message is also underlined in a report where the journalist argues that

> Inevitably the disease spread to women, and with modern day sexual promiscuity AIDS has now become a heterosexual problem which can even affect unborn babies . . . In the meantime, the advice is clean living. (ITN, *News at One*, 23 October 1986)

Later in our sample, such reporting became less evident as pressure from AIDS organisations had some impact.

Heterosexual transmission

In this period, journalists regularly identified themselves closely with the government perspective and on many occasions explicitly endorsed the message coming from the Department of Health and Social Security. Where clear unequivocal support from TV news journalists was most likely was on the issue of the heterosexual transmission of HIV. The government campaign, for better or worse, had adopted this as a central focus of its advertising from 1986 onwards. The idea of a significant threat of a heterosexual epidemic was, however, controversial for many and much debate ensued in sections of the national press (Beharrell, 1993: Chapter 3). TV news had no such doubts, embracing the liberal orthodoxy of 'expert' opinion as if it was an unchallengeable scientific consensus throughout the period 1987–90.

Reporting the launch of another phase of the TV advertising campaign, the BBC correspondent focused the issue:

> But how likely is it that heterosexual intercourse will spread the virus? Figures show of the 1,283 reported cases of AIDS, well over 1,000 are in homosexuals. Only 44 people caught the virus through heterosexual intercourse, and 35 of those got it abroad. But those figures conceal what is now happening. Homosexuals have by and large changed their behaviour because of AIDS. Now experts say that worldwide it's heterosexual intercourse which is the commonest way in which the virus causing AIDS is transmitted. In America in the year ending last August, new AIDS cases in all categories increased by 46%. But in the same period cases caused by heterosexual intercourse rose by 85%. It's a foretaste of what could happen in Britain. Experts say there's no cause for alarm so long as action is taken now. (BBC1, *Six O'Clock News*, 17 February 1988)

No counter or qualifying arguments were broadcast.

On many other occasions the government perspective either framed the bulletin or was explicitly endorsed by journalists, as in these reports from November and December 1986:

> We are at war with a new virus, MPs were told. The message must get through. (BBC1, *Six O'Clock News*, 21 November 1986)

> The government's message is that everyone is at risk, even babies. (BBC2, *Newsnight*, 21 November 1986)

> The experts agree that everyone is at risk and it is vital to find out about AIDS and how to protect ourselves from it. (ITN, *News at Ten*, 1 December 1986)

The acceptance of the reality of heterosexual transmission was not limited to the early period at the end of 1986 and the beginning of 1987. Even after the backlash in late 1989, which suggested that the heterosexual epidemic had failed to materialise, television news stuck with the dominant medical analysis of HIV transmission. In fact, television news simply did not report Lord Kilbracken's claims (see Chapter 3). TV's news values on this question were even more orthodox than those displayed by specialist correspondents on the broadsheet press. Television news programmes were more likely to report on the danger to the education campaign than to construct 'balanced' coverage which entertained arguments for the demise of the campaign.

In February 1990, *The Day Report* (Day et al., 1990) halved the official prediction of total deaths from AIDS. Rather than questioning the course of the heterosexual epidemic, *Channel Four News* used the report to underline the risk of heterosexual transmission. The newscaster introduced the report as follows:

> Government health officials say the number of people expected to die of AIDS over the next three years will more than halve. The Department of Health is expecting just under six and a half thousand deaths by the end of 1993 compared with earlier estimates of up to 17,000 by the end of 1992. But it's also warning that more heterosexuals than previously expected will die of the disease.

The reporter sums up by arguing: 'Today's figures suggest that earlier advertisements aimed at heterosexuals have had little impact. Senior health officials are pressing ministers to renew the campaign' (*Channel Four News*, 2 February 1990).

TV leads the way

Television news agreed with the government contention that an epidemic among heterosexuals was potentially on the way and supported the idea of an information campaign to change sexual behaviour. However, television was not a straightforward ally of the government. In fact, the television agenda was heavily affected by a coalition of interested parties which we have called the liberal/medical consensus. This meant that television was able to approve of the idea of an advertising campaign while criticising the specifics of its approach. TV news critiques of the government campaign did not generally take the form of querying the information-giving approach as some voluntary sector organisations, activists and academics had (see e.g. Health Information Trust, 1987; Rhodes and Shaughnessy, 1989a, 1989b, 1990; Watney, 1987b; Woffinden, 1988). Nor did reporters suggest that moral prescriptions be emphasised in advertising campaigns. Such views were marginalised on television news. Instead, critiques were focused on the official campaign's lack of explicit terminology and on the government's dilatory approach.

Bulletins were organised around these assumptions and evidence was available in the form of statements from AIDS doctors or non-government organisations. These were legitimised by standard phrases such as 'experts say' or 'doctors believe'.

Sometimes journalists went further and themselves endorsed the pressure on the government. On the announcement of the setting up of the cabinet AIDS committee in November 1986, the BBC science correspondent commented,

> AIDS first appeared in Britain in 1979. Since the early 1980s specialists in the disease have been pleading for more to be done to stop it spreading. Now at last it seems they are being listened to. (BBC1, *Six O'Clock News*, 10 November 1986)

On occasion, the critique of government campaigns as too bland was made by comparison with education materials produced by voluntary sector organisations such as the Terrence Higgins Trust. Even before the launch of the television campaign in late 1986, journalists had made it clear that government efforts would be well short of what much expert opinion thought necessary. An ITN reporter in Downing Street argued that:

> The ads on television however will not be explicit, for example, about the use of condoms and the help some people think they will give in preventing the spread of AIDS . . . and that will perhaps raise questions in some people's minds about how effective this whole campaign is going to be . . . Previous government advertising has been criticised as being too bland especially when compared with some private campaigns containing some very explicit advice, run for example by one of the main charities involved, the Terrence Higgins Trust. (ITN, *News at Ten*, 11 November 1986)

This theme continued to frame the approach adopted by TV news throughout the debate and provided a continuing critical edge to reports of the government strategy. Although there was never again the huge amount of reporting that accompanied the first television advertising campaigns, critical assessment of further initiatives continued.

There was very little criticism of the campaign except in terms of its lack of explicitness: one example of a different type of critique came with the launch of AIDS and drugs adverts in November 1988. But the critics were not from the moral right. Instead professionals in the drugs field were interviewed on both BBC and ITN. On the BBC a spokesperson for the Drug Users Support Group was introduced as a 'critic' who 'claims' as opposed to the higher status 'experts' who in earlier bulletins were said to 'agree' or 'believe'. Her critique is addressed at the use of fear in advertising: 'But critics claim the early drug videos were regarded by some young people as glamorous' (BBC1, *Six O'Clock News*, 21 November 1988).[1]

This critique had less status than those of earlier campaigns, but what is most interesting about it is that no coherent moral critique of the campaigns was featured on television news. Even when spokespersons for the moral right were interviewed, it was in a context which downgraded or dismissed their claims. Indeed, in late 1989 we can find journalists criticising the government for buckling under the pressure of moral right activists.

The announcement at the end of 1989 of government plans for anonymised testing provides a good example. 'As our science correspondent now reports . . . the programme comes amidst concern in the medical profession that AIDS is no longer a top priority for the government' (*Channel Four News*, 21 November 1989). The announcement came at a Department of Health conference in London, and the Health Minister is interviewed to explain the policy plans. The 'story' is, on the face of it, the government announcement at the conference. But it is obvious to the correspondent that the bigger and more significant story is the balance of forces at the heart of AIDS policy formation: 'Doctors here were concerned that the epidemic has slipped in the government's priorities. The cabinet AIDS committee has been disbanded, an advertising campaign cancelled and the HEA has been accused of downgrading its AIDS campaign' (*Channel Four News*, 24 November 1989). We can see here that even though a government press conference is the reason for the news and is carried prominently, the reporter uses the occasion to marshal critiques of government action.

The BBC correspondent demonstrated the same concerns a week later, in a report on International AIDS Day in London. The tone of the report is set by the early citing of AIDS activists as condemning 'the demise of the government's AIDS programme'. The sole interviewee is Sir Reginald Murley, who urges the government to stop its advertising on the dangers of heterosexual transmission. He argued that, inside or outside of marriage, heterosexuals 'have a negligible risk of getting AIDS' (BBC1, *Six O'Clock News*, 1 December 1989). In a later bulletin his views were balanced by a clip of Sir Donald Acheson and the correspondent's introduction, 'But government experts say heterosexual cases are now rising and worldwide they are in the majority' (BBC1, *Nine O'Clock News*, 1 December 1989). However, in both bulletins the correspondents' summary is the same – what now for the government campaign? Reinforcing the logic established at the beginning of the report we hear that:

> The government retreats under pressure from the moral lobby . . . Mrs Thatcher has disbanded the cabinet committee dealing with AIDS and she's withdrawn funding from a major sex survey providing data for future AIDS campaigns . . . the HEA has postponed a major television campaign . . . [whilst] the Department of Health is fighting to preserve its AIDS programme.

Whatever else television news had done it had not established the ground for what the reporter called this 'retreat' in government policy.

Criticising the government

Television reporters were also able to be quite critical of government policy and to promote particular policy changes when policy departed from the expectations or demands of the liberal/medical approach. The most obvious example of this phenomenon is in relation to the debate about the provision of condoms and hypodermic needles in prisons. This was an issue on which there was some division within the state. The Home Office, which has responsibility for prison policy, opposed the distribution of condoms and needles, while sections of the Department of Health and much of the wider policy community supported it. This made it much easier for journalists to attack the Home Office, especially since the National Association of Probation Officers and the All Party Parliamentary Group on AIDS were in favour of policy change.

Reporting of HIV/AIDS in prisons occurred against the background of the widely covered issues of overcrowding, unrest and riot by inmates and industrial protest by prison officers during this period. One report was headlined 'Crowded, cramped, insanitary – life in Britain's jails' (ITN, *News at Ten*, 4 January 1987).

In this context, a report from the All Party Parliamentary Group on AIDS 'calling for the distribution of free condoms to all prisoners' received coverage which endorsed the logic of its arguments.

> They say the prison population is where AIDS is most likely to spread from the homosexual to the heterosexual community. They're angry that the Home Office has cancelled plans to monitor homosexual activity in prisons . . . say the Home Office is failing to face the real facts of prison life and to take the advice of their own experts on AIDS prevention.

The chair of the Group and a prison governor are interviewed, both supporting policy change. The junior Home Office minister in charge of prisons is shown arguing that condoms and needles would encourage and increase illegal activity and therefore cannot be contemplated. The logic of the case for intervention however is expressed succinctly by the reporter's summing up to camera:

> Outside the prison, the government has been promoting safe sex as a more realistic aim than no sex. Homosexuality is common among prisoners who may then return home to their wives and girlfriends, risking spreading the infection rapidly once they're released. The government is unwilling to carry out research which would show just how much homosexuality and drug abuse goes on inside. Illegal activities aren't supposed to happen. Meanwhile, the AIDS virus may be spreading rapidly in prison and no one is monitoring its progress. (BBC1, *Nine O'Clock News*, and BBC2, *Newsnight*, 3 November 1988)

This argument again structured later reports, this time in remarkably similar fashion, on both ITN and BBC. The National Association of Probation Officers 'say Britain's prisons are facing an unparalleled health crisis from AIDS . . . say the number of carriers of the disease and the rate at which it is spreading are well above official figures. They say drug taking and dangerous sexual practices are the cause and they want to see prisoners given condoms and clean needles to try to combat it' (BBC1, *Six O'Clock News*, 30 January 1989). The report summed up: 'Probation officers believe AIDS is already a major health crisis in prisons which could become centres for transmitting the virus to the community outside' (BBC1, *Six O'Clock News*, 30 January 1989).

We have concentrated rather heavily on the coverage of official statements and activities both because they are the staple fare of television news coverage and in order to illustrate the orientations of journalists in relation to government sources. This latter point is important because it is so often dealt with inadequately. However, critiques of the government had their limits. Reporters continued to talk in moral terms about the epidemic and often found it difficult to deal with concepts such as 'homosexuality'. In the following sections we try to show some of those difficulties as well as indicating the relative diversity of some of the coverage of gay men and people with AIDS.

Covering science and medicine

Apart from stories about the government campaign there were a large number of items about a whole range of other aspects of HIV and AIDS.

So far we have concentrated on appearances by government ministers, but the biggest category of interviewees on AIDS were medical and scientific experts. Eighty different scientists and doctors were interviewed in our sample. Fifty-two of these appeared on only one occasion each. There were a very small number to whom journalists returned on several occasions. They included two doctors: Professor Michael Adler of the Middlesex Hospital appeared the most (12 appearances) followed by the government's Chief Medical Officer Dr Donald Acheson (10 appearances). The most often quoted scientific source was Glasgow University's Professor William Jarret, who appeared a total of seven times. The next most often quoted were, like Adler, AIDS doctors: Dr Charles Farthing (five appearances) and Adler's colleague at the Middlesex, Dr Richard Tedder (four appearances). It has often been remarked that medical and scientific experts seem to be permanently fixed at the top of the journalistic 'hierarchy of credibility' (Karpf, 1988). Certainly doctors and scientists were interviewed on television more often than government ministers and HIV/AIDS research was a regular topic for news broadcasts. The very credibility of scientific sources, though, can cause problems for journalists because it is both very difficult, and not thought to be so necessary, to check their authenticity (Miller and Williams, 1993). This problem can be exacerbated by the promotional activities of scientists themselves (Check, 1987).

Take the example of the most interviewed scientist on television news in our sample, Professor William Jarret of Glasgow University. Throughout 1987 TV reporters interviewed Jarret and reported, for example, that 'Medical scientists in Glasgow say they are hoping to start testing a vaccine on patients within 12 months' (ITN, *News at Ten*, 19 February 1987). At a Medical Research Council press conference Sir James Gowans, head of the MRC, stated that 'Phase one trial will start within 12 months. I am quite certain of that' and Jarret announced that he would test the vaccine on himself. TV news reported that 'A new vaccine against AIDS which is being developed in Britain may be tried out on humans within the next year' (BBC1, *Six O'Clock News*, 10 September 1987). Jarret was described by the BBC's science correspondent as 'one of Britain's leading experts on AIDS research' (BBC1, *Six O'Clock News*, 10 September 1987). However, in fact, testing of a vaccine never began nor was one manufactured. Furthermore Jarret had apparently not published a single scientific paper on HIV or AIDS by the end of the 1980s.[2] The Jarret case is an extraordinary example of the pitfalls of the symbiotic relationship which can exist between authoritative scientific sources and the media.

Covering non-official news events

There are other quite different ways of dealing with less well resourced, established or institutionalised sources. It is in this area that we can find some of the most divergent attempts to 'make sense' of HIV and AIDS.

Perhaps what is most interesting about British television news coverage of AIDS is the lack of overt homophobia in the news, either from journalists or from those they allow to speak. One of the central objectives of the government campaign was to avoid the stigmatising of gay men (see Chapter 2). This analysis of television news is similar to that of a study of US television news representations of homosexuality (Cook, 1989). This is not to say that there wasn't any anti-gay coverage but it is to say that there was very little which was overtly homophobic.

However, two 'special reports' on AIDS in Britain in November 1986 show some of the problems that can occur in this area when journalists stray from the path of their regular sources. The purpose of the first report was billed as investigating 'how health experts [in Brighton] are coping with the spread of the disease and to find out how much people actually know about it'. But the report did not actually explore this area. Instead it was introduced as follows:

> AIDS can hit heterosexual men and women and drug addicts, but male homosexuals are the biggest group at risk and in Brighton that's meant they're being openly blamed for the disease.

This provides an opportunity for one man in a pub to comment: 'I think it's disgusting basically . . . Well, there are a lot of gays in Brighton and it's a very easily transmitted disease from what I know and innocent people are catching it all the time.' The journalist makes no attempt to challenge this and instead emphasises that: 'Brighton caters for the second biggest homosexual community outside London with clubs like Mr G's offering drag shows just off the prom. Here they resent being blamed for the spread of a virus they didn't invent.' This is said over shots of customers queuing and entering Mr G's as well as shots of a drag act in the club. Two gay men are then interviewed in the club bar in a spurious 'balance' with the man in the pub. Although 'public prejudice' is designated a problem by the reporter, the expression of this prejudice is left as no more than something which gay men 'resent' (BBC1, *Nine O'Clock News*, 11 November 1986).

The second special report was introduced as investigating 'what's being done to control and perhaps cure' AIDS. Again this is not addressed in the report even though, at the beginning of the report, a doctor is interviewed and points out that prevention is the main priority. The journalist takes this as a recognition that prevention is important only for 'non-deviants'. 'Damage limitation to prevent the spread of the disease is a high priority *if only* to protect those like prison officers who come face to face with AIDS cases' (our emphasis). 'Damage limitation' here refers to attempts to confine the epidemic to gay men, IV drug users and prostitutes. It thus seems logical to examine the supposed threat of those with HIV to prison officers, nurses and ambulance staff. We are told that some nurses at St Mary's Hospital in London 'have walked out rather than risk infection' and that ambulance staff 'have their fears too' (BBC1, *Nine O'Clock News*, 12 November 1986).

In this analysis, as Watney has argued, the threat of AIDS is 'regarded from the frightened perspective of the rest of the population whom these groups [are] erroneously held to threaten' (Watney, 1992: 153). The threat of AIDS to gay men, IV drug users or prostitutes is not considered worthy of mention in such reports.

Yet reports such as these were very rare on television news. Part of the reason for this is that most of the credible and trusted sources of news on AIDS have opposed such victim blaming and negative coverage. When journalists didn't, for whatever reason, use or have access to those sources then the coverage became much more negative.

Reporting AIDS in Africa

One notable area where this happened almost without exception was in the reporting of AIDS in Africa. Here the credible and authoritative government and official sources in African governments were routinely ignored or openly doubted and coverage regularly framed African AIDS epidemics as hopeless and the result of backward 'African culture' (see Husband, 1975; Laishley, 1975; Philo, 1993; UNESCO, 1980; Van der Gaag and Nash, 1987. For discussion of public response to coverage of AIDS in Africa, see Kitzinger and Miller, 1992).

Television news explained HIV in Africa in terms of African culture, poverty, ignorance and 'promiscuity'. In the period we examined, news reports on 'African AIDS' mainly gave cultural explanations for the spread of HIV infection. This allowed journalists to examine the effect of poverty on health provision and to explore the 'primitive' societies in which African men won't use condoms, where 'promiscuity' is a way of life and where people still believe in witch doctors whose backward methods help to spread HIV.

The uncontrolled nature of African sexuality was a recurring theme in both news reports and audience discussions. Here ITN puts us in the picture: 'In Zambia some women's groups want to ban some of the more suggestive tribal dancing. It's one of the few admissions that a promiscuous heterosexual lifestyle is a major cause of spreading AIDS' (ITN, *News at 5.45*, 7 May 1987).

Later the BBC tells us that the problem is the 'traditional resistance of African men to using condoms' (BBC1, *Six O'Clock News*, 19 February 1988). The trend continued in January 1990 in a report on 'AIDS orphans'. 'A million of them in Uganda where health experts say there's a high level of promiscuity' (ITN, *News at Ten*, 2 January 1990).

But back in 1987, *Channel Four News* managed to fit three ways in which primitive black Africans were 'spreading AIDS' into two sentences: 'The spread of AIDS is not caused by sexual promiscuity alone . . . AIDS is encouraged by tribal doctors' traditional medicine and a widespread lack of proper medical facilities' (*Channel Four News*, 2 February 1987).

But while this was the dominant picture of AIDS in Africa, there was some information on the news in this period which could have been used to give a different understanding of the problem of HIV in African countries. On a handful of occasions reference was made to an alternative way of understanding AIDS in Africa. This view sees the role of the West through the lens of its colonial history and argues that the Western blaming of Africa for AIDS has more to do with racism than with medical knowledge or science. What is extraordinary about these references is that some of them are used by the journalist as further evidence of the backwardness of black Africans. For example:

> Here, where tribal doctors still have not heard of AIDS, there are deeply rooted fears and suspicions that the West somehow wants to blame Africa for the start of the AIDS epidemic. (ITN, *News at Ten*, 7 May 1987)

Television news discussions of poverty and 'under-development' in Africa rarely addressed the causes of the massive disparities between rich and poor nations – such as the prevailing political and economic order. Instead explanations, where they were provided, often referred to internally gener- ated causes of poverty such as corruption, natural disasters or 'tribal warfare'.

However, we did find one example where AIDS in Africa was reported in the context of the global order rather than in terms of individual irresponsibility or cultural backwardness. This was three years after the end of our sample, but it is instructive because it shows what can be done if different sources are used or established sources are allowed to answer different questions. This particular item was reported by the BBC science correspondent, although at least some of the research and interviews were conducted by a news assistant. The item reported the publication of *AIDS in the World: A Global Report* (Mann et al., 1992). It featured interviews with Anthony Pinching and with Jon Tinker of the Panos Institute. Tinker framed problems related to AIDS in terms of social inequality:

> All over the world HIV is a misery seeking missile. It homes in on social deprivation, on poverty, on disrupted families, on disadvantaged ethnic minorities, on women who have no control over their lives, on wars, civil wars, refugees. Wherever there is misery and disadvantage, that's where HIV homes in on.

Given this context the reporter concludes by underlining the problem of lack of resources rather than relying on the more usual cultural deficit model:

> Spending by the developed world on helping less developed countries tackle AIDS actually declined in 1991. Only 6% of total spending on AIDS prevention went to countries with 80% of the world's infection. (BBC1, *Six O'Clock News*, 28 January 1993)

This short item indicates how different the reporting of AIDS could be if it utilised different sources and abandoned some of its own conceptions of backward African culture. However, what makes this item doubly extraordinary is that it was not rebroadcast on the *Nine O'Clock News*. Instead, it was replaced by a report filed from Zimbabwe by the BBC's Southern Africa correspondent. Although the report was pegged to the launch of the same report, the content could not have been more different.

According to the reporter, the problems in Zimbabwe stem from 'ignorance, but worse still an unwillingness to listen is very much a part of the crisis'. We are then told that some Zimbabweans use 'any excuse . . . from polluted water to evil spirits. Anything but the truth' to explain AIDS. Given this context the reporter has no problem interviewing a white farm owner who distributes condoms to his black workers, 'but not all the men use them'. The reporter concludes:

> Some in authority in Zimbabwe, who should know better, are still reluctant to tackle the problem of AIDS. Those who are trying are seriously under-resourced. Two major obstacles in a country where for deeply rooted cultural reasons there's a refusal to accept that sexual promiscuity can kill. (BBC1, *Nine O'Clock News*, 28 January 1993)

In this version it is African culture and ignorance which is to blame for the incidence of AIDS and even the lack of resources is blamed on African officials.

Alternative sources in the news

When journalists used official sources or others in the AIDS policy community they were much less likely to report the epidemic so negatively. It was also the case that alternative and radical sources made some impression on the news. AIDS activists featured, for example, in a small number of bulletins (11) as a result of demonstrations or rallies. Sometimes this was as a very brief backdrop to other news events, for example, the statement: 'Demonstrators temporarily sealed off Westminster Bridge today calling for the government to do more to stop the spread of AIDS. White crosses in Parliament Square marked what they said was the demise of the government AIDS programme' is used to support the reporter's contention that 'the days of bold campaigns in Britain may now be over as the government retreats under pressure from the moral lobby' (BBC1, *Six O'Clock News*, 1 December 1989). On other occasions demonstrations were the rationale for the whole news item. For example a demonstration in January 1988 for more money for AIDS treatments and research featured comments from two people with AIDS and from the actor Ian McKellen with no 'balancing' comments (ITN, *News at 5.45*, 24 January 1988). Later Michael Cashman and Kathryn Aponowicz from *EastEnders* are interviewed and comments from one of the people with AIDS from the earlier bulletin is repeated. He says: 'We're classed as second class citizens by society because this is regarded as a moral problem as opposed to a human problem' (ITN, *News at Ten*, 24 January 1988). Such coverage, while not extensive, did not disparage people living with AIDS or HIV. In fact it proved possible for other alternative sources to further influence the construction of news bulletins.

Covering the Terrence Higgins Trust

The best example of this is the coverage of the Terrence Higgins Trust (THT), representatives of which appeared 22 times. This was more than any other organisation except government ministers. Of these 22 appearances, Nick Partridge of THT appeared on 16 bulletins. The only person to appear in more bulletins was Secretary of State for Health, Norman Fowler, who was featured 34 times. The THT quickly established itself as an authoritative source for the media and was able to present itself successfully as a source of expert information and advocate for people with HIV or AIDS.

There is only one occasion in our three-and-a-half year sample when the THT is used to 'balance' a victim-blaming interviewee. This followed a speech by Princess Anne in which she referred to AIDS as 'a self-inflicted wound' and spoke of 'innocent victims . . . who may have been infected knowingly by sufferers seeking revenge'. THT 'the leading AIDS charity' (BBC1, *Nine O'Clock News*, 26 January 1988) is quoted as saying 'we are all innocent victims. The Princess will have offended many people' (BBC1, *Six O'Clock News*, 26 January 1988). Nick Partridge is interviewed on both BBC and both ITN bulletins. ITN reported that the THT 'said they were appalled – The human race as a whole was the innocent victim' (ITN, *News at 5.45* and *News at Ten*, 26 January 1988).

Perhaps because of the comments of the Princess, the BBC reporter went on to introduce Partridge with the words 'the talk of innocent victims infuriated Britain's homosexual community' (BBC1, *Nine O'Clock News*, 26 January 1988). Apart from this, the THT was never introduced as a gay organisation. This was seen at the time as a success. Nor was the THT in any way disparaged in the entire sample period. Instead it was used and described by television news as an expert source or simply as a charity, as in the following introductions:

> The Terrence Higgins Trust was set up to help the victims of AIDS. (*Channel Four News*, 3 November 1986)

> One of the main charities involved, the Terrence Higgins Trust . . . (ITN, *News at Ten*, 11 November 1986)

> The Terrence Higgins Trust, set up in memory of the first British man to die from AIDS, pioneered public awareness of the threat. (ITN, *News at Ten*, 4 December 1986)

> A charity which helps AIDS victims . . . the Terrence Higgins Trust say . . . (BBC1, *Nine O'Clock News*, 5 March 1987)

> . . . groups like the Terrence Higgins Trust, which helps AIDS patients . . . (BBC1, *Six O'Clock News*, 5 May 1987)

The Terrence Higgins Trust, the biggest AIDS charity . . . (ITN, *News at 5.45*, 2 July 1987)

Tonight the major AIDS charity, the Terrence Higgins Trust, criticised government policy on AIDS. (BBC1, *Nine O'Clock News*, 28 October 1987)

The main AIDS charity . . . (BBC1, *Six O'Clock News*, 30 November 1988)

By 1989 TV news was no longer introducing or describing the THT other than by name caption on the screen – their expert status was an unspoken assumption.

Covering people with AIDS

People living with HIV or AIDS have featured prominently in television news. Issues such as discrimination, prejudice, fear and ignorance as well as the medical and financial problems involved have been featured. In contrast to much early press coverage, many of these TV reports were 'sympathetic' and often overtly educational in intent. Television could counter misconceptions and introduce expert sources from many areas of AIDS experience.

The largest group of interviewees (47) were of people with AIDS (PWAs) whose route of HIV transmission or sexual identity was not specified. Only four interviews involved male PWAs who were introduced as gay, whereas there were 16 haemophiliacs, a dramatic reversal of the actual proportions of gay men and people with haemophilia who have HIV or AIDS. A number of interviews with parents were shown – five whose children were haemophiliacs, a further nine whose children's status was not specified. There were no parents or partners of gay men interviewed; however there were three interviews with the wives of haemophiliacs. At this broad level we can already see distinctions between the treatment of people with AIDS according to whether they are, in media parlance, deserving or undeserving victims. It is remarkable that in over three and a half years, television news did not interview the partner or lover of any gay man nor any of their other family members. Such domestic settings were reserved only for heterosexuals.

Distinctions between 'innocent' and 'guilty' victims surfaced explicitly in some news coverage of haemophiliacs with HIV. On ITN a headline referred to 'The innocent victims of AIDS' (ITN, *News at 5.45*, 12 October 1987). Meanwhile on the BBC: 'And a plea from the people who got the AIDS virus by accident: Our families must have more money.' It is as if other people acquired the virus deliberately. The newsreader explains that people with haemophilia face the threat of AIDS, 'through no fault of their own' (BBC1, *Six O'Clock News*, 12 October 1987).

But not all of the coverage of people with AIDS was so negative. Only a minority of reports used such discriminatory labelling and on occasion the distinction between innocent and guilty was seen as a problem by the reporter, as in this comment: 'Some believe it is wrong to discriminate between different categories of victim.' Although this does introduce a spurious balance with moralist 'views' it is used to introduce an interview with Jim Wilson of the Terrence Higgins Trust who is able to make the point, 'Immaterial of how a person contracted the disease, once they've got full-blown AIDS their needs are all very much the same and they [the government] should be catering now towards those needs' (ITN, *News at Ten*, 16 November 1987).

Interviews with male patients in hospices and special wards were common in television news reports. One of the more positive examples was an ITN report from America which featured an AIDS hospice in Kansas. Three people with AIDS were interviewed. One said:

> To be in a situation like this is wonderful because you can die with dignity and you can't die with dignity in a hospital. There's no way, you just kind of lie there and fade away. Here you're loved and you're cared about and it's like your family is with you when it finally happens. (*Channel Four News*, 12 November 1986)

The sympathy of the reporter is apparent: 'when his parents found out he was an AIDS patient they were unsympathetic and cruel. For Gerry this place and the friendship of his fellow sufferers was a heaven-sent refuge.'

But there are limitations to this approach. The journalist introduces the interviewee by contrasting his appearance with how he used to look before AIDS. Such comparisons have routinely been used by journalists. They establish the image of AIDS as decline, decay and wasting:

> A self-portrait on the wall constantly reminds 37-year-old Gerry of how he used to be before he was infected with AIDS. Now this talented and trained artist is living in a hospice for dying AIDS patients in Kansas City. He used to be a body builder. (*Channel Four News*, 12 November 1986)

Early perceptions of AIDS were linked to particular images of homo-sexuality and drug abuse. It is easy for sexuality and culture to appear as reasons and causes for AIDS, which carry the inevitable and dreadful price of death.

The way that television news covered people with AIDS was the result of the information available to them in the form of interviews or potential interviews, their own strategies for getting the news, news values and the strategies employed by their sources. All of these factors contribute to the definition of an event as news as well as subsequently informing how the event should be covered. In the coverage of the AIDS epidemic, it was possible for journalists to have access to the same material and yet, for reasons associated with the journalist's own orientations, report dramati-cally different stories. On the other hand, once an event is defined as a story, the activities of the source of the story can very tightly define the logic of how to cover it.

In the former case, the coverage of the Health Minister's visit to a San Francisco hospital and his 'first meeting ever with a hospitalised AIDS patient' (BBC1, *Nine O'Clock News*, 21 January 1987) is a useful example. On the BBC the patient whom Fowler meets was described as follows: 'Ken

... is a homosexual and a former drug user. Many of his friends have died of the disease. He now has it himself.' We are told that 'The patient was recovering from a bout of pneumonia but no one yet has recovered from AIDS.' And after the British Minister has left we were shown Ken 'talking of his earlier life':

> It was a good time, it was reckless abandon and it probably was very irresponsible but it was a good time and we thought nothing of having casual sex or of using recreational drugs, we didn't give it a second thought. But you know when you lose a lot of your friends or a lover or eventually, when it hits the heterosexual community, it will be children and wives and things like that, it wakes you up.

The reporter closes with: 'By the statistical averages of these cases he has about one year to live' (BBC1, *Nine O'Clock News*, 21 January 1987). Here the person with AIDS is a warning to others rather than of interest in his own right. For the journalist this is plainly a guilty victim allowed simply to confess his past sins.

A quite different view of the same man and a different message from his meeting with the Minister came across in the ITN report that night. This time the same person is used by the journalist to make the point that distinctions between innocent and guilty are wrong. The reporter comments that Ken 'is angered though by people who say it is just a homosexual disease and AIDS isn't their concern':

> I wish I could tell all the straight people that, look, it's a virus, it's not running around checking sexual preference or race or class or anything, you know, it's just making people sick and it will make anyone sick. (ITN, *News at Ten*, 21 January 1987)

These two quite different reports emphasise the way in which media factors such as news values and journalists' own orientations can heavily impact on reporting. In the next examples, it is interesting to note that once an event is defined as a news story it can have its own seemingly inexorable logic.

A protest against the siting of an AIDS hospice in the Scottish village of Torphichen supplied the rationale for one bulletin. The item was headlined: 'The villagers ask – An AIDS hospice? Why us?' A second newscaster announces: 'AIDS units are to be set up in hospitals in Glasgow, Edinburgh and Dundee. But the villagers of Torphichen don't see why they should have an AIDS hospice forced on them. A report next.' The report has already been structured by the objectors' point of view and this has the effect of treating their opinions and threatened actions as reasonable and legitimate. The narrative begins with their question, their objection and continues with their perspective: 'Residents say the prospects of the presence of the hospice there will destroy the community' and 'fear the presence of AIDS victims will blight their small community'. Several objecting residents are interviewed, including two GPs, and, despite interviews with two members of the hospice trust, the item ends by underlining (rather than challenging) the 'logic' that AIDS and those associated with it are to be feared and shunned: 'The AIDS outbreak is spreading rapidly so the debate at Torphichen is one which will eventually be repeated in communities throughout the country' (ITN, *News at Ten*, 16 July 1987).

However, reports such as this which access small, poorly resourced groups with a very low level of institutionalisation can also work in the opposite direction. A good example is coverage of the London Lighthouse hospice. Here the report is little more than praise for the activities of the Lighthouse and people living there are allowed to attempt a redefinition of more familiar images of people living with HIV or AIDS:

> It may be a place for people to come to die but it's actually a place for people to come to live well as well while they die, while they go through the dying process. I think that's where the focus needs to be. It's a place where people can come and be educated about how to live in the moment, how to get as much out of the moment as possible.

The project had a well known supporter and benefactor in Ian McKellen the actor, who was allowed both to praise Lighthouse and to appeal for more support for the hospice movement:

> It's a national emergency. It's happening in our capital city. There are thousands of people directly affected by a disease . . . people are dying and people are getting ready for death and their families are deeply affected by it . . . It's terribly depressing to realise that there ought to be a London Lighthouse in Birmingham and Edinburgh and Glasgow and Belfast now. But at least it's set a wonderful example, to see the smiling faces here and realise that AIDS in the end is not about death, it's about life and the liveliness of people here, people who have AIDS and the people who are helping them . . . there are saints in this building. (BBC1, *Six O'Clock News*, 22 September 1988)

Here the bulletin is structured to present the views of people living with AIDS and their supporters, rather than those who would see them as a disruption to 'their' community.

Conclusion

Television news demonstrated striking similarity in the way it presented the government health education campaign. The output of all network television news agreed on the basic necessity of the campaign and of its central premise: the danger of an epidemic of heterosexual transmission. The growing political influence of the moral right's attack on the health education strategy owed little to television journalism.

The closeness of television news journalists to key sources in the AIDS policy community from late 1986 was reflected in the specific criticisms which news reports did make of the government's efforts: that they were not explicit enough and that they were too little too late. The case for a more radical policy in the prisons was made in the circumstances of open divisions between ministries and between government and expert advisors.

In short, government announcements and press conferences were guaranteed coverage – usually on all bulletins on all four channels. The coverage, though, was not always favourable to the government.

The relatively restricted range of these orthodox sources also helped to account for the poorer reporting on television of the detail of health education and sexuality. In particular, news reports continued to speak in narrow and contentious moral terms about the epidemic and often to display little understanding of the debates about terminology and representation.

Medical and scientific 'experts' were routinely accessed and very rarely questioned, even when, as it turned out, some were prone to economies of truth. Television news rarely accessed and reporters rarely endorsed overt homophobia. They were, however, more likely to allow moralist perspectives to structure their reporting when they abandoned their regular sources in the policy community. The importance of a range of alternative sources was illustrated by the success of the Terrence Higgins Trust in accessing news accounts. In covering people living with HIV or AIDS, some television journalists were prone to allocate blame, both in their choice of interviewees and in the distinctions they made between innocent and guilty victims. However reporters were also vulnerable to alternative sources of AIDS information. Such vulnerability worked both to access coverage which assumed that the problem of AIDS was the people living with it, as well as, on other occasions, to challenge preconceptions. This could allow some quite positive portrayals of people with HIV and AIDS and endorsement of arguments for more funding for care.

It is very hard to argue from this that television news has been straightforwardly and uniformly negative in its coverage of the AIDS epidemic. To be sure, there have been some very negative portrayals and prejudicial coverage, but television news did manage to do some new things. Part of the reason for this has been the success of organisations such as the THT and the campaigning of gay and AIDS activist groups as well as the commitment of large parts of the medical establishment to a liberal/medical approach rather than a moral one.

It is also very difficult to talk of television news coverage on AIDS as objective or neutral. Television news did bolster certain conceptions of the epidemic and very largely marginalised the views of the moral right. In fact television was committed to particular viewpoints on AIDS, although these could be negotiated by individual reporters, by source strategies and by news values. It does not make sense, in these circumstances, to talk of objectivity. However, there is a pervasive tendency in media studies which concludes that because an objective account of the world is not possible, the notion of bias is equally useless. Alternatively, 'texts' are seen as having no meanings outside the 'readings' of them made by audiences. These approaches lead to relativism and the inability of the social scientist to comment upon the world in general, or upon the meaning of media texts in particular. We do not share these assumptions. It should be apparent from the above that we think that television news was very definitely promoting some views at the expense of others.

Notes

1. The only other example in our sample took a specific advert to task for its assumptions about its audience and its lack of sensitivity towards people living with HIV or AIDS. The item was introduced as follows:

> The government's latest anti-AIDS campaign says that any difference between HIV infection and AIDS is only a matter of time. But AIDS workers say that's not true and have warned that the government's message will take away patients' will to live.

The reporter goes on to say: 'The main AIDS charity, the Terrence Higgins Trust, has condemned the campaign and disputes some of the government's figures . . . One man who has AIDS yet leads an active life and runs the Frontline self-help group said the government is encouraging people with the virus to simply give up hope':

> When I was first diagnosed I was told that I had 15 months to two years to live. I accepted that and I got on with it. I have since met people who have been diagnosed the same as myself in England and in America, people who have gone on for about ten years. (BBC1, *Six O'Clock News*, 30 November 1988)

2. Such claims and their coverage, which often failed to make the distinction between a vaccine and a cure, had the more than unfortunate consequence of raising the hopes of people with HIV and AIDS or those who were worried about it, many of whom apparently phoned Jarret's laboratory wanting to know about the vaccine/cure. Nick Partridge of the THT commented on this case that: 'Because AIDS is a clear public health threat, anything that can be labelled as a breakthrough is bound to have a big impact. In their rush for front pages and scientific prizes, journalists and scientists often forget that they're dealing with the lives and deaths of real people.'

The story of Professor Jarret's record was revealed by Duncan Campbell on Channel Four's *Scottish Eye*, 5 p.m., Sunday 1 March 1992 and in Campbell's 'AIDS messiah with feet of clay', *Scotland on Sunday*, 1 March 1992: 6. See also Marcello Mega and Alan Hutchison 'University defends work of top AIDS scientist', *Scotsman*, 2 March 1992; Cameron Simpson, ' University hits out in AIDS row', *The Herald*, 2 March 1992; David Hamilton, 'AIDS pioneer fury at TV "failure" attack', *Sunday Express*, 8 March 1992. A defence of Jarret is mounted by fellow researchers and the university vice-principal, to which Duncan Campbell replies in 'Lurid line on AIDS research', *Scotland on Sunday*, 8 March 1992.

5

AIDS on Television: Form, Fact and Fiction

David Miller

There is certainly self-censorship. We call it editorial control. (Mick Rhodes, Head of Science Features, *Network*, BBC2, 23 February 1988)

Between 7 March 1983 and 30 August 1990 over 250 non-news television programmes on AIDS were broadcast on British network television. The importance of both factual and fictional non-news programmes in the coverage of AIDS/HIV was highlighted in 1987 when the government identified them as part of their public health campaign. In March of that year the three television networks collaborated with the Department of Health and Social Security (DHSS) in AIDS Week which was primarily aimed at 'young people', and included chat shows, question and answer programmes and music as well as public education slots. AIDS Week marked an unprecedented degree of co-operation between the media and the government in peacetime. Broadcasters had been brought in as part of the official public health campaign as a result of the 'state of national emergency' declared by the government. The alarming projections about the spread of the disease convinced the broadcasting organisations of the need to co-operate with the government's educational effort.

This chapter examines non-news actuality and fictional output of television including the programming of AIDS Week, drawing on interviews with television production staff and broadcasting executives. It provides an overview of the themes of non-news programming on AIDS; examines why television programming took the form it did and highlights the relative strength of differing approaches to AIDS.

The chapter starts with an account of the amount of coverage, summarises the relations between broadcasting and the state in the late 1980s and discusses AIDS Week. It then follows the discussion of phone-ins during AIDS Week with a review of factual programming including audience participation shows, educational programmes, current affairs and documentary and science programming. Fictional formats are then discussed including drama series and plays. The chapter concludes with a discussion of struggles over the language and imagery deemed appropriate for covering AIDS.

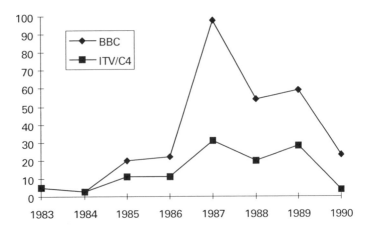

Figure 5.1   *Non-news television programmes on HIV/AIDS, 1983–90*

The development of non-news coverage

Non-news programmes dealing with HIV and AIDS on British television developed along the same lines as TV news interest in the topic (see Figure 5.1) At the beginning there was little attention paid to the disease. In 1983 ITV and Channel Four, as well as both BBC channels, had only a handful of programmes dealing with HIV/AIDS and fewer programmes about AIDS were transmitted in 1984. In 1985 coverage began to increase sharply with a more gradual rise in 1986. 1987 was the pinnacle of coverage which included the special events that comprised AIDS Week. There was an overall decline in 1988 but in 1989 Channel Four, ITV and BBC coverage rose again largely due to the controversy over the targeting of the government campaign on AIDS. Between 1989 and 1990 there was a steep decline in the interest shown by non-news programmes on all four channels.

Broadcasting and the state: the state of play in the late 1980s

The election of the Conservative administration in 1979 led to increasingly bitter conflicts between broadcasters and the government throughout the 1980s. The New Right philosophy of Mrs Thatcher was a break with the post war settlement and marked the end of the politics of consensus which had arguably characterised post war British politics. By the end of 1986, when the idea of co-opting the broadcast media in AIDS education was first raised in the DHSS, there was heightened tension between the government and broadcasters, in particular the BBC. Government policy intentions for the future of broadcasting made the Corporation exceedingly sensitive to the official mood. Norman Tebbitt had recently attacked BBC coverage of the US bombing of Libya and the Special Branch had raided the offices of BBC Scotland following the broadcast of an episode of the *Secret Society* series on the Zircon spy satellite (Philo, 1995). It might be argued that the softening up of the broadcasters made it much easier for the government to secure consent for co-operation over AIDS Week. However, in our view the appeal to the liberal/medical consensus and to the ethos of public service made by the DHSS over AIDS is better seen as a return (even if only temporarily and exceptionally) to the territory of consensus politics, precisely the territory which the government had, in other areas, so clearly abandoned.

AIDS Week

The ten days of AIDS Week on television were 'probably the first event not concerned with the monarchy, sport or parliamentary politics to dominate the schedules' (Alcorn, 1989: 196). The Head of Daytime Television at the BBC, Roger Laughton, saw AIDS Week as 'an unprecedented week of public health programmes' in response to 'an unprecedented public health problem' (*BBC Television Presents the Facts on AIDS*, BBC news release, 17 February 1987).

The origins of AIDS Week

By late 1986 pressure was mounting for a greater governmental response to AIDS and the television response was also being raised. On the 29 October Tory MPs were reported as urging ITV and the BBC to give 'free television time' for AIDS education programmes (*Daily Mirror*, 29 October 1986). The Cabinet AIDS Committee met for the first time on 4 November, and discussions between the television networks, prompted by Sir Kenneth Stowe, Permanent Secretary at the DHSS, came up with the idea of a four channel 'simulcast'. In mid-November Secretary of State, Norman Fowler met with the Chairman and Director General of the IBA and of the BBC. Fowler (1991: 259) later noted that: 'Television comes in for a lot of stick from politicians of all parties, but in this case they were magnificent . . . The meetings were short and the only request was "how can we help?"'

Five days later BBC, IBA and ITV executives, newspaper editors and radio representatives were summoned to the Cabinet Office for a meeting of what was called the AIDS Publicity Liaison Committee with officials of the DHSS and others. At the meeting the idea of AIDS Week was discussed. Geraint Stanley Jones, the Director of Public Affairs at the BBC, said the BBC 'would be interested in discussing with the IBA and the companies an AIDS information week' (Memorandum from Clare Mulholland, IBA Director of Programmes to David Glencross, November 1986). Clare Mulholland 'emerged [from the meeting] with the impression that the DHSS is somewhat overwhelmed by its task'. Indeed at the beginning of December the Health Education Council held a workshop for health education practitioners on 'Regional Responses to AIDS'. IBA Senior Education Officer Susan Elliot attended and reported that the meeting

> threw into sharp relief the slow-wittedness and general incompetence of the Government response to a health problem about which the basic facts have been known for three years. The frustration and anger among the 20 or so taking part was tangible. (Memorandum on 'HEC workshop "Regional Responses to AIDS" 5.12.86', 8 December 1986)

By mid-December discussion and planning within the BBC was advanced enough for an internal meeting to conclude that the original suggestion of a four channel 'simulcast' would 'produce party political irritation'.[1] A two channel broadcast was approved. By 12 January the IBA had ruled out a long ITV/Channel Four simulcast but accepted the principle of a short one and had set the date of Television Week for the end of February (Alcorn, 1989: 197). In the end ITV and Channel Four did broadcast the same 90-minute programme, but not at the same time (ITV 21.30, Friday 27 February; Channel Four, 23.15, Saturday 28 February). AIDS Week was launched by a joint BBC/ITV press conference on 17 February.

Broadcasters, the state and AIDS Week

Broadcasters had a curious double-edged relationship with the state over AIDS Week. The AIDS crisis represented the welcome return of consensus after a prolonged onslaught from successive Thatcher administrations. Broadcasters were happy to assist in what was presented to them as a national emergency in which the government, exceptionally, needed help. As Clare Mulholland of the IBA saw it:

> There were doubts about this and that but no one really doubted that this was a genuine emergency . . . There was no question of the DHSS or the government running it. People accepted fairly early on that they were being appealed to by government for help and that's what they responded to. (Interview with the authors)

The broadcasters suspended the normal rules of competition and the drive for ratings, and all the television companies co-operated in scheduling AIDS Week. The spirit of common purpose brought broadcasters together and many became personally committed and involved.

However, it was consensus at a price. The AIDS crisis appeared to be a safe consensus issue – a public health emergency on which dissent was likely to be minimal. However, it was also highly problematic as it involved the representation of sex and sexuality which, under the guise of taste and decency, had been a matter of controversy between the state and broadcasters for much of the post war period. Moreover, those largely affected were stigmatised groups (gay men, IV drug users, sex workers, black

Africans). AIDS, therefore, presented a series of problems in how broadcasters would address their audience and present the government's health education message on AIDS while appearing to maintain their independence from government.

In practice the sense of mission during AIDS Week allowed the broadcasters to move beyond previously accepted conventions for the portrayal of sex, and in particular of condoms. Public 'offence' at the change in policy had less impact. For example, the BBC broadcast a series of public service announcements before the 9 p.m. watershed in February 1987, leading to a number of complaints from parents. Malcolm Walker, Head of Presentation, responded robustly.

> I have sympathy with those who have no wish to see the AIDS films broadcast at an early hour. But we are confronted with an issue that really is too important to ignore. The Department of Health believes that these films should be aimed at those aged 13 upwards, and if we are to reach such a young age group, the films must be transmitted at times of day when we know they will be watching. I know this means that even younger children will see the films, but if the message saves even one life in the future, surely this must outweigh the chance of causing offence to a relatively small number of people. (*Radio Times*, 28 February–6 March 1987)

However, doubts about the government's motives and the extent to which broadcasters were violating their own standards were not far from the surface. John Fairley, Director of Programmes at YTV, was appointed to co-ordinate the independent television contribution to AIDS Week. In February 1988 he said:

> The problem that we felt then and I think I feel a lot more [now is] that we became sort of evangelists for condoms. We were trying to sell a point of view which broadcasters don't do and we'd never got into that game before and I think I rather – overall – regret it. (*Network*, BBC2, 23 February 1988)

Some broadcasters worried that the government might use their co-operation as a precedent to pressure the media into line in other areas of policy.[2] Such sentiments were publicly expressed by independent television executives and seem to have been most keenly felt at Channel Four. In 1988, Gwyn Pritchard, commissioning editor at Channel Four, highlighted the dangers for the future:

> I think we ought to be terribly careful when people say 'well yes, now that AIDS is on the screen you've got to look at it only this way. You've only got to raise these questions' . . . I think some people.. with the best intentions, and from a side of the political spectrum which one would least expect . . . are going to end up saying 'because of these particular conditions we should avoid looking at certain things' . . . I think that's a real danger for us as broadcasters that we shouldn't fall into. (*Network*, BBC2, 23 February 1988)

It was such sentiments that contributed to the commissioning of documentaries on Channel Four which challenged both the scientific orthodoxy and the government line on HIV transmission (see below).

AIDS Week programmes

AIDS Television Week was launched on 27 February 1987 with LWT's 90-minute *First AIDS*, billed as a 'pop and showbiz extravaganza'. The *Daily Telegraph* argued that 'LWT had found a way of getting the desperate message across through a combination of frankness, clinical precision, humour and lack of pretence' (*Daily Telegraph*, 2 March 1987). Later that evening at 9.30p.m. the BBC's 12-minute simulcast (on both BBC channels) *AIDS – The Facts* was broadcast. In the course of the ensuing ten days, 26 separate programmes were broadcast across the networks, with some additional regional programmes. These included five special editions of audience participation shows, broadcast late at night, two science documentaries, three current affairs programmes, an edition of Channel Four's *Seven Days* religious programme and the BBC's *Heart of the Matter*, on hostility towards homosexuality. The largest category of programming was explicitly educational with two series of short programmes, *AIDS Help* on ITV and *AIDS Brief* on Channel Four, together with the BBC's *AIDS – The Facts*. On Monday 9 March, the day after the last AIDS Week programme, ITV began the serialisation of the four part drama *Intimate Contact* and from Friday 13 March for five weeks BBC2 broadcast an education programme *Facing Up to AIDS*.

Mary Whitehouse of the National Viewers and Listeners Association (NVLA) was reported as saying that ITV's opening programme *First AIDS* 'should never have been screened' because, as she pointed out, 'the message was either carry a condom or you get AIDS. At no time was the word marriage mentioned' ('Thumbs up for TV's AIDS war', *Daily Express*, 28 February 1987: 5). In so far as there was a 'tone' to the programmes on AIDS Week, this was it. Firmly within the liberal orthodoxy on AIDS, if somewhat ahead of government pronouncements, 'punitive ideologies were criticised and an implicit ideology of a supportive society and individual responsibility was encouraged' (Murphy, 1987: 39).

Murphy shows that 'AIDS Week was presented as a debate . . . between a perspective which saw a duty to the sick and those at risk . . . and a punitive, deviant controlling response' and 'the former was the preferred response' markedly, outweighing the punitive approach (ibid.). During AIDS Week there were, for example, more than four times as many statements supporting societal or individual responses to AIDS as those suggesting punitive actions (Murphy, 1987). The preferred view of AIDS allowed a number of television firsts: Norman Fowler (dressed in his gardening jumper) became the first government minister to say the word 'condom' on television; Donald Acheson, the Chief Medical Officer claims the record for the first use of the term 'anal sex'; condoms were unrolled over fingers, cucumbers, bananas and even, by Clare Rayner and Ian Dury, on a dildo (see Garfield, 1994b: 128).

The educational thrust of AIDS Week was matched by a clear bias in favour of liberal responses to AIDS by presenters of public participation and other shows. A steady stream of 'experts' in the studio could also be called upon to 'correct' callers.

> *Caller*: It's an unnatural act despite what Dr Nick said about it; the homosexual act is unnatural, perverted and incredibly filthy.
> *Canon Wright*: I cannot take that view . . . I'm pretty convinced that homosexuality is normal, that is the way God made us.
> *Presenter*: [to caller] Marjorie, that's a man of the Church saying that to you.
> (*Open Air*, BBC1, 23.35, 4 March 1987)

According to Murphy (1987: 21), 'Experts use their authority and the facts in an attempt to normalise the disease away from deviance and blame.' This liberal approach meant that almost all of the programmes concentrated on heterosexual transmission and tended not to give advice to gay men (or lesbians). There was also little comment in AIDS Week on more structural responses to the crisis, such as legislation to prevent discrimination.

While the educational efforts of AIDS Week were located within the liberal orthodoxy on AIDS, we should not overemphasise the homogeneity of non-news programmes across the schedules. The rest of this chapter examines the range of factual and fictional television programming on AIDS, showing that different formats enabled and constrained programme makers in distinctive ways. We start with audience participation and educational programming since these were a key feature of AIDS Week.

Audience participation shows

Audience participation shows, such as the phone-ins discussed above, were the space where moral and punitive approaches to AIDS were most evident. These shows were new to British television in the mid-1980s, following the advent of breakfast television. Programmes such as *Day to Day* (later *Kilroy*), and *The Time, The Place* adopted the format and style of the American *Oprah Winfrey Show* in featuring the studio audience in discussion. Broadly analogous were programmes such as *Open Air* in which viewers were invited to phone in with their own perspectives or questions which were answered by a series of guests or 'experts'. While programmes with studio audiences could afford to go out live, phone-in programmes were subject to a delay of some minutes, leaving time to edit out unacceptable content. Furthermore, during AIDS Week, both *Day to Day* and *Open Air* were moved from their daytime slots and broadcast in the late evening. Nevertheless, such programmes depend on people speaking out freely, even if only for a very short period of time. To the extent that editorial control is attenuated, the possibility of alternative perspectives arises. In the case of AIDS, this allowed the comparative over-accessing of punitive and victim-blaming views as compared with the preferred liberal response of the programme makers (see the examples above). This is contrary to some recent work which has praised such shows as a kind of public sphere (e.g. Livingstone and Lunt, 1993). Such views are also an integral part of programmes which (specifically in relation to AIDS) were set up to function as educational. The agenda of such programmes is constructed as an opposition between ignorance and prejudice, intolerance and enlightenment.

Educational programmes

Almost all of the television programmes about AIDS during 1987 – and a large proportion afterwards – were designed to be educative. In programming terms, however, only a limited number of programmes were classified as educational. In the ITV system, educational programming is the business of the Educational Advisory Council, which sets priority areas and targets to which the independent companies respond with programme proposals. Channel Four especially has a responsibility for commissioning educational programmes, defined by Robin Moss of the Independent Television Commission (ITC) as 'those programmes which ITV and Channel Four propose should be educational and which the ITC approve as educational' (interview with the authors). Since 1982 the IBA (then the ITC) has required all ITV and Channel Four educational output to be accompanied by some form of back-up or support such as helplines or printed information.

In the period under discussion, health education was the highest priority of educational broadcasting. Programmes are made on social issues, such as homelessness, but health and environment feature more prominently in the educational output. As Robin Moss of the ITC explains:

> We would rather not have too much of that [social and political programming] because there are big issues like 15,000 people a year dying prematurely from smoking related disease, like AIDS and sexual health . . . Numero uno is health education, followed by environmental education and so on. (Interview with the authors)

The reason for this is that health and the environment are seen as less controversial, often regarded as non-political topics around which there is some measure of consensus. This is partly because of the credibility and authority of medicine and science. It can result in criticism of established interests in programming which sees its function explicitly as educational. As one educational TV producer put it, 'we do have a definite sort of health policy commitment. We are not in there to make a programme to scare people.' 'In my end of broadcasting,' he continued, 'we are all covert liberal lefties'. On AIDS this had the effect of making it easier to include material which in a current affairs programme might require to be 'balanced'. Thus moralist perspectives were seen as beyond the pale of acceptable opinion in educational programming. According to one producer:

> I don't feel an obligation to show both sides of the question or to try and be objective. I don't know how you square that up. I am not a propagandist, I would never bend the facts or distort them or anything like that, but I always feel that pressure that you are supposed to be trying to open people's thinking up.

Thus in December 1986 Susan Elliot, Senior Education Officer at the IBA advised those making programmes on AIDS to 'be aware of racism and anti-gay feeling and fight both' (memorandum by Susan Elliot, IBA on 'HEC workshop "Regional Responses to AIDS" 5.12.86', 8 December 1986).

Precisely because of their educational status it was possible to go much further in such programmes in discussing sex, sexual practice and sexuality than in other television forms. One example is the filming of a female advice worker putting a condom on with her mouth as part of health education for sex workers. This was done in the context of a discussion about sex workers' clients refusing to wear condoms.

However, educational broadcasting was, and is, not a completely open space. Education and especially schools broadcasting found it difficult to deal with homosexuality. In 1985 the BBC Schools Department was commissioned to produce a play on two gay teenagers. *Two of Us* was delayed for two years and then shown at 11.30 at night. It was a further two years before it was shown to a schools audience (*The End of Innocence*, BBC2, 5 December 1995). By and large such controversies are avoided by self-censorship. It is rare for things to get to the final stage before interventions are made. According to the producer of *AIDS Update '89* the closest that the series came to an act of censorship was the removal of one word from Muriel Gray's commentary about Clause 28, which outlawed teaching about homosexuality in schools. Her use of the term 'infamous' to describe the clause was edited out on the instruction of the executive producer.

Current affairs and documentary

By contrast with educational programmes, current affairs and documentary programmes are more centrally concerned with political controversy and debate. They are therefore more likely to include a range of opinion. As with television news, such programming could be extremely critical of government when its actions did not live up to the demands of the liberal perspective (see Chapter 4). This was especially the case with issues such as haemophilia and AIDS in prison. However, the vast majority of current affairs and documentary programmes were organised from within the liberal perspective. Alternative representations of HIV and AIDS were sparse and confined in the main to minority viewing slots. Alternative programming had three main variants. First, programmes which argued for a moralist approach to AIDS either within the structure of the programme or openly. These programmes were rare. Secondly, programmes which challenged the scientific orthodoxy on HIV and AIDS, such as a series of programmes on *Dispatches*. Thirdly, programmes which provided a critique of dominant representations either explicitly as in programmes specifically dealing with representations of AIDS (*The Media Show*, *Network*, the *Late Show*, etc.) or in providing an alternative frame of reference or critique of government policy from the perspective of those with HIV. These programmes were also rare, the latter type exceptionally so. It is very difficult to point to any mainstream television documentary or current affairs programmes (*World in Action, Panorama, This Week*, etc.) in our sample which provided a critique of the dominant approach from the perspective of people with AIDS, or allowed for debate amongst gay men or IV drug users on how best to respond. In fact the politics of AIDS was one notable absence in current affairs coverage. For example, BBC's flagship *Panorama* broadcast five editions on AIDS between 7 March 1983, the first documentary on AIDS, and January 1989.[3] None of them dealt directly with the politics of AIDS. This neglect was partly because of the lack of *party* political controversy in the area.

Documentary and current affairs programmes are entrusted with different missions. Furthermore, the mode of address of programmes on AIDS varied. They variously attempt to explain what is being done to stop AIDS at the level of science, inform the public on recent medical developments, educate the public about matters of transmission and protection and monitor government conduct (or sometimes the conduct of other organisations or institutions). Especially in the more documentary film type presentations, an individual or group of people affected by AIDS is shown attempting to deal with the effects of the virus. Such films tend to be more open to the perspectives of those with HIV or those around them.

Compared to television news, current affairs programmes were more likely to include a wider range of voices on AIDS. However, voices from beyond the liberal/medical consensus were often downgraded and marginalised by the programme's inferential structure. For example, Thames Television's *This Week* set out to tell, in the words of the programme title, 'The truth about AIDS'. Broadcast in August 1990, as a direct response to the argument that heterosexuals were not at risk of acquiring HIV, the programme featured interviews with Reginald Murley, sponsor of Family and Youth Concern and Lord Kilbracken. The reporter gives a strong clue to the stance of the programme in the introduction: 'we look at the argument that heterosexuals have nothing to fear from AIDS and the scientific evidence to the contrary'.

The programme was woven around the comments of several women with HIV, all of whom had acquired it through heterosexual sex. All but one, as the commentary explains, had their identity protected because of the stigma, discrimination and hatred they faced because of their HIV positive status. These women are living refutations of the comments of Murley and Kilbracken and are used to underscore the message that HIV can be passed heterosexually. But the fact that their identity had to be protected is also used to show that HIV has encouraged prejudice and ignorance. As presenter, Mavis Nicholson puts it:

> Some women have had to go to the ultimate length of changing their name and moving home . . . Normally, ill people would expect comfort and sympathy. These are often treated as lepers.

Murley and Kilbracken are then interviewed and their contributions rejected by the views of experts and statistics. Nicholson then concludes: 'So, there seems no getting away from it. Heterosexual sex is spreading the AIDS virus.' The programme concludes with footage of the one HIV positive woman who had gone public and issues a call for a fight against prejudice and ignorance:

> Liz will have to go back into hiding in order to carry on her life. Unless our attitude changes, the truth about AIDS is that it will become a scourge for homo and heterosexuals alike. A scourge surrounded by almost medieval ignorance and superstition. Better it be an enemy that we fight in the open as Liz was trying her best to do.

Here, moralist views are accessed only so that they can be discredited. The entire programme is organised within the scientific orthodoxy and the liberal perspective.

Criticism of the government

When government actions departed from those anticipated by the liberal view, criticism could be trenchant. In the two examples discussed below, government policy came in for severe attack and government spokespersons were shown in the main as misleading, complacent, untrustworthy and callous. In the first ('The fatal factor', *First Tuesday*, Yorkshire Television for Channel Four, 1 March 1988), government policy on HIV-infected haemophiliacs came under the spotlight. In the second ('A sentence of death', *Brass Tacks*, BBC2, 20 September 1988), prisons policy was examined.

The first programme opens with a visit to a lawyer to draw up a will for one HIV-infected person with haemophilia:

> Alan White suffers from a rare blood disease. He's a haemophiliac. Until recently his was an outstanding success story. He has a young family, a career, everything to live for. But through his National Health Service treatment he's been infected with the AIDS virus. Today Alan and his wife Christine have come to prepare for the possibility of his premature death.

Later, accounts of victimisation and discrimination were given:

> On this estate in Hartlepool the family of a dying haemophiliac was victimised. [name of person] died of AIDS at the age of 20 . . . The punishment wasn't over for [his] parents. They were the victims of fear and discrimination in their own community. Their hut was daubed with graffiti.

> *Father*: It had been done in the night. The wife came in crying. She said have you seen what they've done outside on the wall. Somebody had written 'Beware of AIDS here'. Our lives just changed . . . We were just frightened. You could be going out in the town centre shopping and someone would look at you and walk away and cross the road. We used to come in and cry. In fact we once felt like committing suicide.

Doctors involved with looking after people with haemophilia were interviewed and the programme establishes that they are not to blame for their patients' infection. Instead we are told that the government knew about the dangers of importing blood, especially from USA in the early 1970s.

The programme shows that government negligence has led 1,200 haemophiliacs to become infected and the government has then turned its back on them, releasing only a small amount of money for hardship payments. Unlike coverage in the press and on TV news, no explicit distinction was drawn between innocent and guilty victims of AIDS and the blame is laid squarely with the government.

The passion and horror of this otherwise exemplary piece of investigative journalism is somewhat dissipated by the total lack of similar documentaries prosecuting government inaction, cynicism and misinformation on behalf of IV drug users, sex workers and especially gay men with HIV.

In a similar fashion, Brass Tacks' 'A sentence of death' examined prison policy and the negligence of the government in preventing the spread of HIV infection by not providing condoms and safe injecting equipment:

> Are the authorities acting quickly enough? Tonight *Brass Tacks* provides evidence of a serious failure in the Prison Service to face the AIDS problem.

Prison governors, prisoners, prison pressure groups, the World Health Organisation (WHO) and the government's own Drugs Advisory Committee were marshalled to criticise the government's insistence, in the person of junior Home Office Minister Douglas Hogg, that no steps be taken to make penetrative sex or injecting drug use safe. The programme concludes:

> The authorities will have to acknowledge the extent of illegal activities in prisons, in order to tackle them openly and create a climate in which ignorance and secrecy can be overcome.

The programme begins and ends with the situation inside Modelo prison in Barcelona where an ex-prisoner 'Paco' is shown with his wife and young children:

> After his test in prison last year, Paco discovered that he was HIV positive. Two months later his wife found that she too had the infection. She was seven months pregnant and she had never injected drugs. This family's tragedy shows clearly why the issue of AIDS in prison should be a crucial concern for everybody, not only those inside.

Here is the paradox of the liberal approach, which disavows prejudice while at the same time viewing AIDS from the perspective only of 'non-deviants'. In this view 'we' need to be concerned about prisons not because of the lives of those inside them, but because of the danger to 'us': 'the most frightening prospect is that AIDS unchecked inside prisons will continue to spread outside into the wider community'.

Alternative representations

Alternative representations were most likely to appear on Channel Four, late at night or in documentary film series (as opposed to current affairs). It was also here that one of the very rare programmes adopting a moralist perspective was transmitted. Reporter Christine Chapman put forward the argument that the key to combating AIDS was to sacrifice sexual freedoms and put an end to 'permissiveness'. The programme, an edition of the 'access' series *Diverse Reports*, concluded with a clear statement advocating moral approaches:

> AIDS . . . says we can no longer enjoy sexual freedom without seriously damaging our health, and the lives of others. Unfortunately, it's very unlikely that you'll hear that said, so we've made our own television advert to sell the message. ('AIDS is a four-letter word', *Diverse Reports*, Channel Four, 17 September 1986. For a discussion see Watney, 1987b: 115–21)

Documentaries

Very different approaches were taken by two documentaries: an edition of *Forty Minutes*, on 'London Lighthouse' and *Remember Terry*. Both were 'soft' in news terms, revolving around sympathetic portraits of human beings in difficult situations.[4] The former programme focused on the nursing staff of 'London's first purpose built AIDS hospice' while the latter was about Terry Madeley, the 'first man to come out with AIDS on British television'. Because these were documentaries, they were not required to maintain the appearance of balance and could endorse particular views about AIDS. Their documentary status also meant that they differed from the tightly argued, didactic perspective of current affairs access programming such as *Diverse Reports*. It would be possible to argue a similar line to these programmes in an edition of *Diverse Reports*. But conversely, it would be much more difficult to produce a documentary of the style of 'London Lighthouse' or *Remember Terry* from a moralist perspective. This is partly because of the style and form of the programme, and in particular its sympathetic approach to its subjects. It is also because the range of acceptable views in documentary production more easily excludes and ignores punitive voices as compared to news and current affairs and discussion programmes. Both documentaries managed to move into territory unexplored by other programmes on AIDS.

Forty Minutes' 'London Lighthouse' examined the relationships between nursing staff and 'residents' in the hospice. According to the voice-over:

> London Lighthouse was developed in response to a crisis but it has become a focus for a range of radical new ideas about nursing and health care.

New nursing staff are shown at an induction meeting and we are told:

> their induction encourages them to challenge the conventional role of the nurse. They wouldn't wear uniform and they would refer to those staying on the unit as residents rather than patients. But the overriding principle was that the nurses would let residents have as much say as possible in how they were cared for.

The film follows the progress of the nursing staff and patients as they go about trying to make this model of care work. The emphasis is on the way in which the crisis of AIDS has forced a re-evaluation of nursing practice that may be of benefit elsewhere. But there is also a sense in which working with people with HIV is seen as a privilege. There was no question of accessing the views of those who might object to Lighthouse or those who might advocate punitive measures against people living with HIV or AIDS.

Fronted by Patti Caldwell, *Remember Terry* was able to go further than 'London Lighthouse' because it focused on a person with AIDS rather than carers. It could expose 'the uncertainty that follows an HIV positive diagnosis, the constant stress of hospitalisation, drugs and remission in a way that no previous programme has done' (Alcorn, 1989: 207). The programme features 'Terry's mum Lil' who is shown as passionately devoted to her son:

> *Lil*: It's quite a journey, but I don't mind that. If it makes him feel better, then I'm there. That's what I'm here for, Patsy. After all, he's mine. If it were any of the others I'd do the same thing, wouldn't I. What I do for Terry is done with all the love in the world. I wouldn't change him anyway, nothing of him.
> *Patti*: Lil and Terry's relationship is extraordinary. She herself has had two heart attacks and a stroke and yet she visited him almost every day he's been in hospital – a round trip of two hours, four buses and a walk at each end.

The programme allowed a glimpse of the complex process of dealing with death which faces many people with AIDS:

> *Patti*: Last night your, your lover phoned up and was just really really sad and he was convinced that you were giving up.
> *Terry*: But that doesn't mean my wanting to die has changed.
> *Patti*: Do you want to?
> *Terry*: Yes . . . Yesterday – I've already said it, haven't I – that someone said that if there was a button in front of you that you could press and you'd die like that, that's not changed. I'd press that button with no hesitation at all. I would. I don't – I'm not frightened of death. I'm not going to meet Mr Anderton after I'm dead . . . [*laughter*] . . . or his God. What can I say? I'm not depressed, but the quality of my life is so low and I think – I mean it's all very heroic when people stumble around and look like victims or the caricature press victim, but that's not for me. It's not vanity or anything. If life doesn't have quality, then I don't see the point of life.

The programme ended with Terry's funeral service, which Caldwell herself had helped to plan and at which she gave an oration. *Remember Terry*:

> *is* exceptional in the way that it foregrounds the bonds of friendship between producer and subject, implying that it is in no way unusual for television to jettison its subjects after filming. It questions the role of the reporter as an objective viewer, since Patti Caldwell is involved quite deeply in the action. (Alcorn, 1989: 207; emphasis in original)

Limitations

While both films set out to treat their subjects sympathetically, they try to address the perceived assumptions made by the assumed straight audience. In the case of *Remember Terry* the programme shows that Terry is also an 'innocent victim' by revealing that 'Privately, he never saw himself as promiscuous. He believes he caught the AIDS virus six years ago, when the dangers of gay sex were unknown and AIDS hadn't even been identified.' To reinforce the point, Caldwell asks for more detail:

> And then you settled down with your lover, didn't you?
> *Terry*: That's right. We decided that we wanted to be monogamous, we didn't want any kind of open relationship.

Similarly, in 'London Lighthouse', a young female nurse is the only one to be introduced with more detail than simply name and rank. We are told that she is married and has a child, with whom she is seen travelling to child care. This introduction functions to indicate that she is heterosexual, so that 'we', the imagined audience, can identify with her. Presumably 'we' would be unable to identify with any of the gay male nurses on the staff in quite the same way. Furthermore the programme is mainly focused on the reactions of the staff to the stress and trauma of looking after people with AIDS.

> In the first three months five people died at Lighthouse. The nurses were finding both the fact and the manner of these deaths distressing and, as expected, they were having to give each other a lot of emotional support.

While some of the residents are interviewed about their views on their own care and are shown in negotiation and discussion with the staff, the film does not foreground how the residents themselves have dealt with living with HIV or with the nursing regime in Lighthouse.

Science programming

Science programming on British television tends to take the form of either magazine format programmes (*Tomorrow's World, Antenna*) or documentary reports (*Horizon, QED, Equinox*). Science programming on AIDS between 1983 and 1990 tended to concentrate on natural science and, in particular, 'hard' laboratory science at the expense of 'softer' varieties, such as epidemiology or social science. The predominant question was the extent to which, and how quickly, we can be saved from AIDS by scientific intervention. Scientists were presented as moving carefully and rationally towards truth. Here, as in other examples,

> science is presented as a generator of certainty, when it is properly conducted. Uncertainties and ambiguities are the result of incompetence of the scientists, or inadequacy of the apparatus, or of the limited tests conducted so far. Residual uncertainties will be eliminated by future tests. (Collins, 1987; see also Hornig, 1990 and Murrell, 1987)

BBC2's *Horizon* provided clear examples of this in 'A strange and deadly virus' (24 March 1986) and the later 'Can AIDS be stopped?' (4 March 1987). Here the story of the scientific response to AIDS was presented as a straightforward matter of scientific progress, in which reasonable-sounding theories are tested and then abandoned if falsified. Thus the US Center for Disease Control is portrayed as a rational and objective actor: 'Immune overload was not the answer, so the CDC pushed on.' Elsewhere we hear of the difficulties in naming 'AIDS': 'It was such a curious disease, they struggled to find a name. Eventually they called it AIDS.'

This of course neglects to mention that 'they' originally called it 'GRID' or Gay Related Immune Deficiency. This might have complicated the picture by introducing questions about the social and political agendas of science. The story of the discovery of HIV is so identified with the scientists that on one occasion the virus and its relatives are even referred to as the property of a particular scientist – Robert Gallo – in the phrase 'his family of viruses'. Of course the ownership of HIV was indeed a cause for serious conflict between the US and French governments and it was later acknowledged that 'Gallo's virus' didn't 'belong' to him at all. The politics of the scientific fight against AIDS did not feature in these programmes. If it had, it would have complicated the narrative push of the detective story of HIV.

One consequence of the concentration on 'hard' science is the neglect of personal, ethical and (openly) political questions and their interaction with science. In particular questions about the intervention of people with AIDS in treatment programmes and ethical questions about the use of double blind trials with human beings have tended to be invisible in science programming. The emphasis on science and the generation of certainty means the exclusion of 'politics' and 'emotion'. Yet, many scientist interviewees frequently resort to heavily loaded 'scientific' characterisations of human sexual and social behaviour. Editions of *Horizon* did not question the copious use of terms like 'normal sex', 'promiscuity', or even 'rampant promiscuity among many gays' who 'were found to have an astonishing number of sexual partners' (*Horizon*, 24 March 1986, 4 March 1987).

In the midst of this simple acceptance of the orthodoxy on HIV and of the official version of the scientific endeavour (not to mention the public relations of some scientists) one of the editions of *Horizon* did include a comment by an epidemiologist which strongly hinted that the simple faith in science was being overplayed:

> We've got a third world problem and a problem in the bits of the West that are like the third world, like in bits of the United States where there's a lot of heterosexual AIDS . . . AIDS is a problem of poor people like a lot of other diseases . . . There's two whole totally separate sets of problems. The science problem – that I'm optimistic about. Sooner or later we're going to have vaccines, therapy probably . . . The political problem is not so easy. It's something that needs to be attacked on a worldwide level. ('A strange and deadly virus', *Horizon*, 24 March 1986)

However, this viewpoint is not developed as the programme is only interested in the 'scientific' problem. The pre-eminence of 'hard' science was not the only restriction in science programming preventing alternative ways of seeing AIDS. The BBC did make a different sort of programme for the

Horizon slot about gay men and AIDS. Titled 'Sex and gay men', it was to have gone out in March 1986. The introductory commentary stated:

> AIDS is especially difficult to contain because 90% of its victims are gay men. For any public health campaign to be effective it would have to go into intimate details of homosexual sex. And to reach everybody at risk, it must be mounted on such a scale that everyone else, whether they like it or not, will be informed as well. In this film gay men talk frankly about their sexual lives and whether they've been affected by the first four years of AIDS.

However, this film was 'banned and an attempt to reach those who were the majority of those suffering from AIDS failed. The BBC even destroyed the negative' (*The End of Innocence*, BBC2, 5 December 1995; see also Howes, 1993: 361).

It was very rare for British science programming to examine either disputes within science over AIDS or the extent to which science by itself (as opposed to political, economic and social programmes) might be an answer to AIDS. Of the two, disputes were more likely to be covered. Where they were mentioned, as in the following example from *Tomorrow's World*, doubt was cast upon challenges to the orthodoxy:

> You may have seen the recent publicity about a prominent American scientist who argues that the virus thought to cause AIDS is not the culprit at all. Peter Duesberg of the University of California has even offered to be injected with the virus known as HIV or Human Immuno-deficiency Virus. Most scientists are quite convinced that he's wrong and that HIV does cause the disease. (*Tomorrow's World*, 14 April 1988)

Viewers may have seen publicity about Duesberg's theories, but they wouldn't have seen it on the BBC, since neither BBC news nor current affairs programmes devoted any time to Duesberg's theories in the period up to 1990. Duesberg's arguments were thoroughly covered not on science programmes, but on Channel Four's current affairs series *Dispatches*. In 'The unheard voices' (13 November 1987) and 'The AIDS catch' (13 June 1990), independent production company Meditel challenged the orthodox version of the science of AIDS.

The first thing we should note is that these documentaries were both about science and about the politics of science. Underlying them is a view of science which questions its straightforward objectivity and points to its social and political assumptions. According to Chuck Ortleb, publisher of the *New York Native*, who is interviewed on the programme:

> I think if you start interviewing all of the scientists . . . you'd find out that there is a lot of doubt out there. Publicly they're afraid to speak up, because they'll be punished. They will lose their grants, they will lose their jobs. Science in America, at least AIDS science, is really religion and if you dare challenge authority, you lose your livelihood. That's the way science works. (13 November 1987)

The later programme also suggests that the media have a close relationship with the government on medical issues. Jad Adams argued:

> Medical journalists in particular seem to think that the public are best served by giving them unadulterated information which comes direct from the government. It's something which no other journalist does: if the government say something, the first thing they do is ask a question about it. (13 June 1990)

This allowed the programme to advance an alternative explanation. The hypothesis as outlined by Duesberg is that HIV is a harmless passenger virus and the reason people are dying is because of immune suppression due to 'lifestyle' factors. For our purposes, we can note that such views were accessed only on Channel Four partly because of its responsibility for minority viewing, and partly because, as we saw above, Channel Four executives became sceptical about co-operating with the government following AIDS Week. Science programming was the most limited of the non-news forms of television. Critical voices were rarely heard. In fact, television news accessed the voices of people with AIDS more effectively than science programmes.

Dramatising AIDS

AIDS has provided some limited opportunities for drama. In Britain, as in the US, AIDS has 'remained a topic that television drama could only address with some difficulty' (Buxton, 1991, cited in Treichler, 1993: 189). The bulk of dramas on AIDS (*An Early Frost, Intimate Contact, Sweet As You Are* and *Buddies*) were broadcast between 1986 and 1987. AIDS has also featured in soap opera (*Brookside* and *EastEnders*, but not *Emmerdale* or *Coronation Street*) and in long-running series such as *Casualty* or *The Bill* as well as in episodes of imported US drama such as *LA Law, Midnight Caller* or *thirtysomething*. In the period up to the end of 1990 only one full length single drama had focused on HIV/AIDS. *Yellowbacks* was in the political thriller genre.

The bulk of the dramas featured either the reactions of family members, friends or colleagues to HIV diagnosis or the problems of heterosexual or 'innocent' victims in dealing with HIV and social responses, including issues such as discrimination. In the main the programmes addressed themselves to questions of intolerance, ignorance and prejudice and how they might be overcome at an individual level, rather than examining structural problems or collective responses. They have tended not to address AIDS as a political problem – even where prejudice and discrimination are seen as emanating from institutional sources (rather than individual attitudes).

However, there have been some clear variations in the dramatic portrayal of AIDS which relate to formal features, to struggles over the process of production, to historical changes in the production environment, to the vagaries of broadcast regulations and to perceived audience sensitivities. The fictional programmes examined here include series with self-contained episodes, soap opera and other series in which the storyline carries over from episode to episode, serials and single plays.

Drama series

The most limited fictional treatment of HIV and AIDS has been in action-adventure series, especially those which feature one or two leading characters in episode-long narratives, with little continuous story or character development between episodes. Here the demand for action and for problems for the hero(es) to solve tends to militate in favour of using AIDS as a discrete problem for the lead character. Story values themselves help to make sure that the problem is people living with AIDS rather than AIDS per se or societal responses to it. Thus, a widely criticised episode of *Midnight Caller* featured a bisexual man who, knowing he has HIV, has unprotected sex with a former girlfriend of the hero. In the end he is saved from being shot by one of his (female) victims by a police officer (Howes, 1993: 513). Such problems more rarely afflicted those series where the evolving storyline allows for the development of character and where the narrative does not depend on action-adventure conflicts. Series such as *Casualty* and *The Bill* (or in the US, *thirtysomething* or later, *ER*) were sometimes able to treat HIV as a problem for the person living with it as well as for the central characters. The person with HIV could thus be the object of concern, pity or compassion, rather than simply hatred. Series like *Casualty* and *The Bill* follow a larger number of central characters rather than one or two 'heroes'. They deal with a variety of self-contained cases (injuries and illnesses or suspected crimes) played by actors who appear for a single episode. This allows space for the central characters to develop in the context of particular challenges. In particular, coping with crisis and drawing on human reserves of compassion and care are central (even where there is conflict over this between characters). But such a format allows much less space to develop the character of those with 'problems', whether because of HIV or something else. This means that unless a central character is diagnosed HIV positive, the narrative will tend not to develop the problems faced by a character living with HIV, but will concentrate on how the central characters deal with the problem posed by someone with HIV.

Soap opera

Similar limitations are evident in soap operas when new characters appear for the sole purpose of interaction with an established character. However, because soaps do not come in self-contained chunks but develop storylines, the potential to examine the impact of HIV on both central and marginal characters is correspondingly greater. At *EastEnders* one of the originators of the HIV storyline said that it had

> broken the barrier that no public health campaign has managed to do in alerting young people to changes in behaviour and seeing themselves as being potentially at risk . . . [This is because] we have more time to do things much less crudely than a lot of educational drama.

This potential has not always been fulfilled. British soaps have dealt with AIDS (or completely ignored it) in a variety of ways, but no British soap has yet included a central gay character living with HIV or AIDS.

EastEnders gave gay character Colin a mysterious illness but played with audience uncertainties about his having HIV before revealing that it was ME. Channel Four's *Brookside* introduced a gay character (Gordon Collins) earlier than *EastEnders* and executive producer Phil Redmond predicted further developments in the handling of such 'social issues': 'As we look forward from 1987 towards the next five years, we . . . must cover in a realistic and responsible way issues such as AIDS – something that was not even heard about when the programme started five years ago' (Redmond, 1987: 7).

Yet *Brookside* did not seriously deal with AIDS in the ensuing five year period. The only involvement was that Gordon Collins became a volunteer AIDS line helper and Gordon's lover Chris lent his flat to a friend who was dying of AIDS (Geraghty, 1992: 144). Christine Geraghty suggests that the reason the mainstream soaps have found it so difficult to exploit the potential of the serial to develop complex characterisations and storylines in relation to black, lesbian or gay characters was because 'both soaps take the family as the basis of their structure' (Geraghty, 1992: 137; see also 1991). She argues that 'the notion of model families at the heart of the soaps implied the existence of deviants from that model' (1992: 139). Therefore: 'The white working-class family, however extended and open, does not readily or realistically (in the programmes' terms) accommodate black people or lesbians and gay men, for instance, and yet their presence was essential to the programmes' claims to deal with current social issues' (1992: 140). It is as if the structuring of the narrative around the family is of itself enough to prevent positive representations of 'deviants'. However, it is not only the narrative which determines such characterisations, nor is it the structural constraints imposed by the format. As we show below, the negotiations over storylines and scripts in the process of production (the process of policing meaning) are crucial in determining the shape and scope of characterisation and plot.

Much of the early coverage of AIDS followed a liberal educative approach in similar fashion to factual education and information programmes. This approach is also a staple of the 'social awareness' of both *Brookside* and *EastEnders*, and can tread an uneasy line between the demands of 'entertainment' and 'realism' together with the need to provide 'education' (Buckingham, 1987: 83–4).

Education and entertainment

AIDS was one issue where the 'more trusted or authoritative' characters adopted a 'teacherly' role in relation to other characters who are 'taught' a lesson as 'a kind of surrogate for the viewer' (Buckingham, 1987: 84). In particular Dr Legg (in *EastEnders*) often occupied the 'teacherly' role, being 'seen to advise the characters on a range of medical and psychological problems'. As a result of becoming a counsellor for the Samaritans Kathy Beale 'in turn has increasingly come to adopt the role of "expert" adviser, for example condemning Dot for her bigoted and hysterical response to the threat of AIDS' (Buckingham, 1987: 84).

In 1987 Dot realises that Colin and Barry are lovers rather than simply flatmates, during a conversation with Barry as he dries the couple's one pair of sheets in the launderette. As soon as she finds out, her attitude changes and she starts to worry that she may have been infected by drinking a cup of coffee from Barry's flask.

> *Dot*: And now God's finally got fed up and He's sent this dreadful plague down on you all and you still won't learn will ya?
> *Barry*: Ah hang on. Are you trying to tell me that AIDS is God's punishment for being gay?
> *Dot*: Well of course it is, what else could it be?
> *Barry*: Well how comes the only people almost guaranteed not to get it are lesbians! (*EastEnders*, BBC1, 31 March 1987)

Dot then exits the launderette and spies Dr Legg in the square. She approaches him and asks if he will give her 'that test for – you know – AIDS'. Dr Legg reassures her :

> *Dr Legg*: . . . just let me put your mind at rest. You can only catch AIDS through sexual contact, a blood transfusion or, and I don't think this will affect you, sharing a syringe with someone who has it.
> *Dot*: Ohh none of that lot affects me.
> *Dr Legg*: Well, you can't catch it from coffee cups, shaking hands or just being in the same room as anyone.
> *Dot*: What about service washes?
> *Dr Legg*: Dot, what did I just tell you. You catch it directly from blood or sexual contact. Of course, if it really worries you, you can put your mind at rest by making any sexual partner use a condom. (*EastEnders*, BBC1, 31 March 1987)

At which point Dot gets embarrassed and hurries off. *Brookside*'s Paul Collins (father of gay character Gordon) went through a similar learning process, in which he was reassured that he could not become infected with HIV from ordinary social contact. Such interactions function as means of conveying information and inviting the audience to identify with the information provider or be taught a lesson. Here, AIDS rather visibly enters the storyline for the purpose of health education, having very little purchase on the narrative and the development of characterisation. It could be interchanged with many other 'social issues' which fleetingly appear.

Only the BBC's *EastEnders* went further than this and (from 1990) made some efforts to portray a more complex picture of a character living with HIV. Mark Fowler, the son of the central Fowler/Beale extended family, returned to the series after a long absence. Played by a new actor (Todd Carty) his HIV status was the rationale for his return to the series. Although educative material similar to previous *EastEnders* coverage did appear, more complex representations were possible. With a central character being infected, HIV became a key part of the storyline. Counselling, Mark's fears about dying, the problems of negotiating sexual relationships and of disclosing one's HIV status were all examined. Later there was discussion about the practicalities of having children. At the beginning girlfriend Diane tried to get Mark to go for counselling with the Terrence Higgins Trust. In the end he was late and missed the appointment, but Diane went anyway, and expressed doubts about her ability to cope with Mark's HIV status.

> I think I should look after him, take care of him, but I don't know if I can . . . Sometimes I just feel like running away, leaving him. God that must sound awful. It's just I have enough trouble sorting out my own life, without having to worry about somebody else's . . . Then I start feeling guilty. As though just by thinking about running away I'm letting him down. It's like everything depends on me. I'm the only one he can turn to . . . I spend half my time feeling sorry for what's happening to Mark and the other half feeling guilty for wanting to run away.

The counsellor prompts her:

> *Counsellor*: What do you think you would be running away from?
> *Diane*: Mark.
> *Counsellor*: Anything else?
> *Diane*: I love him. I don't want to watch him die. He's only 22. It's not fair. It's just not fair. (3 February 1991)

Later Mark starts seeing a new girlfriend, although he plainly finds it difficult to relate to her. Diane confronts him in the square:

> *Diane*: I said, have you got yourself a new girlfriend?
> *Mark*: Maybe.
> *Diane*: Well, that's nice.
> *Mark*: Yeah, I think so.
> *Diane*: Don't you think you're being a bit irresponsible?
> *Mark*: Don't you think you're being a bit of a pain in the neck?
> *Diane*: I saw the way she looked at you. She isn't just gonna want to hold hands in the movies you know?
> *Mark*: Who says I do?
> *Diane*: So you intend to sleep with her, do you?
> *Mark*: I don't plan things like that.
> *Diane*: Yeah, well maybe you ought to, in your condition.
> [*Mark ignores this.*]
> *Diane*: I was just trying to point out that . . .
> *Mark*: Diane, there is such a thing as safe sex, remember.
> *Diane*: Yeah I know, but does she? Does she know you're HIV positive? Don't you think you should tell her?
> *Mark*: [*drops wheelbarrow in exasperation*] I'm gonna tell her all right. Not that I think it's any of your business Diane, you're the one who did a runner and left me in the lurch, remember?
> *Diane*: I didn't. I was just trying to . . .
> *Mark*: Yeah, that's fair enough then. That's your lookout. But it doesn't mean I've got to spend the rest of my life in – It doesn't mean I've got to spend the rest of my life in a state of terminal celibacy. I'm sorry if you can't see it like that. But that's the way things are – tough. (25 February 1991)

Here the problems of HIV are considered from the perspective of the person living with HIV as well as from that of those around him. This is a considerable advance on the presentation of HIV as a problem which enters a series for one or a few episodes.

The return of Mark Fowler: working AIDS into the storyline

The return of Mark Fowler to *EastEnders* occasioned much discussion in the script group meetings at the BBC and according to *EastEnders* insiders 'we were very stuck for reasons as to why this aberrant young man might want to come home'. HIV provided a solution to this narrative dilemma. One member of the script group at a 'very unusual meeting' said 'well maybe he's come back because he's HIV'. There was 'probably for the only time in the history of any bi-weekly a unanimous but rather silent agreement . . . It was then largely a matter of waiting for this idea to be passed by the powers that be.' Some expected the idea to 'slip sideways' or for the presentation of '865 reasons why you can't do this'. This was said to be normal practice:

> Censorship at the BBC is conducted in very discreet and subtle ways. It's largely self-censorship. It's not about anybody walking in and saying 'you can't do that'. It's about very senior people humming and hahing, saying 'are you sure you want to do that?' And then on cue everybody says 'well, no, maybe we don't, you're absolutely right' . . . You don't get to do even a percentage of what you want to do. (member of script group)

However, in this case the HIV storyline went through because, according to one insider, AIDS

> had lost some of its immediate slightly hysterical interest, and, if you like, the smoke had cleared a bit. There was more knowledge. There were more statistics available and it was less a thing of the moment, more of a permanent and disturbing phenomenon, that some people were attempting to come to grips with. And I think that atmosphere enabled that idea to go ahead.

Once the idea was approved, the programme makers felt they had to move tentatively, because of the tenor of public debate around AIDS and centrally because of the debate around soap operas in the tabloid press: 'It was a story we thought the press would jump on, so we were a little more careful with it.' This had the result that *EastEnders* went mainly to the Terrence Higgins Trust for information and advice:

> Normally we speak to as many different experts involved as we can. Because this story was regarded by the producers as being top secret, we had to be fairly narrow and quite discreet. So we actually came to a private and very discreet understanding with the Terrence Higgins Trust, that we would use their facilities, their library, their counsellors, people who were HIV, either symptomatic or asymptomatic, that we would restrict ourselves fairly carefully to the Terrence Higgins Trust.

The Trust arranged basic level training for all of the script-writers and talked to the actors involved. It was also in day to day contact over particular issues and was sent copies of the script to look over, particularly those concerning the counselling sessions. In return for its expertise the

Terrence Higgins Trust sought and received guarantees about the nature and direction of the storyline. According to Nick Partridge of the Trust:

> The one guarantee that we insisted on if we were to spend time talking about it and helping on a technical level, was that if Mark were to be diagnosed positive, then he would live with that for a very long time and effectively if there were contractual difficulties over the next two or three years he would do a midnight flit – as he had done before – rather than being killed off.

Such guarantees fitted fairly easily with the narrative demands of having a central character with HIV. As one script editor at *EastEnders* explained:

> We have a young actor to play this part. It is an important point in his career. We have a theoretically much loved regular character and he is an asset to the programme. We do not intend to kill him off. Therefore we are limited in our ability to portray HIV through that particular character. He cannot go into a rapid decline, because this is the BBC sacrificing their own asset. We will have to be very careful of falling into the trap of portraying HIV as something that does not affect people's health and that it is easy to live with and you get away sometimes scot free. It's useful for us in that it's very easy for us to resist the opposite, which is to say HIV by definition is a total and absolute disaster, there is nothing positive about it; that people will necessarily become ill very quickly, fall apart and all the rest of it . . . There is an impulse – which I think is probably the right one, both creatively, politically and pure doing the business of making a good entertainment programme – to make this as positive a story as we can. That it's about a 'heroic' attempt to live in a positive way despite the fact that a young man has HIV.

In addition the programme makers perceived that it was necessary to build Mark up as a strong and positive character before he was confronted by negative reactions to HIV. This was achieved by keeping his HIV status from other characters.

> We have been very careful to limit the number of characters in the programme who know that this young man is HIV. Because we do not want to go straight in and OD on people's general negative reactions – disgust, ignorance, fear. We want to make sure that that character is well established, sympathetic and that we've stripped away as much of the hysteria and antagonism as we can before we commit ourselves to look at a very negative reaction to someone with HIV. I think that's something we're duty bound to do if only in the name of realism, otherwise we're living in toytown.

Furthermore, Mark's own views were to be the subject of challenge as he learned more about HIV. This arose particularly from making it clear that Mark had acquired HIV heterosexually:

> Mark is a 'normal' white working-class male. He doesn't like gays, he doesn't like junkies. Therefore he was rather insulted and offended by the suggestion that he fell into either of those two categories. Now we do not have the intention of reinforcing prejudice against homosexuals and intravenous drug users and discriminating against them. And it will be an important and I hope interesting part of the story that, in the course of learning about himself and his condition, Mark will be forced to confront his prejudice against homosexuals and intravenous drug users.

The demands of narrative and the development of characterisation allowed *EastEnders* to do things that other drama series did not. However, with the potential freedom offered by a regular ongoing plot line, there are limitations which make the realistic portrayal of HIV, or indeed matters of sex and sexuality in general, somewhat problematic. These relate to the conventions governing prime time viewing: 'We can't show people undressing, we can't show people swearing, we can't show them having a pee for that matter, not that it's of any great interest.' In addition, 'you can't use language that describes sex. It's all done by innuendo.' Naturally this interferes with the communication of even straightforwardly educational information.

> British television is incredibly prudish. Three-year-olds are watching it. You can't talk about rimming and fisting and water sports and all the other things that you should do or might want to do and you just have to accept that. You're not being paid to conduct a revolution in British television. Well, not every day!

According to *EastEnders* sources there was only 'one occasion where something we wanted to do was stamped on'. This was in relation to dramatising the dilemmas of safer sex. This was hampered, in the first place by the fact that 'when this programme was set up, there was an interesting absence, there were no bedrooms'.

> We wanted to dramatise the dilemma of Mark and in particular his girlfriend, in terms of what they'd do when they go to bed. It's very difficult to do that when they're sitting on the sofa.

Internal negotiations produced a compromise: 'I think we've got as far as getting them to agree that the conversation takes place in the bedroom. This is an advance, believe me.' The production of soap opera is also constrained by the demands of ratings. In the case of the HIV storyline the fact that the ratings did not drop was seen to reduce the pressure of the programme makers:

> It is a relief, although it's not the be-all and end-all of these stories – for what it's worth we hit number 1 three or four weeks running at the start of that story. The viewers did not switch off, which I think was quite important if only politically. If they had switched off we would have been on weaker ground within the BBC.

Ratings are one element of pressure on programme makers. Another constant source is from the 'public debate' about soap operas to be found in the tabloid press.

> The *Sun* – and not just the *Sun* – represents a certain pressure on programme makers, who after all are trying to please an audience. Many of their viewers will read the *Sun* or will share the opinions of the *Sun* and that's a pressure on programme makers. And it doesn't mean that people sit down and say 'Oh my God what's the *Sun* going to say about that', it infiltrates in a more subtle way.

The internalisation of the pressures of ratings, prime time and tabloid comment are by themselves more than enough to limit the representation of

HIV in soap opera. They help to explain the decision to deal with hetero-sexuality and AIDS rather than having a central gay character with HIV.

Serials and plays

Serials, single plays and films share with soap opera the time and space to develop characterisation. They are different in that the narrative comes to a close, whereas the soap opera continuously unfolds. Furthermore, serials and especially plays are seen as *creative* works, which are the responsibility of an author, rather than a team of script-writers. This means that they can explore issues in a less didactic manner and are less pressured. In general, serials and plays are less limited than soap opera in their representation of sex and sexuality, in that they are on television later in the evening. There are bedrooms in *Intimate Contact*. The key element of creative fiction is that it explores emotional responses and interactions, rather than recording factual states of affairs, which is the purpose of actuality television. Peter Goodchild, Head of Drama Plays at the BBC made this point in response to criticism of *Sweet As You Are*:

> Overall I think – which is the most important thing that drama can do, because drama does work in that completely other way than straightforward information – what I think did come from *Sweet As You Are* is the sheer bombshell effect of that kind of pronouncement [about HIV status] on a relationship – guilt or no guilt. That, I think is the kind of memory that people will actually carry with them and will change their attitudes towards the seriousness of what's at stake. (On *Network*, BBC2, 23 February 1988)

To the extent that AIDS is a central part of the storyline, emotional and interpersonal responses can be examined in depth. Where AIDS is inci-dental or one of many lines of narrative development (such as in drama series and soaps), such complexities are more difficult and easy moral lessons or didactic information giving are more prevalent.

Straight AIDS

Both of the most prominent British plays which focused on AIDS (*Intimate Contact* and *Sweet As You Are*) featured heterosexual men who acquire the virus from a female prostitute or a female student respectively. In *Intimate Contact*, a four part mini series, first shown a few days after AIDS Week, the plot centres around middle-class businessman Clive and the effect of his HIV diagnosis on himself, his family and his social circle. Eighteen months before the opening of the drama Clive had unprotected sex with a prostitute in New York. When it becomes known that he is HIV positive he is ostracised at work and by his friends. His wife, Ruth, is asked to leave her golf club and stop working in the local Oxfam shop. Her insular, con-servative and homophobic outlook is challenged by this and more importantly by her meeting with a gay couple at the hospital Clive attends.

Later she also gets to know a working-class man with an HIV positive son with haemophilia. Thus, *Intimate Contact* is more concerned with the 'snobbery and hypocrisy of his family's responses, than with his illness' (Watney, 1994: 217). In similar vein *Sweet As You Are* focuses on the reactions to the discovery that the main character (played by Liam Neeson) has HIV, in particular of his wife (played by Miranda Richardson). Consequently in both plays the emphasis is on seeing the problem of AIDS as a problem of ignorance. This of course puts it very firmly within the orthodox view on AIDS.

Representing gay men

British television has failed to put gay men at the centre of AIDS dramas. Gay men with AIDS have featured at the centre of imported dramas such as *An Early Frost* (transmitted 3 May 1986) and *A Death in the Family* (transmitted 10 March 1990). However, they too have tended to ignore both the impact of AIDS as a disease and the problems of gay men living with HIV, concentrating on the reactions of families and society more widely. *An Early Frost*, for example, features a yuppy lawyer and his lover. 'We see how AIDS affects a young man's mother; father; sister; brother-in-law and grandmother. There is no consideration given to the fact that this is happening to him – not them' (Russo, 1987: 277).

When he finds out he is HIV positive he returns to his family to die, 'with limited signs of the gay community or of its support' (Treichler, 1992: 143). As Treichler argues, *An Early Frost* illustrates television's tendency to 'dissolve the gayness of the gay person with AIDS into a homogenised and universalised person facing death' (Treichler, 1992: 144). Even so the production was not without its problems, precisely because it dealt with homosexuality.

> *An Early Frost* was rewritten 13 times before the network censors were happy. No touching allowed, not even in the privacy of the male lovers' apartment. No shake of the hands, even though the family members can't keep theirs *off* one another. (Howes, 1993: 214, emphasis in original)

Alternative perspectives

Perspectives which challenge the orthodox view (where they have been aired) have tended to be shown late at night on minority channels such as Channel Four. An early example was a British screening of Arthur Bressan's US-made *Buddies*, which tells the story of a young middle-class gay man who 'buddies' an older gay man dying from AIDS. As Simon Watney puts it:

> The man with AIDS is an ex-hippie, whose outlook and identity had been forged in the early 1970s period of Gay Liberation. The film movingly describes his buddy's gradual recognition of the extent of anti-gay prejudice in the USA and its

baleful influence on the course of the epidemic, and his new friend's life-expectancy. It is an extremely ambitious allegory of the difficult social relations between different generations of gay men, and the divisions of class within the gay communities in the US. (Watney, 1992: 154)

The inability of mainstream television even to portray the perspectives of gay men, never mind portray them well, is pointed up by the existence of alternative representations such as *Buddies* or *Chuck Solomon – Coming of Age*, both shown late at night on Channel Four.

Single plays

Roy Battersby's *Yellowbacks* was the only drama on AIDS between 1983 and 1990 (and indeed until the end of 1995) that dealt with the 'political' implications of AIDS. It was in the tradition of the political thriller and projected a dystopian future in which repressive state powers to control disease have been radically extended. The depiction of an imagined near future was extrapolated from contemporary currents of opinion, particularly around compulsory testing and segregation of people with HIV and AIDS. It drew on elements of documentary practice and in some ways resembled a drama-documentary.

The use of metaphor in this nightmare vision of the future is what marks *Yellowbacks* out as different from the dramas discussed above. The play is set in a crumbling disused hotel (itself a metaphor for Britain, according to Battersby) and centres around the interrogation of university lecturer McPherson (played by Bill Paterson) and Battersea GP, Dr Juliet Horwitz (played by Janet McTeer) by agents of an unidentified official agency. The interrogations occur simultaneously. McPherson is upstairs being cross-examined by Mr Caesar with no physical violence or threat of violence. Downstairs, meanwhile, Horwitz is being subjected to threats and intimidation by a team of younger more junior interrogators, Peter Pike and Cheryl Newman (played by Tim Roth and Imelda Staunton). Each is asked for information about the whereabouts of Martin Pitt who, it emerges, was the lover of McPherson and with whom Horwitz was close. He is also infected with a communicable disease, which, although it is not identified as such throughout the play, is clearly intended to be AIDS. Pitt has allegedly being deliberately falsifying test results in his work in one of the labs and urging sexual relations with the powerful as a legitimate weapon. McPherson and Horwitz are held under the Dangerous Diseases Act which apparently includes secret powers to detain suspects, as Horwitz discovers to her terror:

Horwitz: You're saying that a warrant has been issued for the seizure of my patients' records under some unpublished section of the Dangerous Diseases Act? Who issued the warrant?
Newman: The Regional Health Authority.
Horwitz: No Regional Health Authority has that power.
Newman: They all do now. I'd show you the section in the codes of practice but unfortunately they're classified. You'll just have to take my word for it.

Horwitz, it emerges, has been party to a conspiracy to falsify test results in order to protect people from the full rigours of the law which include compulsory testing and 'voluntary' incarceration in a 'sanatorium'. Civil liberties organisations (with whom both McPherson and Horwitz are involved) also believe that people with the infection are forcibly taken to secret camps in large lorries topped with yellow tarpaulins (hence Yellowbacks).

Although she is forced to drink large quantities of alcohol, intimidated and made to stand hooded against a wall supported by her fingertips, Horwitz does not give them any information about Pitt. We also find out that Pike has arrested Horwitz against procedures and that there is a marked class divide between him and his seniors, symbolised by Caesar. In conversation with another official, Norman Jarvis, Pike requests a fake Viral Immunity card (which would show that she was infected) with which to intimidate Horwitz. Pike argues that Caesar will fail to crack McPherson and that Horwitz will lead them to Pitt, thus putting him in the clear for breaching procedures.

> *Pike*: He won't get him, will he? Won't get anybody, he's a fainthearted tweed, he's cavalry twill. All that's a long past world and I'm buggered if I'm going to be looking up Caesar's nose much longer and neither are you, Norman . . .

Jarvis agrees to give Pike a fake VI card and Pike responds:

> *Pike*: Nice one, Norman you're an Englishman. Pitt, Horwitz, McPherson, what are they eh? And Caesar come to that? Dopeheads, yids, poofters and school ties. You name it, we got it. That's disease Norman, that's the real plague and it's here innit? Here's to clean-up time, and a working-class government.

The spectre of fascism is explicitly raised. Finally, McPherson finds out that Horwitz is also under interrogation and reveals that Pitt is in fact already dead. The play closes following McPherson's claim to Horwitz that there are no camps and no yellowbacks. But it is not clear whether he is telling the truth.

In the late 1980s and early 1990s there was a series of disputes about the dramatisation of political controversies. State pressure on investigative journalism during the 1980s pushed journalists and others into dramatisations as one of the few places left on television for critical programming (see Kilborn, 1994; Kerr, 1990). One key reason for this was the difficulty of finding interviewees willing to talk on camera. However, of more relevance here is that there is an expectation of creativity in the writing of a 'play' which applies to some extent even when the documentary takes precedence over the drama. In *Yellowbacks* the drama was pre-eminent. Roy Battersby, Director of *Yellowbacks* argues that:

> the thing drama has always been able to do – and I think at this point in Britain it is even more important that it can do it – is that drama can deal in metaphor . . . Drama deals best with the truth of the imagination – you can't argue with something that comes with the imagination, it has its own authenticity – whereas

a lot of docudrama becomes reduced by nit picking. If something is realised in a drama it has its own completeness and authenticity. Drama is a unique way of telling the truth to power.

Because it was a single play *Yellowbacks* was able to provide a strong critique of state responses to disease and illness. Repressive state action did not feature in any of the other dramatised representations of AIDS. Nor did it feature much in factual programming.

Language and imagery: some concluding comments

Some television formats can allow a greater complexity as well as permit space for alternative representations. However, there are also some limitations of programming on AIDS which did seem to have the potential to affect programming across a range of formats. Both language and imagery have caused problems. Treichler notes that 'generally, "penis" and "anal intercourse" are considered to be the most sensitive words' (Treichler, 1992: 151). Of course which words are considered sensitive varies according to perceptions of audiences and programme forms. Dildos and condoms are acceptable on education programmes, 'homosexual' is more accepted than 'gay' on science programmes and on *EastEnders* discussion of sexual matters has to be carried out by euphemism. The ability to use explicit or accurate words also depends on the (geographical, cultural and ideological) closeness of television production to the centre of editorial control. Thus a BBC Wales radio producer was 'reprimanded . . . because a programme on AIDS included what the corporation said were "earthy and coarse" descriptions of homosexual acts' (*Guardian*, 13 November 1986). These had slipped through the editorial hierarchy partly because they were in Welsh! However, imagery has caused the most problems in representing AIDS. The lack of bedrooms on *EastEnders* and the inability to show almost any image of a penis make sensible representations of sex and sexuality very difficult.

However, television forms do not determine content in any mechanistic way. Instead they provide potentialities which can be explored. Furthermore television forms are the subject of struggle and the focus of media strategies. The precise content of television coverage of AIDS depends also on the balance of forces and the particular cultural, regulatory and political climate, which is likely to vary between nations. Notwithstanding the problems of using imagery on British television which had previously been shown in other European countries, it was the BBC which produced a screen version of David Leavitt's novel *The Lost Language of Cranes*, basing the action in London, rather than the original New York. None of the US networks would touch it and the version made for transmission in the US had to be partly reshot with the actors wearing boxer shorts in the sex scenes (Gilbert, 1992). Similarly a positive film about a man with AIDS, *Chuck Solomon – Coming of Age*, was turned down by the PBS network, but later shown by Channel Four (2 October 1987, 11.20p.m. repeated 18 December 1989, 1.15a.m.) in Britain (Treichler, 1992: 151).

Equally, there are ways in which the content of portrayal has changed in the opposite direction. Peter Goodchild, Head of Drama Plays acknowledges:

> I can think of one particular film which we made – it's called *Reservations* – about two years ago which had as its centre the libertarian attitude to young people and I'm absolutely certain we wouldn't be making that now. (*Network*, BBC2, 23 February 1988)

Changes in portrayals of AIDS continue to take place against the background of a series of assumptions about what a broadcast audience will take. Furthermore, the perception is that new types of programming, especially radical content, are difficult to create in the face of the danger of creating a 'backlash'. As Head of Science Features at the BBC Mick Rhodes puts it:

> We must accept that lurking just behind us is a great big black cloud . . . There is a very obvious problem of deeply offending the other people who are watching, and creating a backlash. (*Network*, BBC2, 23 February 1988)

Here is the key area, where the agenda of tabloid newspapers influences broadcasting practice. The seriousness with which notions of 'offence' are taken does mean that innovation and critique tend to be stifled by the self-censorship encouraged by the perception that the audience is reactionary or the knowledge that the editorial hierarchy is unwilling to take risks. As Jonathan Grimshaw has put it:

> I've been involved with making programmes about AIDS with producers and in the middle of the debate about the programme the producer has said 'Oh well we wouldn't be able to get away with this', or 'we wouldn't be able to get away with that'. Now, self-censorship seems to be something that broadcasters are increasingly imposing on themselves. (*Network*, BBC2, 23 February 1988)

Such pressures are a perennial feature of the broadcasting landscape and emerge more clearly in areas of controversy such as AIDS. We examine them in more depth in relation to news reporting in the next chapter.

Notes

1. Although according to Fowler:

At the department we went through the advertising carefully and at one stage we toyed with the idea of a ministerial broadcast. Indeed the opposition agreed to give up its right to reply. But we had not even had a ministerial broadcast for the Falklands War and the idea was dropped. (Fowler, 1991: 258)

2. As it turned out, such worries were well founded. In 1988 the Northern Ireland Office (NIO) used the AIDS campaign as a precedent in its attempts to have the BBC continue to broadcast its adverts for the confidential telephone, by which people can inform on suspected members of illegal organisations. The NIO argument was that these were simply public service announcements which should be carried in the same way that AIDS adverts had been carried by the BBC. The BBC succumbed to this argument and broadcast the adverts for a short

period only, to stop a few weeks later following threats purporting to come from the Irish National Liberation Army (information on the NIO from interview with senior BBC Northern Ireland executive, 1989).

3. 'Love's pestilence', 7 March 1983; 'AIDS: the race for a cure', 2 December 1985; 'Living with AIDS', 26 January 1987; 'AIDS: the fight for control', 29 June 1987; 'The killer inside', 30 January 1989.

4. There were a number of other similar programmes in the sample period, such as 'Suzy's story', *QED*, BBC1, 2 March 1988 and 'Diary of a frontliner', *Forty Minutes*, BBC2, 18 February 1988.

6

Sourcing AIDS News

David Miller and Kevin Williams

The media are central actors in the political process which no organisation, from the central institutions of the state to the smallest campaigning group, can ignore. The Head of Information at the British Medical Association (BMA), for example, stated that the organisation would not have 'any influence at all if we didn't have influence with journalists. I'd say they're essential to the running of the BMA.' There is a variety of reasons why the media are important for different organisations. For larger organisations such as the BMA, media strategies are useful in attempts to influence government policy and promote the interests of the medical profession. Other organisations use the media to increase their membership or promote particular activities and interests. They may use the media to target public opinion generally or to reach a very specialised audience of perhaps only two or three people. The form of contact with the media can range from leaks and off the record briefings to press conferences and publicity campaigns and events. The complexity of public relations politics is in the myriad of agendas and audiences which the strategist may try to influence. This chapter examines the factors that shaped the media strategies developed around AIDS. These include the resources available, co-operation and competition between sources, varying targets and tactics, contests over promotional strategies within organisations, the role of the press office and dilemmas of policy influence versus campaigning. We also examine the failure of the Health Education Authority's promotional strategy, the success of the strategy of the Terrence Higgins Trust and the influence of the media on promotional strategies.

How do they do that? The question of resources

AIDS information in the period of our study was provided by bodies as diverse as the Department of Health, the Health Education Authority (HEA) and the BMA through to the Terrence Higgins Trust, Body Positive and smaller AIDS charities such as AVERT and OutRage! Some of these groups have the provision of AIDS information as their sole objective; others provide such information as one part of their promotional activities. It is important to note the structural inequality between organisations in the

Table 6.1 *Spending on public relations and publicity (£1,000s)*

	Public relations			Advertising/publicity		
	DHSS/DoH	HEA	THT	DHSS/DoH	HEA	THT
1985/86	1,100	NA	–	NA	NA	NA
1986/87	1,200/936~	NA	–	19,200	NA	NA
1987/88	994	NA	–	28,800	5,271.5*	NA
1988/89	NA	NA	–	10,799	NA	70
1989/90	890	NA	–	16,762	NA	107
1990/91	1,250	NA	–	21,489	NA	173/72
1991/92	1,491	NA	–	24,083	NA	79
1992/93	NA	NA	–	22,000	NA	77
1993/94	NA	NA	–	23,700	NA	104

NA = not available

~ Figures from 1985/86 'include costs of salaries, accommodation, common services and other non manpower items' as does the higher figure in 1986/87. The lower figure in that year and all subsequent figures refer to 'professional manpower' (*Hansard*, 16 November 1987: 433 and 4 November 1987: 775)

* including £3 million on AIDS

The figures for the Terrence Higgins Trust are taken from successive Trust *Annual Report and Accounts*. Except for 1993 the figures do not refer to complete financial years. The figures for 1987/88 refer to the 9 months ended 31 December 1988, the figures for 1989/91 refer to the calendar year and the figures for 1992/93 are for the 15 months ended 31 March 1993. Additionally the figures for 1989/90 and 1990/91 cover 'communications, leaflets, posters etc.' whilst the lower figure from 1990/91 and succeeding years refer to 'publicity'.

field. These inequalities are the outcome of the financial, institutional and cultural resources available to source organisations (Schlesinger, 1990). Access to a secure financial base is a key resource for any organisation which wants to pursue particular aims and affects their ability to allocate separate budgets to campaigning or information work. Comparison between the general promotional spending of the Department of Health, the Health Education Authority and the Terrence Higgins Trust gives an indication of the disparity in relation to AIDS (see Table 6.1).

The lack of financial resources imposes clear limits on the kinds of informational strategies it is possible to launch. Press relations at the Terrence Higgins Trust have been, according to a spokesperson: 'very reactive . . . [because] the number of people and the resources we work on are very small'. The Conservative Family Campaign relied to a great extent on the efforts of one individual, its 'chairman', Graham Webster-Gardiner. According to Dr Adrian Rogers of the Campaign:

He [Graham Webster-Gardiner] would go into [Conservative] Central Office. He'd go where every proper campaign should be and he would have meetings with the leader of the House of Lords and he'd try and get to meet a whip or two. He really worked extremely diligently. We became, in a very small sense, influential. We had over 30 sponsors. (We have less now.) Then we went for the mailing of our members to see if we could fund Graham as a full time chairman, but we didn't have enough money – nowhere near enough.

The question of financial resources is related to the degree to which an organisation is institutionalised. Government departments clearly exist on a more secure footing than do lesbian and gay activist groups or AIDS charities. AIDS charities are comparatively recent organisations and often their goals are discrete in that they are related to information giving or providing care and support. A cure or vaccine, for example, will mean that some will cease to function. The Department of Health is, on the other hand, an established institution in the field of health policy. Organisations whose very existence is insecure have as one of their primary information goals the active pursuit of legitimacy and resources. A result of the dependence of the Conservative Family Campaign on the voluntary work of one person was that:

> We are now in a situation where he [Webster-Gardiner] has indicated that he is unable to continue putting in that amount of work. We've been so successful, we've become nationally known and yet – unlike any other nationally known organisation – we've got no offices and no full time employees. If he's not going to continue, nobody else has the time or the location to do so. So our future is pretty bleak.

While the Campaign was able to establish itself as a source of information, its lack of finance limited its efforts to operate within the information environment. However, while legitimacy and financial resources are important, source organisations are also dependent on cultural resources. There is a need to conform to the practices and routines of the policy making process and the nature of media production which determines the way in which information is provided. As with financial and institutional resources, cultural capital can be increased by strategic and tactical means. Presentational skills can be useful in notching up cultural capital with the media, and 'resource poor' groups which lack institutional and financial resources may use these skills to improve their standing. According to Nick Partridge of the THT:

> Between '85 and '87 it became clear that I was good at talking with journalists and particularly doing television and radio work. Also, the majority of that work has to be done during the day and the number of volunteers who were available to do that with the right skills and qualities and confidence are very very limited.

The THT's attempts to develop its presentational skills were made within the context of negative cultural evaluations of homosexuality. Partridge attributed his success to the fact that

> I'm not threatening in a way. I am 35. I'm middle class. I speak in BBC type English. I'm very acceptable. I am the kind of homosexual you'd want to take home to your mother and that is a great relief to [journalists], especially the ones who are desperately trying to show their liberalism.

This was in contrast to another THT spokesperson with whom journalists had much more difficulty . . . Because he wears much more leather than I do. He has a moustache. He's much more an outwardly gay man. Similarly, I think if I were a stereotypically effeminate gay man, that similarly would have been a problem, much more of a problem, and we would have been ignored.

The decision to 'go public' is that much harder for lesbians and gay men who have to consider the implications of being out in public life. As Nick Partridge put it:

Particularly in '85 and up to '87, the risks you ran in appearing on television on a regular basis, talking about AIDS issues and by default talking about gay issues as well, were fairly substantial . . . It's not something you decided to do lightly. Any lesbian or gay man has to think very carefully about . . . being out on television, it has implications for your lover, particularly for your family. While you may well be out to your parents, you might not be out to your grandparents and to your broader family. You have a range of things you have to think about. So the number of people prepared to come forward . . . is limited.

Such problems were compounded for people who were publicly HIV positive. Organisations for people with HIV receive frequent requests to provide people with HIV for television programmes, most commonly to discuss issues of discrimination. One of the key problems of appearing on television programmes designed to combat prejudice and discrimination is the possibility that identifying publicly as HIV positive will lead directly to the interviewee facing an increase in discrimination. Jonathan Grimshaw was a founder of Body Positive in 1985, an advisor on television programming and (during 1986–87) he frequently appeared on television in his capacity as a person living with HIV. He took 'a conscious decision to come out of the spotlight'. As he put it:

It's been enormously stressful. Certainly the time I was doing it, you are genuinely taking risks in being very publicly identified as somebody with HIV. A lot of people who did appear had very unpleasant experiences and although I didn't have any negative experiences – I wasn't attacked or beaten up or any of those things – it was constantly at the back of one's mind that one could be.

Thus in the provision of AIDS information, some individuals had to confront the real risks attached to some popular attitudes to homosexuality.

In the pursuit of cultural capital, 'credibility' is a valued resource. For one AIDS specialist, his status as a doctor underwrote what he said, but he perceived that this status could be dissipated if he spoke too freely.

I think the problem is that . . . it's known that I am – in their perception – permissive and slightly liberal and not prepared to stand for discrimination. [In] a sense [you] have lost some of your credibility once you have a label round your neck and it's quite difficult to claw that back . . . You lose what was originally seen, potentially, as a sort of independent voice. (Clinician)

The availability of financial, institutional and cultural resources is vital to the goals and consequent strategies adopted by different organisations. Government departments do not normally engage with the media to raise financial resources from voluntary donations or recruit members. Charities and resource-poor groups may need to do both in order to survive. Thus the resources available to any organisation are constituted and reconstituted by the strategies formulated by organisations and individuals to win power and influence, and it is to these we now turn.

What do sources do? Competition and co-operation

Studies of source-media relations emphasise the contest between sources and in particular the crucial role of official sources: powerful institutions with greater financial, cultural and institutional capital. However, the relationship between official and non-official sources is not only one of competition. Persuading other groups to share certain policy positions or at least to work together on matters of mutual interest is also important. This much is clear from public alliances. However, sources can also work together covertly – while publicly giving the impression of being independent or even sometimes antagonistic to one another. Furthermore, sources may use others (knowingly or otherwise) to promote a message or carry out an action which, for whatever reason, they themselves feel unable to. Organisations or factions within them can feel constrained by their position (as a government department, a charity, a scientific body, etc.) not to step outside the norms of 'appropriate' behaviour. The consequence is that the influence of some sources on public debate may not be reflected by their profile in media accounts.

In the early stages of the government response to AIDS, the DHSS invited doctors at the sharp end of the treatment of people with HIV and AIDS, as well as representatives of people with HIV and gay men, to participate in committees which fed into media strategies and policy making.[1] These groups had different inputs into the development of the government's AIDS policy but the crucial point is that a low or non-existent media profile is not necessarily an indicator of a lack of power in public debate or policy making. Indeed, the definitions of state and governmental bodies can be influenced by less well resourced organisations. Conversely the formation of the definitions of less powerful organisations can be affected by their relationship with state and governmental bodies. Some HIV/AIDS organisations in the voluntary sector have charitable status and receive funding from central government, which can constrain what they can say and how they act. Pressure groups on the moral right, such as Family and Youth Concern or the Conservative Family Campaign (which are not funded by central government) have called on the DoH to withdraw funding from the Terrence Higgins Trust (*Cut off funding to Terrence Higgins Trust call*, Family and Youth Concern press release, 22 November 1989). This has some impact on the planned public profile and media strategy of the THT, which has to take its credibility seriously especially when it may affect THT funding arrangements with central government. As Nick Partridge has put it:

> We have to be the responsible party, that's our role. One: it protects our charitable status, secondly our combative up-front campaigning has to be in the context of charity and . . . I want this organisation to remain a trusted source of information.

For organisations closer to the centres of political power, such as the Health Education Authority, the link with the Department of Health is not simply financial. The HEA can be required to take direct instructions from the Department. These impact on the day to day working practices of the Authority which is nominally 'independent' of government.[2] This meant that the Authority could not always say what it wanted to on AIDS:

> On some things, in the AIDS field in general, the HEA was very circumscribed, so we would just refer people to [leading clinicians] Michael Adler or Tony Pinching. Once you've been referred to Pinching or Adler you've got the contacts and you phone them up direct . . . And the HEA . . . were not allowed to say anything outside the area that we were being paid to deal with, which is public communications . . . So all we could do was parrot stuff that the Department of Health press office had, and had published anyway. So as a source of hard information, the HEA couldn't give journalists very much. (Public affairs official, HEA)

Consequently, the HEA did much of its media work behind the scenes, which often meant referring journalists to sources of information who were sympathetic to their line and more free to comment.

The influence of groups such as Family and Youth Concern and the Conservative Family Campaign was also greater than its media profile would indicate. Moralist pressure groups such as Family and Youth Concern concentrate on lobbying and 'educational' work in preference to targeting the media. This is not to say that they do not issue press statements. Indeed, they have been able to secure prominent space in mid-market tabloids for articles by sponsors such as Sir Reginald Murley. Nevertheless, their main work is distributing propaganda materials to educational establishments,[3] and lobbying Whitehall. Both organisations see the media and public opinion as important but secondary. Dr Adrian Rogers of the Conservative Family Campaign stressed that: 'We've always fought a total rearguard action with public opinion. The main thrust of the organisation has always been to attempt to influence those in power and the Conservative Party.'

Nick Partridge of the THT notes that these groups 'have access to a ministerial and prime ministerial level which we will never get close to' (cited in Woods, 1989). The access to the policy making process of groups such as the Conservative Family Campaign was influenced by personal and ideological connections with the Conservative government. Such access, however, did not lead inexorably to influence. They were able to gain access to meet government ministers, and they had some supporters in government, but this did not necessarily translate into policy change. Meetings often ended unsatisfactorily. Robert Whelan of Family and Youth Concern described a meeting with the then Health Minister, Virginia Bottomley, as a 'waste of time':

There were three civil servants sitting there, we were not introduced. They knew who we were but we didn't know who they were. They were making notes all the time we were speaking, they had briefed the Minister of course . . . They sat there like the three wise monkeys . . . The Minister says what the Minister is told to say and if the Minister objects the Minister is moved. Now Virginia Bottomley herself is a very charming woman. She is a wife and a mother, she must realise the implications of that sort of [health education] material.

The perception of organisations such as Family and Youth Concern is that their access to ministers was frustrated by the civil service (particularly the Department of Health) which they saw as deeply hostile to their agenda.

Different goals, different target audiences

Sources attempt to use and manipulate the media in order to influence a wide variety of debates, agendas and audiences. This is one reason why media strategies vary enormously. Media strategies are not only formulated to influence public opinion – a commonly held assumption about informa- tion activities. Sources use the media to raise funding, boost membership, satisfy membership expectations, resolve disputes between or within organ- isations, improve the standing of an organisation or individual within their own constituency, influence business practice or local or national govern- ment policy. Accordingly, the audience for a particular strategy can be the entire population of a given state or bloc of states, the membership of a pressure group or decision or policy makers. In some cases the target may be a very small group of people indeed, such as key officials in a govern- ment department or a single member of an official committee.

Some of the first professionals involved with AIDS were clinicians who were treating increasing numbers of HIV positive people. They became frustrated at the lack of government action. Government officials indicated that they thought AIDS was a very important issue but 'this is such a sensitive issue that the Department couldn't possibly start making official comments' (clinician). Clinicians were important sources of expert knowl- edge for medical reporters and they began to realise that they could use this relationship to bring pressure on the government. The then medical editor of the *Sunday Times* was one journalist who was targeted:

[He] had done some silly story about a new treatment and I told him so. So when he rang up with another new treatment I said: 'this is not a cure and it's misleading patients and making the government think that a cure is round the corner so they don't need to put money in. There is a substantial problem and we need money for the epidemic. Why don't you start running stories about resources?' And he followed that advice and ran a good piece in the *Sunday Times*. (Clinician)

The consequence was that the clinician was 'able to steer that on to the agenda, together with [television current affairs programmes] which led to a context where the pressure started to generate'. Other clinicians also took a high media profile using their position as authoritative information sources to pressurise the government. One said that he 'began to realise that nothing was being done at all . . . [and] that one could, if one spoke in the correct way, use the media to exert leverage on the government'. In his view such leverage was, at least to an extent, successful:

> I do think that people like myself who could see that one had to translate issues into strategy and therefore get money for HIV services – I think that was very effective . . . I think that those early media interventions were very effective – not in getting money personally for research or anything – but in getting money put into health education and into services. But it took a hell of a long time. The government didn't mount a health education campaign until 1986 – we were seeing our first cases in 1983–84.

Thus a small number of clinicians used their relationship with a handful of leading medical reporters to place pressure on key actors in government. Struggles within government meant that this pressure could be welcomed as a means of pressurising another section of the Whitehall bureaucracy. Indeed on occasion the Department of Health encourages pressure groups to criticise another branch of government or even the Department itself in order to encourage action for which it needs support even if it can't say so publicly.

Other sources were less interested in trying to manage the news agenda to influence policy. The goal of activist groups such as OutRage! was also to impact on media representations and public understanding of the gay community and AIDS. According to Chris Woods of OutRage!, this was a new departure for lesbian and gay activism:

> We were in completely virgin territory. Gay activists had not been involved in this kind of media work even in the early seventies with the Gay Liberation Front. They sort of invited the media as an afterthought to those actions whereas OutRage! set out right from the beginning to build its action around media coverage. Actions were gauged a success according to the volume of media coverage that was gained from them, not the number of lesbian and gay demonstrators that turned up to that action. We could do an action with half a dozen people.

Such tactics also have another purpose, or at least result, in the effect they have on the activists themselves. For Keith Alcorn of OutRage! 'direct action actually gives people something to do with the anger that they develop as a result both of the stories which the mass media do produce and the stories which they ignore. So that's one of the things which informed our thinking when OutRage! began.' Chris Woods also noted the 'self-respect that something like OutRage! can give individuals who until that point felt completely disenfranchised and disempowered'.

Similarly the British Medical Association saw its own constituency as an important audience to target:

> We felt that there was more than one target audience, for our message, and it wasn't just the press and the public . . . Doctors were as important a target audience as anybody else, with as much prejudice and so on that had to be combated. (Public affairs official, BMA)

Providing information to medical practitioners was not only a matter of combating ignorance but also a necessary component of building an effective strategy to influence parliamentary and public opinion.

> If you've got the medical profession's attitudes wrong, then you're in real trouble. So we began as quickly as we could and as positively as we could with the medical profession itself. They were given priority. But then very soon afterwards, you have to make sure that you bring into line Members of Parliament. Because it's no use doctors thinking in the right way, if Members of Parliament start legislating for absurd things like giving everybody an HIV test, and then shipping people to an island somewhere if they prove to be positive. And then comes the general public and the press. (Public affairs official, BMA)

To reach doctors the BMA used specialist and professional media and journals rather than mainstream press and television:

> We'd spend a great deal of time in the early days, just filling as many pages as possible of the medical journals, with as much information as we could to doctors on AIDS, and their attitudes about AIDS and HIV patients, their responsibilities and so on. And we made sure that the issue was raised, that there were features written, that doctors who dealt with patients who are drug addicts were writing features. We encouraged them to, we helped them to. And generally encouraged the journals to make it an issue, and to make it of interest and importance. (Public affairs official, BMA)

As we have seen (in Chapters 3 to 5) the coverage of AIDS in the media varied between different newspapers and television programmes and between different genres of reporting. Sources recognise that in order to use the media to reach their target audiences or influence a particular agenda they have to deal with different journalists in different ways. At the HEA, journalists were divided according to the papers they wrote for into the 'easy group' and the 'difficult group':

> We always send the same information, the same materials to everybody. We give everybody the same opportunity to come to press briefings, to talk to us, whatever. So we don't in any sense discriminate, [although we] perhaps work harder to get the difficult group, you know, ring them up personally and so on, and spend more time with them. [However], if I wanted to get a particular piece of information or point of view across, I would proactively get hold of some of the people I know – the BBC or the quality newspapers – and say 'Look, do you think there's an idea here for a piece, for a programme', whatever. And I wouldn't do that with the difficult group, because I'd always be nervous that things would go wrong. So in a sense, we were less – are less proactive with the 'difficult' group than with the 'easy' group, and use them less in a proactive way. (AIDS division official)

Similarly at the THT distinctions were made between groups of reporters. According to Nick Partridge:

> I always take the calls from *Sun* journalists although my palm does get a little sweaty because you never quite know what it's going to be. Is it going to be 'the car that had AIDS', that sort of stuff? . . . The majority . . . of them are well-spoken, articulate . . . I do my 'Well, you've got to understand what the difference

between HIV and AIDS is' bit and I think this is never going to get into the paper. Never mind, you treat them with a modicum of respect and you hope, maybe when that journalist has moved on to somewhere else where he or she has more freedom of action, what I've said will have sunk in . . . it will have an effect there. But I long since didn't bother sending press releases to the *Sun*.

A number of other tabloids were also seen as lost causes:

Don't bother with *Today* any more, don't bother with the *Star*. Most things we'd also put out on PA [the Press Association] anyway and they may pick it up there, but it's not worth the photocopying and postage, quite honestly. I answer the phone and I certainly keep in touch with the agony aunts on those papers but that's as far as it goes.

The BMA had a different approach to the tabloids, seeing them as a key channel to reach heterosexuals:

If you're talking about so-called safer sex in heterosexuals, then the *Sun* is the place to get your message over. And for the *Sun* to be telling all its millions of readers that, provided you have so-called straight sex, that you're safe, is really a disservice of magical proportions. But I have to say on other things to do with health education, they've been absolutely wonderful, and if we can get something into the *Sun*, they're marvellous. So I can never, ever understand why people say haughtily 'don't invite the *Sun*'. It's an absolute joke.

Nevertheless, the BMA also operates an informal hierarchy, which reflects its perception of the importance of different journalists within news organisations. BMA press officers referred to the 'top health journalists' as the 'A-team', usually those who cover the NHS and health policy. Those who tend to cover medical issues such as the progress of particular diseases like AIDS was referred to as the 'B-team'. The presence of the 'A-team' was seen as indicating that a news organisation was giving the story 'more credence'.

Source tactics: from government briefings to pressure group 'zaps'

A range of interactions between the media and social institutions are reflected in the strategies deployed to influence the media. The main contact between sources of information and journalists is on the phone. Nearly all of those press and public relations officials we spoke to put the proportion of their time on the phone as between 80 and 90%. The reliance on the phone has increased in recent years as the British press has decamped from Fleet Street and moved almost *en masse* to the East End of London (whether Wapping or Canary Wharf).[4] One information specialist noted:

The move to Wapping has been quite a culture change. For example, a *Sunday Times* journalist said to me 'we should meet up for a chat . . . But it would have to be on a Wednesday because I really only come up to town on a Wednesday.' That means they do all the work on the phone.

Nevertheless press conferences, launches and briefings retain a certain utility. They tend to play a bigger part in the repertoire of government and other institutionalised sources such as the BMA, which reflects the degree of authority and credibility enjoyed by these organisations. If they are organised by the Department of Health, such events are guaranteed at least a mention in the press; BMA and HEA conferences and launches are likely to attract national newspaper journalists, while the THT would only definitely get the gay press to its launches. However, the Trust was able to exploit the greater pull of official press conferences and launches by turning up unannounced and distributing THT literature at official functions. According to Nick Partridge:

> I have [gone to] almost all HEA press conferences to a point at which Mukesh Kapila [Deputy Director of the AIDS division at the HEA] got very angry with me. [I was] perceived as undermining their press conferences by arriving with a pack of press releases from the Trust and leaving them on the chairs. It seems to me to be direct action really. I know that the draw that the HEA has is much greater than the draw THT has so in the press conferences we've run there's never any guarantee that the journalists are going to come along to them. So I use that and make myself available to comment on what the HEA has just presented.

Off-the-record briefings, quotes or information may be used by any source but it is government sources who are best able to use them to strategic advantage. They have access to more information and, crucially, are the locus of decision making. For resource-poor groups and activist organisations, 'lobbying' is either a luxury they can ill afford or is eschewed for ideological reasons. For example, lesbian and gay pressure group, Stonewall 'opts for discreet lobbying, a measured assimilationist approach concentrated on the corridors of political power', while OutRage! 'likes to take to the streets. It organises "kiss-ins", "mass turn-ins" and "queer weddings", events tinged with humour that belie serious intent. It organises marches and vigils and demos at which it carries banners and blows whistles. And it gets its name into the newspapers' (Garfield, 1991: 4).

OutRage! has been considerably more sophisticated than many other activist groups in the area. From the beginning, the organisation has aimed to orchestrate lesbian and gay activism to maximum effect by targeting the media. The news media themselves have often been the targets of groups such as OutRage! or ACT UP in a tactic known as 'zapping' the media. In Britain ACT UP have conducted 'die-ins' outside newspaper offices which have printed particularly homophobic items. In September 1991 OutRage! under one of its cover names 'Socialist Lesbians and Gays' picketed the *Guardian* over an article about gay men and AIDS which had included statements such as 'there is an inbuilt fatalism to being gay; biologically maladaptive, unable to reproduce, our futures are limited to living for today because we have no tomorrow. A gay man is the end of the line.'[5] Socialist Lesbians and Gays stated

> It's time to call the liberal press's bluff. We demand an immediate right of reply to the offensive and hate promoting article Gay Abandon . . . You didn't believe the

ever-so-liberal *Guardian* would print such insulting and abusive anti-gay rubbish? Well now you have it, on a scale to make the *Sun*, *Daily Star* and *News of the World* cry into their beer with jealousy. ('Guardian target for campaigners', *Capital Gay*, 13 September 1991)

In the US during the Gulf War ACT UP activists invaded both CBS and McNeil/Lehrer news studios as the news was being broadcast. At CBS they shouted 'Fight AIDS, not Arabs'. On the McNeil/Lehrer news show, which broadcasts on the smaller PBS public service system, 'activists chained themselves to desks. They arrived opportunely, during an interview concerning carpet bombing. The activists spoke for several minutes on the AIDS crisis and the work that needs to be done to save lives, not slaughter them' (Carter, 1992: 18). These actions recall those of the lesbian activists who invaded the BBC news studios on the day that Section 28 of the Local Government Act was passed (see Howes, 1993).

Charities cannot afford to pay for glitzy launches or even be sure of attracting more than a handful of journalists to their press conferences. ACT UP or OutRage! do not conduct daily lobby type briefings since they do not have the institutional or cultural resources – even if they had the ideological disposition to do so. However, in recent years, publicity and the cultivation of both formal and informal contacts with the media have been seen as increasingly important and organisations of all kinds have allocated more and more time and money specifically to media relations activities. This has resulted in source organisations investing more in media training for its employees or members. It has also meant the influx of a new type of employee. The growth of the promotional professions, and the contracting out of tasks to public relations, marketing and lobbying agencies has grown considerably. This development has been characterised by increased suspicion and tensions within source organisations. These are grounded in perceived or actual conflicts of interest between the information or promotional professionals and other parts of the source organisation, especially when the newcomers gain privileged access to information or resources. These conflicts and clashes of interests are part of the wider tensions within source organisations which can influence the framing of media strategies.

Bureaucratic organisations house large numbers of competing interests and agendas. In a government department one of the main functions of the press office is to manage such divisions and present a unified face to the outside world (Miller, D., 1993; Miller and Reilly, 1995; Miller and Williams, 1993). If divisions within government become public, this will in itself result in media interest. The production of the mass media campaign on AIDS was characterised by protracted conflicts within government (see Chapter 2) which often spilled over into media controversies. Stories about 'government interference' in the Health Education Authority became commonplace. So much so that, as one member of the HEA put it, 'the best stories about the HEA are "Government bans", "Government forces changes", "So and so leaves"'.

The gatekeeper role of the press office

The culture of an organisation, its internal lines of communication and responsibilities and its institutional cohesiveness, are fundamental to its ability to generate and execute a coherent media strategy and successfully carry it through. Government departments are populated by a variety of professional groupings who are jockeying for position. Conflicts of interest and intent exist. We can identify the groupings of administrative civil servants, ministers and information officers as important in relation to public profiles. There are also a number of specialist advisors in government departments, such as scientific professionals and doctors in the Department of Health, who may play a role in the framing of media policy.

The status and therefore potential effectiveness of the information division or press office of government departments is partly determined by its relationship with ministers (cf. Schlesinger and Tumber, 1994). In fact this relationship is seen as one of the most important by information officers:

> If the ministers are publicity conscious and think it matters then consequently the press office will have high status. If you get ministers who aren't very interested in publicity and don't think it matters then equally it doesn't matter what the press office does. (Information Officer, DoH)

Since all publicity campaigns and most press statements have to gain ministerial approval, government ministers are clearly a key influence on departmental information policy. Paradoxically, however, a publicity conscious minister is likely to give the press office a freer hand than a minister sceptical of the value of the media. At the Department of Health, treating press officers as clerks is seen to be a problem mainly affecting other government departments:

> I think our status in this department is higher than some departments. Some departments will not tell the press office anything and the press office is used to make announcements when they are ready, they have had no hand in the form or content of the announcement, or if there are questions they are referred up and the press office will give out exactly what it is told to give out even if it is mumbo jumbo. It seems to me if you have got that kind of outfit, why bother having press officers instead of clerks? You don't need to pay people a few extra bob to do it. Certainly there are press officers – quite highly paid ones – that do that. (senior Information Officer, DoH)

The importance of the press office in the Department of Health is illustrated in a 1990 internal guide to the Minister's private office. This stresses that *'Ministers attach a very great importance to media coverage.* Consequently the publicity for any announcement, speech or visit should be given early consideration in consultation with the Press Office' (DHSS, 1990: 29, emphasis in original). As in other departments (cf. Miller, D., 1993) administrative civil servants can be mistrustful and suspicious of the press office. Part of the mistrust of information professionals is that they are seen as being too close to journalists. Many press officers have a background in journalism which can reinforce suspicions that their closeness with the world

of journalism will prove too beguiling and the press officer will be powerless
to stop themselves leaking information. In the case of health education this
conflict is exacerbated because the professional grouping has a fairly low
profile and status in the media. One information specialist in the HEA:

> [has] had the feeling in the past that sometimes people haven't informed the press
> office because they don't trust us not to give information out. You have to coax
> people and say 'okay, you seem to feel this is a controversial issue. Please just tell
> me what's happening with it. Tell me the story first and then I'll decide what we
> should do about it. We won't volunteer any of this information, but if a journalist
> were to ask us this, this and this, this is what we would say and then, only if they
> pressed us would we say this.' There are people here who have to be persuaded
> that it's wise to tell the press officer the whole story first. (public affairs official)

This information specialist was prepared to be 'economical' with the truth:
'That's what we do . . . That's what the job is.' However the problem for
the press office and the public affairs division was that they sometimes felt
they were kept in ignorance of policy and often did not know anything
about information they would have been happy to withhold. This margin-
alisation in policy making meant that HEA relations with the media were
often impaired because the press office was unaware of what was going on.

A press office can sometimes act as a barrier to the provision of information to the media if it is unable to put its hands on the information
required. Many enquiries from journalists mean trying to locate the relevant
person in the source organisation who can answer the query or provide a
response. Delays can lead to difficult relations with journalists. This is
recognised by senior information officers in the Department of Health:

> Patently there are times in this department where if you were to ring the correct
> civil servant direct you would get the stuff and they would get a better story and
> they would get it quicker. (senior Information Officer)

However, the Department of Health also seeks to discourage direct links
between civil servants and the media. The aim is to control access of
journalists to the Department by encouraging them to go through the press
office. The information division in the Department encourages civil servants
to mistrust the media:

> We go to some trouble to encourage that mistrust. We want to get the press to
> deal through us. Our argument is that – sometimes it is a serious argument and
> sometimes true – we have a much greater chance of knowing the full picture. Also
> we are used to dealing with journalists, we can say x is a rat, x is not. (senior
> Information Officer)

The Department of Health is cautious in its dealings with the media, trying
to regulate access through a narrow channel. At the BMA, suspicion of the
media is seen largely as being in the past:

> The BMA has had a press office since 1948, so there's no problem about it.
> There's no question that we talk – we use the media – absolutely no question at
> all. It's been 13 years since somebody said to me, do you think we run this place
> for the press, because the answer's yes, we do. And I think if we're taking

decisions that don't stand up to scrutiny by journalists, then we've taken the wrong decision. (public affairs official)

This is certainly a change from the 1950s when the BMA's PR operation was in its infancy and there was doubt and opposition to using the news media. Then the BMA's public relations office was small, consisting of a PR officer, his assistant and five support staff. Publicity at this time was 'used chiefly as a tactical weapon for nudging the Ministry [of Health] into certain positions or whipping up a show of unity in the profession' (Eckstein, 1960: 73–5). Eckstein notes, however, that the BMA did breach the secrecy of negotiations with the government over the implementation of the National Health Service. A series of public meetings to mobilise 'mass indignation' was organised. However, publicity was 'rarely used for any broader strategic purpose by the Association' and the BMA waged 'few publicity campaigns simply because it seldom has any pressing need to wage them'. Members of the Association considered such activities vulgar. But as Eckstein points out, the BMA's lack of media campaigning was also a reflection of the limited audience for medico-political issues in Britain at the time: 'the BMA and its political affairs simply are not very newsworthy, and this in turn can be explained by the absence of any important disagreements on medical policy in Britain'. There was also no pressing need because the BMA's voice was represented in a 'reliable and usually friendly' way inside the Ministry of Health and its goals did not touch on matters of high policy. The main audience for the organisation's PR work were Members of Parliament, with whom the BMA sought to forge close links. Publicity is now much more central to the daily operations of the BMA. The tag of vulgarity has less force and there has been a sea change in the consensus on medical and health policy since the 1950s which has also meant a radical change in the need to wage publicity campaigns to influence government policy.

The job of the information professional also entails trying to police and monitor disclosure from and about their organisation. To do this it is necessary to cultivate relationships inside as well as outside the organisation. In a way, then, the press officer is engaged in impression management. Success, as a Department of Health information officer put it:

is partly the attitudes of the ministers; it is partly the calibre of the people in the press office . . . No press officer can get on without getting on well with the officials, so it is partly how well you communicate within the Department and it is partly how you are seen outside by the media.

Information divisions are usually arranged hierarchically, and reflect the sources of power inside an organisation. In government departments, where statements need to be approved by ministers (DHSS, 1990), PR work will inevitably be more bureaucratic than at an organisation such as the BMA, where the press office has more input into the decision-making process. A senior member of the BMA's information team contrasts the two organisations:

The Department of Health puts out more press statements in a day than we put out in a week, or month I should think . . . you've got to agree something when you can get into see the Minister, you go off with it and you promote it. And the talented press officers at the Department of Health . . . will then have what it takes to elaborate on it and to help the journalists accordingly. Whereas here it's quite different. We . . . often develop the line ourselves, clear it with whoever it needs clearing with, and then we'll brief the staff here, and then we'll go sell the line.

Another BMA press officer says that 'it is not at all unheard of for this Division . . . to, not necessarily change BMA policy, but certainly bend it, maybe in a very different direction. [The Director of Information] will say "you're not going to get that past the British public" – [meaning] think again . . . present that in a different way' (public affairs official, BMA). For government information officers political direction is much more important. Press officers in the government departments are much less free to develop policy than in an organisation like the BMA.

Pressure groups and publicity – campaigning or policy participation

For resource-poor groups such as charities and pressure groups, media appearances can lead to jealousy or to accusations that a critical edge has been lost, demands have been watered down, that publicity is becoming an end in itself or is sought for personal vanity (cf. Gitlin, 1980; Goldenberg, 1976).[6] As Nick Partridge of the THT put it: 'Some do criticise us for being too nice, too respectable. And obviously there are also those other "Oh her, she's just a media queen" – that sort of dismissive thing that can take place.' The THT also came under attack from critics of AZT. Organisations such as Gays Against Genocide picketed THT offices alleging a corrupting relationship with Wellcome PLC, the makers of AZT.

There are also tensions between the campaigning objectives of activist groups and their desire to participate in the debate around the policy process. For some the danger is becoming too much part of the system. As Chris Woods of OutRage! argues in relation to Stonewall:

> people like [Ian] McKellen and [Michael] Cashman are the sort of high profile gay and lesbian politicians who decided that the way forward was through conventional lobbying methods which is where Stonewall comes in and I don't criticise that. What I do criticise is their assertion that it is the only way to actually achieve political change or the only way to actually mobilise people around the issues. What started off as a revolutionary movement in the late sixties and early seventies, had by the end of the eighties been subverted to the point that it was political conformity. To be gay was to be politically conformist.

The emergence of lesbians and gay men as a political constituency is seen by Woods as creating a number of dilemmas of media strategy:

> When we get an opportunity to speak to the media, we're often forced into the position of having to speak in soundbites . . . As a community, for the last

20 years politically it has suited us to promote ourselves as a homogeneous collection of individuals who have the same agenda. Now, as organisations like OutRage! develop their own politics and other groups as well, those debates that have always gone on within the community are actually coming closer to the surface . . . Now that creates all sorts of potential problems for media management and media manipulation because you can see the media picking up on these things, they're starting to see these debates come to the surface and rather than seeing that as a sign of political maturity which it actually is, this is a community that's actually arguing amongst itself to define itself, they're picking on that as a weakness and trying to exploit that. So often you find yourself in the position which is the last thing you want [of] trying to control the debate and simplify it to a point where the media can be controlled, and that is going to be a continuing problem in any kind of media work that we do.

This dilemma of maintaining a balance between critical campaigning and influencing the policy process has been acknowledged by those in the field of AIDS activism. The need to have some form of 'respectable' organisation to negotiate with the powerful was clear to OutRage! The pressure in these circumstances is to 'go legit', or as Cindy Patton has remarked of AIDS activists, make the journey from 'grassroots to business suits' (Patton, 1990). But there is also a recognition that such a move could blunt the cutting edge provided by direct action. In these circumstances OutRage! created a series of 'affinity groups' to work on different campaigns and, if necessary, become involved in negotiations with the powerful, while leaving OutRage! free to continue with direct action. This 'good cop–bad cop routine' was employed to greatest effect with actions against the Metropolitan Police and the creation of the London Lesbian and Gay Policing Initiative. According to Chris Woods:

we realised it wasn't enough just to get up there and shout and point at the police and say this is a mess. We had a list of a dozen demands, everything from them amending their equal opportunities policies to them stopping arrests to co-operation on murder enquiries. What we did in the background to focus the energy we were generating around that campaign, we set up the London, Lesbian and Gay Policing Initiative of which OutRage! was just one part, which was open to all London lesbian and gay organisations, which has now become the main negotiating body with the Metropolitan Police. Nobody ever talks about the involvement OutRage! had in creating that but it was a direct result of Outrage!'s campaign . . . a very cynical 'well OK we can't just make a noise, we're not nice people and the Met aren't going to talk to us. How are we going to get them to talk to the community?' We'll set up this institution – and we did it.

OutRage! also attached importance to improving the organisation's credibility with the media by the production of well researched information for journalists. As Peter Tatchell of OutRage! has put it: 'We produce very good quality press releases that back up what we say with hard facts and statistics. It makes it much easier for people to take us seriously' (cited in Garfield, 1991: 5). The management of credibility and the simultaneous safeguarding of radical potential inscribed in this approach is quite new and distinct in both AIDS activism and lesbian and gay politics (at least in

Britain). It shows a very sophisticated understanding of media and pressure group processes and has allowed OutRage! to develop into a formidable direct action organisation.[7]

The strategy of the HEA – failure of an official source

The struggle around the provision of AIDS information to the British public illustrates the practical problems that influence the ability of official and non-official sources to shape media accounts. The HEA's campaign placed great emphasis on the mass media. Its strategy involved two components: advertising, and media relations. The HEA recognised the importance of targeting specific media outlets, editors and reporters to create a positive climate to support its advertising campaign. This was spelled out in the 'total public communication strategy' drawn up for the HEA by the advertising agency Boase, Massimi, Pollit (BMP). A proactive public relations campaign was envisaged which sought to 'brand' the HEA as the 'most useful source of AIDS information' (Boase, Massimi, Pollit, 1988). However, the implementation of this strategy was influenced by several factors, including health educators' distrust of the mass media, the HEA's relationship with the Department of Health and the low status of health education in the eyes of the mass media.

Distrust of the media

Health educators have tended to be suspicious of the media, resulting in a certain reluctance to deal with journalists. As Holmes has noted they regard the media as 'untrustworthy' and as 'sources of conflict and misinformation' (Holmes, 1985: 18). This suspicion of the mass media was illustrated by the way in which some health educators in the HEA reacted to enquiries from journalists. A public affairs division employee said that many health educators' 'idea of a journalist was somebody from the *Sun* . . . A journalist to them was a hack of lowest order'. According to another member of the public affairs division

> a story would break in the press and they'll then come and say 'But how did the journalists know about it?' and you have to say 'Because that's what journalists do' and there is the attitude here that 'Oh, so and so's such an awful journalist, they're always pestering us and they're always finding things out and blowing them up . . . ' and you say 'No, no, no, that is a good journalist.' It is always that culture clash, really. (Public affairs official)

Because of this the HEA's public affairs division – which was responsible for formal relations with the press through its press office – had to educate many senior HEA staff on the need to be open and accessible to journalists. Attempts were made to encourage them to read the newspapers and watch TV regularly in order to gain some understanding of the differences between media outlets. But, as one member of the HEA said, 'there was a resistance' from health educators. The cautious approach of many HEA staff influenced journalists' perceptions of the HEA's usefulness as a source of both HIV and health education information. Although many correspondents had what they described as valuable informal sources inside the HEA they would refer disparagingly to formal contacts. As one tabloid medical correspondent said: 'they never really had anything I wanted'.

As we saw in Chapter 2, there were also tensions in the HEA between those with a media or advertising background and those with a research or health education background, which could affect the genesis of media strategies. In addition the HEA developed a complex bureaucracy. Symptomatic of this was what many of our interviewees (HEA staff together with voluntary agencies and activists who worked with the HEA) described as a 'meetings culture'. This had the effect of drawing out decision making. According to one public affairs official:

> The HEA has problems with bureaucracy. It can take a long time to get the simplest piece of information. It can take a long time to get hold of people here. It is very much a meetings culture. Whereas I feel that if we have a journalist on the phone wanting to talk to someone from the AIDS programme then I think we really need to respond fast to that because we want to have the HEA view put across. Also we want to make contact with that journalist and I think that should take priority over being at a meeting.

HEA/DoH relations

Another factor influencing the development of the HEA PR strategy was its relationship with the Department of Health. The HEA took over responsibility for HIV/AIDS from the Department, which did not look favourably on the HEA trying to establish itself as the 'most useful source' of HIV/AIDS information. The Department, according to some HEA sources, got 'shirty' about this strategy, being unwilling to give up its 'expert' role. These concerns were formalised in a *Memorandum of Understanding* drawn up between the DoH and the HEA in 1989. While accepting that the HEA has a right to give advice in public and private where appropriate, the document circumscribes the conditions under which public statements can be made.

> The HEA was not established to be, nor is funded as, a campaigning 'pressure group', although it is conceivable that issues might arise on which it would attempt to influence strongly the direction of government policy through 'pressure' and be seen to be doing so. It must judge such instances carefully. It is important that Ministers, through the Department, are informed in advance of advice to be given in public. (DoH/HEA, 1990: 7)

Clearly, this had implications for the HEA's information strategies: news releases had to be checked by administrative civil servants and clearance was often delayed. Quite often, according to HEA sources, a 'terribly straightforward and anodyne press release' would 'disappear down a black hole in the Department of Health'. Sometimes, 'press releases didn't get out at all'. Such delays discouraged the HEA from issuing statements. As one senior member of the HEA told us, it was:

> A very hard part of my job to give interesting quote-worthy comment, which wouldn't have the government down like a ton of bricks. It was a very difficult line to tread. Sometimes I erred on the side of being too bland, and sometimes I erred on the side of finding a ton of bricks on my head.

The lack of quotable material and the restrictions placed on the HEA made it difficult for the HEA press office to establish effective relations with journalists who despaired of what they saw as the authority's 'fence sitting'.

Status of health education

Health education as a profession has relatively low status (Ling, 1986). Health educators are near the bottom of the journalists' 'hierarchy of credibility'. Doctors and scientists have much greater authority and therefore credibility for journalists.

The failure of the Health Education Authority to make itself the leading source of AIDS information, illustrates some of the potential problems for official sources in trying to manage the media. Chief among these in this case was the relationship with the sponsoring Department of Health. But the failure of the HEA strategy does not indicate that its critics on the Christian right were successful or that other organisations pushing similar lines to the HEA also failed. For example, we can look at the success of the Terrence Higgins Trust.

The strategy of the THT – success of an alternative source

The Terrence Higgins Trust was formed in 1983 to provide information on HIV/AIDS. The Trust's origins were in existing lesbian and gay organisations such as the London Lesbian and Gay Switchboard (see Terrence Higgins Trust, 1987; Schramm-Evans, 1990). By the late 1980s the Trust had established itself as the leading AIDS voluntary agency and had won the right to be consulted by journalists as a credible source of information as well as an advocate on the needs and interests of people with HIV. According to a THT spokesperson: 'Overall certainly no other voluntary organisation has been as widely quoted and widely used as a resource.' This is supported by an analysis of press coverage of AIDS, carried out for the HEA (between April and July 1993). It found that 'The Terrence Higgins Trust is easily the most visible organisation amongst [those] we looked at' (McKeone, 1993: 4; see also Chapter 4).

Part of the THT's success can be explained by reference to its media friendly approach and the strategies it used to try and manage the media. However, it is also the case that the Trust was very useful for journalists anxious to balance a story on government policy or respond to the latest statement or activity of the moral right. Such opportunities, while not necessarily in the interests of the Trust, did enable it to become a regularly used source of information. In some respects the failure of the HEA to make itself into a leading source on AIDS was encouraged by the fact that the Trust was already a source of AIDS information, and the unwillingness of the HEA to comment naturally helped to turn journalists toward the Trust. The THT's success with the media proved to be a problem. As Nick Partridge explained:

> One of the problems that we suffered from, particularly around '87 was that the public image of the Trust was much bigger than we actually were as an organisation. The common sense and dignity of Tony Whitehead and other people that we put up to talk meant that we were rapidly established as a sensible organisation to go to. I haven't really had to do much scouting around or what I call pushing the Trust at all, it's always been much more reactive, people come to us and it's only been very occasionally we run press conferences for instance.

The Trust, along with other voluntary agencies, has been able to change the representation of AIDS in ways that move beyond the medical approach of the orthodoxy.

> One of the important things that we've done is from 1984, we've helped to create a three way debate about what in the past would have been seen solely as a medical issue and would often have been debated between an interviewer, and a doctor. We've always managed to make that a three way debate in which you've had a doctor, an interviewer, and somebody affected one way or another by HIV. I think it's something we had begun to see and many programmes looking at cancer had a voice from people with cancer talking about their issues but not as strongly as has been seen in AIDS.

The Trust, in pressing for more open discussions of safer sex, has played an important role in the broadening of discussion in the media about sex, sexuality and sexual practices.

> We managed to do things that had never happened on television or radio before. Tony talking about masturbation on *Woman's Hour*, I've talked about fist fucking on BBC 1 with a huge audience – that has never happened before – incidentally it's never happened since. I think about '87 it was a blip which has now been screwed down tight but I've been able to extend talking about sex on television and radio a great deal to the point where certainly things like *Sex Talk* would never have been possible without the kinds of things that I did on *Open Air*, and others have done, the need to talk about safe sex. (Nick Partridge)

However, the Trust's success with the media, and in promoting change in public opinion and culture, has not necessarily been matched by success with government, where relations were sometimes uneasy, not least when the funding of the Trust was cut in 1991. Furthermore success in the media strategies of the Trust does not mean that people with HIV are free of discrimination or that they are able to call upon proper services and support. While activist groups can be successful in reaching some of their goals, their continued existence testifies to the goals and target audiences that remain to be influenced. Nevertheless, we can see that media (and to some extent state) practice has been changed by the intervention of the Terrence Higgins Trust – as well as other AIDS organisations – in the provision of information and opinion.

Influence of the media on source organisations

The relationship between sources of information and the news media has been described as a 'dance' in which the sources take the lead (Gans, 1981). But sources also attribute power to the news media. Furthermore the media may be used for information or intelligence gathering by sources. Most organisations which have more than the bare minimum of resources collect press cuttings (for example, the DoH, BMA, HEA and THT all do so). Additionally consultation with journalists can be a good way of getting information. Clearly, sensitive information about opponents' activities, troubles and intentions can be of great use in the planning of promotional strategies.

> We have an intelligence service or try to have and we find something that is about to happen and we can see that the Department is going to have to announce what it plans to do in some way. We grab it and pinch it and bring it to the Minister's attention, and suggest how it might be done. (senior Information Officer, DoH)

Contact with journalists can also reveal information about one's own organisation. The activities of rivals can be monitored, leaks can be traced or more confidently planned. On the other hand journalists may sometimes be the only way which a press officer or administrative civil servant can find out about the activities of their own organisation. This kind of information gathering seems to have gone on in the HEA and in the Department of Health. One Department information officer told us that he would rely on a leading broadsheet medical journalist for information about government policy: 'you know and everyone knows that he knows more about AIDS than anyone else around. [So] I go to [him] for information about policy, no problem at all'.

Press officers also use journalists for sounding out ideas. In this respect media institutions can influence the organisations on which they report. In some ways journalists are involved in mediating the world to the sources as well as mediating the sources to the world.

> Sometimes [journalist X] will ring up and say 'What's going on' and I'll tell him and I'll say 'And while you're here, I want to try out an idea on you.' So I have a good working relationship, good enough with the journalists, actually to be able to try out the line, and say what do you think if we did it like this. And [he] sometimes says, 'It would be quite useful, but if you did it on Thursday, that would be even better, because . . . ' (Senior public affairs official, BMA)

The media can impinge on an organisation in the sense that they can supply the information and set the agenda for the discussion of internal issues. Campaigning media coverage can, for example, bring about changes in policy or the organisation and structure of government or pressure groups. It can also identify issues which organisations define as unimportant or with which they are unfamiliar. Often journalists are consulted on the reception a particular policy development or presentational gambit is likely to receive from news organisations or public opinion.

In some institutions the very fact that an individual appears regularly in the media can have a deleterious effect on her/his standing in the institution. According to a leading AIDS clinician:

Someone like myself who was on quite a lot of government and MRC committees was also trying to retain academic credibility with one's peers. What being on the television does is to actually undermine part of your authority with your peers because you're seen as a pop person, trying to sort of get in the limelight, being ambitious and certainly there was – if you take an institution like this – a lot of jealousy and reservation about someone like myself doing a lot with the media. It's that balance between feeling you have something that you should be saying and that you can say it reasonably well and that you've thought it out and also retaining some authority at a political or institutional level and still be seen as a serious person. That is the thing that is the hardest.

Similarly, decisions on health education campaigns in the Department of Health or the Health Education Authority were influenced by the spectre of the media consequences. According to HEA sources, personal testimony adverts were very difficult because of press interest in the identity of those featured:

amongst the tabloids, the personal so-called human interest side of any story always seemed to be more important to them than the substance. So we've actually had to not go ahead with certain advertising strategies that we thought would be good, because of them. We went through a lot of painful meetings with the support groups, people who work with HIV and AIDS, to try and ensure that we protected whoever came forward with their story, from being interfered with by the press. But really we came down to the thought there was no way we could protect them sufficiently.

Perceptions of public opinion as mediated by the press can also impact on policy. One advertiser who had access to top level discussion on the early part of the DHSS campaign told us of the reaction of the DHSS committee to the statement of the Chief Constable for Greater Manchester:

At the same time there was the famous quote by James Anderton, about swimming about in cesspits. What was interesting, when that came out the group collectively said that basically this guy is a loony, direct line to God and all that. Then the *Daily Mail* did a survey and found out that 56% of people in this country agreed: they said 'well'. I guess this is where the political dimension comes in: 'hang about: 56% agree with him'. One cannot ignore that kind of volume of opinion.

The media influence policy making, but they also have direct effects on the planning of media or campaigning strategies.

Conclusion

This chapter has highlighted some of the factors that shape source strategies. The financial, institutional and cultural capital of sources are important determinants of their capacity to shape media accounts. However, the planning of media strategies is tempered by the audience that is targeted as well as by the available means for participating in policy and opinion making processes. The struggle for definitional advantage highlights co-operation as well as competition between sources. The example of AIDS indicates that official sources have considerable advantages in their capacity and resources to influence media accounts. However, these advantages do not necessarily result in success, as the example of the HEA indicates. Conversely, a lack of resources does not mean that sources are always excluded from the media. Alternative and oppositional groups can and do gain coverage and even access to the news, and the case of AIDS shows how this happened with the Terrence Higgins Trust.

But strategies and their execution are only half the picture; we also need to examine the process by which media accounts are produced. Divisions within source organisations play a key part in the framing of information policy as well as the interaction between the source organisation and the news media. The role of the press office in policing this interaction is important. The next chapter gives an account of the process by which the promotional strategies of source organisations are transformed into 'news'.

Notes

1. Although Tony Coxon, then Professor of Sociological Research at University College Cardiff who was a member of the DHSS advisory group on health education and AIDS, has argued that the input from social science and those representing people with HIV was marginalised in policy-making decisions (see Social Services Committee, 1987b: 54–62).

2. Although it should be noted that one of the contradictions of the formation of the 'sturdily independent' HEA, as Norman Fowler, the Secretary of State, dubbed it, was that the assignment of the AIDS public education campaign to the Authority was done partly to rid the DoH of the responsibility for a potentially embarrassing issue. Ostensibly the HEA was free to be bolder than the government in its advertising, although at the same time the HEA was considerably constrained by actual DoH control (see DoH/HEA, 1990).

3. According to Robert Whelan they distributed 900 copies of their video *The Truth about AIDS*, which claims that the only safe sex is 'chaste sex' (interview with the authors).

4. All the News International titles are based at Wapping and the bulk of the rest of the British press – Mirror Group (including the *Independent*), the *Telegraph* and the *Mail* – are based at Canary Wharf.

5. The article was written by out gay man Rupert Haselden under the title 'Gay abandon', *Weekend Guardian*, 7 September 1991. See also letters in response, e.g. 'The gay subculture: perverting the truth', *Guardian*, 10 September 1991 and 'Forum', *Weekend Guardian*, 14 September 1991: 12.

6. Such processes were extensively documented by Todd Gitlin (1980) in relation to the Students for a Democratic Society in their campaigns against the US assault on Vietnam.

7. Since the interviews with Woods and Alcorn took place (in September 1991) the profile of OutRage! has been raised dramatically by their targeting of homophobia in the armed services and the Church and the 'outing' of leading gay clergy.

7

Producing AIDS News

Kevin Williams and David Miller

The previous chapter discussed the information strategies used by different groups to influence and shape the reporting of AIDS by the news media. The news media have to negotiate an information environment of competing interpretations and accounts. This chapter examines the main determinants of the news gathering and reporting process which shaped the way in which the news media made sense of conflicting information about AIDS.

News media coverage of AIDS has to be seen against the background of growing media interest in health and medical matters in recent years – a growth matched by the allocation of increased resources to these issues. Specialist medical or health correspondents were responsible for much of the reporting of AIDS in the press and on television. But AIDS was also reported by generalist news reporters and freelance correspondents. The different ways in which these types of reporters defined their role in covering AIDS accounts for some of the variations identified in both the press (Chapter 3) and television news (Chapter 4). However variations in the coverage were also the outcome of the differing organisational environments in which journalists work. Reporters work for different news outlets and therefore are subject to different pressures and conditions. Variations in the reporting of AIDS can partly be accounted for by examining how reporters responded to and negotiated with the working routines, editiorial process and priorities, and news values of their organisation. This chapter examines the rise of health reporting in the British media, the role definition of specialist and general reporters, and the constraints and possibilities opened up by the editorial process, news values and editorial priorities (whether they be ideological, political or economic) and proprietorial intervention. It is the complex and dynamic interaction between these 'media factors' and source strategies that explains the precise content of news media accounts.

The growth of health reporting

In the 1980s the interest of the British press in medical and health issues increased significantly. Entwistle and Beaulieu-Hancock (1992: 375) recorded a total of 2,959 articles in eight tabloid and broadsheet newspapers over a two month period in 1990. This showed a marked increase from 1981 when only 1,397 articles on health and medical matters from seven newspapers for a similiar period were recorded (Kristiansen and Harding, 1984). Most national newspapers now have either designated health pages or sections that provide regular features on health and medicine which go beyond the news reporting of these issues. They allow for a more in-depth discussion as well as providing practical advice (Entwistle and Beaulieu-Hancock, 1992). Television, too, has increased the amount of coverage it devotes to health and medicine (Karpf, 1988), launching a number of educational series in the 1980s (see Whitehead, 1989). Since 1978 the *British Medical Journal* has carried a regular 'Medicine and the Media' page (Karpf, 1988: 2). By the 1980s every paper also had a medical or health reporter or columnist. The *Independent* established a health team under a medical editor and most of the broadsheet papers followed suit. In 1967 medical reporters founded the Medical Journalists Association 'to improve the quality and practice of medical journalism and to improve relationships and understanding between medical journalists and the medical profession', and membership had risen to over 300 by the late 1980s.

AIDS emerged against this background as a mysterious syndrome which combined two staple features of good copy: sex and death. As the celebrated Fleet Street editor Kingsley Martin said in the 1930s: 'in times of peace a first class sex murder is the best tonic for a tired sub editor on a dull evening' (quoted in Chibnall, 1980: 206). AIDS fitted the bill: 'It's got sex. It's got drug abuse. It frightens people. That makes good copy' (health correspondent, Scottish broadsheet). Moreover, coverage of illness constitutes around one in four stories on health related matters in the British press (Entwistle and Beaulieu-Hancock, 1992; Kristiansen and Harding, 1984). From the point of view of specialist medical or health reporters AIDS was a challenge. It engaged their professional interest. As one senior medical journalist said: 'I think we probably got too close to it because it was such an extraordinary story. You don't often have a completely new disease' (medical editor, broadsheet paper). However the reporting of AIDS was not the preserve of the specialist reporter; it was also covered by other kinds of journalists.

Specialist and generalist journalists: role definitions

The majority of medical and health stories are written by non-health specialist authors or are not attributed (Entwistle and Beaulieu-Hancock, 1992). Much of the material on health pages today is contributed by freelance writers of varying degrees of experience and knowledge. While medical and health correspondents tend to focus on news stories, the bulk of the features output is by freelancers. Medical correspondents often are too busy to write features. According to one health correspondent on a broadsheet paper,

95% of the work I write is on the news pages of the paper and occasionally I am on the features pages. Most of the features pages work on health issues is done by freelance people who are commissioned by the editors of those pages and that is a reasonably good situation because there is so much work on my own patch.

The growth of freelance reporters has been in keeping with the growing media interest in health. A long-serving medical editor of a quality paper notes that 'when I started off it was 90% from me. When I got an idea I'd ask a freelance to follow it up. Now freelances phone me with their ideas and I take up a large amount.' AIDS news was covered by general reporters and freelance correspondents as well as regular medical or health specialists. These reporters defined their role in covering AIDS in different ways. They were also subject to different pressures and conditions of work.

Health correspondents were appalled at some of the antics of general reporters or national press stringers in the reporting of AIDS (see Meldrum, 1990). They saw general reporters as being responsible for much of the shoddy journalism:

> General reporters tend to get things wrong because they don't check adequately or they don't talk to the right people. They just talk to dubious characters who have theories that, you know, AIDS came from outer space or something. They don't want to spoil a good story by checking it with somebody who might know better. Don't want to ruin it by discovering it is untrue. (Health correspondent, Sunday paper)

Similar distinctions between types of journalist were often drawn by sources of information. One Department of Health press officer noted, for example, that 'health correspondents were very responsible and good, but because AIDS became a headline story you got a lot of general reporters who really didn't know what they were writing about . . . and just went for the easy line and they didn't bother to check with us'. Specialist news correspondents, by the nature of their jobs, tend to develop a close relationship with a relatively small number of news sources and become dependent on them (Chibnall, 1980; Ericson et al., 1987, 1989). This is one reason why the *Sun* has only a few specialist correspondents. Specialist correspondents were abolished by Larry Lamb during his stint as editor because he thought that they

> were mostly dilettantes anyway, under-employed and equipped with expensive perks like private secretaries. Worst of all, they became members of their respective clubs, which actually encouraged them not to dirty their patch by writing embarrassing stories. If a story was big enough, Lamb held, it could be covered by a general reporter. The alternative argument, that specialists had in-depth knowledge of their subject, did not interest him. (Chippindale and Horrie, 1990: 16)

The close ties between specialist correspondents and the medical profession are important in explaining the media reliance on the 'liberal/medical approach' (see Chapters 3 and 4). By contrast general reporters do not tend to build up regular contacts in particular areas and are thus less dependent on medical sources. In practice the main significant difference is the degree to which 'news values' are likely to triumph over the perspectives of the dominant sources in a particular specialism. This is to some extent a product of general reporters being in more intense competition for space or time than specialist correspondents, who are assured more access.

Reporting by specialist correspondents was also influenced by role definitions. Medical journalists have tended to 'put themselves forward as mere bewildered, puzzled seekers after truth, dependent on such influencers of opinion as . . . expert [sources]' (Loshak, 1986: 8). However, health and medical reporting has always included an element of proselytising about how people should best avoid illness. AIDS appealed to many specialists' sense of social responsibility and this was reinforced in 1987 when the government defined the AIDS crisis as similar to a wartime emergency. In the years before the campaign, when AIDS was more easily seen as affecting the 'deviant' and 'marginal', reports in the media were often initiated by specialist correspondents who saw it as their 'duty and respon-sibility' to cover AIDS. This was often in the face of the indifference and hostility of news editors. Many correspondents felt it was part of their job to convince their organisations of the need to report AIDS. In this sense, they were acting as advocates for growing concerns within the medical community.

However, the close ties between medical sources and specialist reporters before 1985 also reinforced the view of AIDS as a gay syndrome. For example, according to a News International executive, 'there were reputable scientists who claimed AIDS could be passed from saliva, from breathing air, from skin contact'. Naylor (1985) and others have pointed out that media treatment of AIDS as a gay syndrome was a product of the close relationship with the medical profession which sought explanations for AIDS in the lifestyles and behaviour of homosexual men. However, by 1986 and 1987 such explanations were out of favour and specialist correspon-dents were subject to attempts to mobilise them as part of a concerted official campaign to educate the public on AIDS.

Some reporters feared their professional commitment to neutrality would be impaired by promoting the AIDS campaign.

> I think it is very dangerous for journalists to be drawn into a public education campaign. It limits our role. It is something we would like to do personally but I think we have to stick to information because if you get drawn into that then you would get drawn into an awful lot of nasty things. (Science correspondent, TV news)

For others there was little room for education in health and medical reporting:

> I see myself as a reporter. I don't see myself as an educator. I know that what is written in the newspapers has an impact on educating people but I think your writing can become rather dead if you see your main role as educating people. And I also think it is arrogant, as a lot of our readership is knowledgeable about the whole area of the NHS and health and so forth and so I try not to be particularly preachy. A lot of people feel the newspapers are often bullying you

into living a healthy lifestyle. I try not to bully. I try not to be particularly pedantic or hectoring about giving up smoking and all that. (Health correspondent, Sunday paper)

In part the worry was that the government might use such co-operation as a precedent to pressure the media into line in other areas of policy. But, in general, medical or health correspondents had a much more committed view of their role. Many overtly defined their reporting of AIDS in terms of their duty at the time of a public health crisis to involve themselves in official efforts. Some parts of the media accepted this role with ease. Among these were 'people who write for women's magazines . . . and the agony aunts, and the whole pop culture of music magazines has been very supportive of us' (health educator). Particularly during the period of 'crisis' many recognised that what they wrote could affect their readers (either with or without HIV). One broadsheet medical journalist defined her role thus:

It's always first to inform. I think we do have a strong public health role in this one, probably more than anything else. Well, maybe in the same way that we do with smoking . . . As a smoker I am diligent about writing stories about how pernicious, disgusting and unhealthy it is.

This public health role led some correspondents to play a more active role in the issue of AIDS than the professional ideology of neutrality would normally allow. Thus when Lord Kilbracken was reported by the *Sun* as confirming that 'Normal sex is safe' (*Sun*, 17 December 1989) the problem for concerned correspondents whose papers might be expected to follow the Kilbracken line was how best to counter it. One tabloid correspondent told us that her strategy was to

try and get as many experts on the phone to rubbish it. You can't just sit there rubbishing it yourself, you're a reporter of other people, but you're selective about who you're picking up the phone to get.

On the beat

The decision of some medical and health correspondents to define their role in this way was a product of the way in which they have been socialised into the culture of their 'beat'. Their background and working routines can lead them to share the perspectives and outlooks of those they report on. The background and knowledge of medical and health correspondents varies widely but most of them came into the job through three routes: via the medical profession, direct from a science background and via the trade press or apprenticeship on other newspapers. The most common way seems to be from other journalism posts. Medical or health reporters have served their apprenticeship in trade journals such as the *Chemist and Druggist* or professional journals such as *Nursing Times*, *GP*, the *Doctor* or *Pulse*. Others have worked on the provincial press.

There are two ways into the national press; either come up via the provincial press or the trade press. If you come via a provincial paper then to become a specialist you just switch and learn on the job. Otherwise you come from trade, say, medical press to be health correspondent. (Medical reporter, Sunday paper)

Most of these reporters have little or no formal knowledge of medicine or health issues and acquired their knowledge by learning on the job:

Pick it up as you go along. You go to conferences. You read magazines . . . You are given a job and you just do it. (Science correspondent, TV news)

I used to read the *British Medical Journal* and the *Lancet* every week. I think I educated myself on the issues in medicine quite well doing that. (Medical editor, broadsheet press)

The lack of medical or scientific knowledge is not regarded as a serious disadvantage; knowledge being seen by most correspondents as a product of what people tell you rather than the development of specific specialist expertise. On emerging from their apprenticeship on the trade or provincial press journalists are assisted in learning the ropes by senior colleagues. Much of the learning process involves handing down sources or key contacts. Knowledge is more a question of knowing where to go to find out and then writing in accordance with house style rather than building up expertise in a specialist area. Expertise on health and medical matters was not deemed a particular problem:

When it comes to expertise we often know more about what we are writing about than the average GP or even the average specialist. (Medical editor, broadsheet press)

In fact, some correspondents see a lack of specialist knowledge as a bonus:

I know nothing about what I am covering so I have to work on the basis that if I can understand it then Joe Bloggs can understand it. (Science correspondent, TV news)

Some of the senior reporters do have some sort of medical or scientific background. One leading medical correspondent on a broadsheet paper gained a PhD and three years of medical research experience before entering journalism while a reporter on a tabloid newspaper has a chemistry degree which 'certainly helps . . . with the science stuff'. Some medical corre-spondents are doctors by training. Ironically these correspondents often tend to be the most critical of the medical profession. Dr Vernon Coleman of the *Sun* or Dr James Le Fanu of the *Sunday Telegraph* are critics not only of the orthodoxy on AIDS but of the medical profession as a whole. Other medical correspondents were critical of what they saw as these reporters going out on a limb and being deliberately controversial.

Problems of covering AIDS

The reluctance of individual journalists to report AIDS at all was com-mented on by Norman Fowler, the Minister of Health during the late 1980s. 'There were also some journalists who would think nothing of covering a war but who had asked their offices not to send them on stories connected with AIDS' (Fowler, 1991: 250). Specialist reporters varied in their use of gay organisations or AIDS charities as key sources of information. Some were reticent in using such organisations either because of their attitudes to homosexuality or their perception that these sources lacked credibility:

> I am not gay myself and I don't use the gay press. (Health reporter, Sunday paper)

> If I was doing a story on AIDS I might ring the National AIDS Trust and the THT but they wouldn't be the first port of call. (Health reporter, Sunday paper)

A significant proportion of the male medical and health journalists did seem to have had difficulties in relating to out gay men. One voluntary sector spokesperson related that during a lunch appointment with a TV journalist who 'just doesn't understand at all', the journalist asked:

> 'Were you born homosexual, because I've got my two young children and they're coming up to 13, 14 and it does worry me one of them might be gay' . . . And this is a man who's done programmes in which he'll show a throbbing disco floor and talk about the homosexual underworld. That's who you're dealing with, so of course there are going to be problems.

However as the AIDS story developed, medical and health correspondents came to rely on the THT and other AIDS charities more and more. Role definitions and background knowledge were important here but the occupational culture of journalism could provide a countervailing pull. Under this heading, we consider working routines and practices, news values, the editorial process and proprietorial influence.

Working routines and practices

Most reporters identify deadlines and pressure of time and space as the key determinants of what they produce, although this varies between tabloid and broadsheet papers. Tabloid reporters stress the problem of space and style:

> It is much easier writing for a broadsheet because you can write it at length and we have got to sum up in five paragraphs what it means and make sure people understand it. (Medical reporter, tabloid paper)

> We've got to be a lot more careful. We are putting it in a chatty style and getting it all in a nutshell, in a smaller space. It is actually more difficult writing for a tabloid than it is writing for one of the heavies where you can go on and give chapter and verse in a way you can't here because it is going to get cut for space. (Medical reporter, tabloid paper)

Tabloid reporters also single out the nature of their audience as a limitation:

> The heavies . . . unfortunately don't get through to too many people and probably the people they *do* get through to are responsible anyway. We get through to people who don't realise that if you have sex you can get pregnant. You've got

to get it through to them. It is incredible the letters I get, the people who don't know the simplest thing. (Medical reporter, tabloid paper)

Specialists on Sunday papers also stress the production constraints under which they work. They are more remote from the daily news cycle which means they have to produce a different angle on the week's news and have more time to consult a range of sources:

> You have to distinguish between daily papers and Sunday papers. The whole point, the whole *raison d'être* of a Sunday newspaper is to get a different story so you have got to find different sources and different angles. (Medical reporter, Sunday paper)

> Daily papers are fed more stories than Sundays. I worked on *The Times* for a while and a lot of the time you go along to a press conference and write it up and it goes in the next day's paper . . . There are no press conferences on a Saturday and on any other day it always ends up in the next day's papers and so there is nothing left for you. So . . . you do have to read more obscure journals, read in greater depth and speak to more people. (Medical correspondent, Sunday paper)

Constraints of time and space are especially pronounced in TV news. TV news reporters' complaints often resembled those of the tabloid correspondents:

> I was working in BBC news and current affairs and most of what I had to do was really short and snappy pieces with very little time to prepare it. Typically something for a news bulletin might have a minute or a minute and a half on the six o'clock news on Radio Four which roughly translates into a 100 or 150 words, which is less than half a column in a newspaper, so the amount of information you can put across is very short. And even if you had three or four minutes on the *Today* programme or *PM* quite a lot of that had to be filled in with actuality, in other words voices of people, so again the amount of information you could put over is much less than in an average newspaper article and details are lost. (Science correspondent, broadsheet paper)

Time pressures on TV news reporting were seen as more intense than in the press. TV was described as 'a slower medium'. According to one reporter, 'you have to take more time to do a story because you not only *research* it, you not only find out *what* the story is, you not only *write* the story but you also sit in an editing booth for half a day and put the pictures to the story' (science correspondent, TV news). Some of the 'conventions' of TV news were seen by specialist correspondents in television as hampering their ability to cover AIDS and encouraging less knowledgeable reporters to cover it:

> On television you really can't do more than one story a day – because you can't appear more than once a day. So if two medical stories come up on the same day you find someone else to do the other one. (Science correspondent, TV news)

The visual nature of television also produces particular problems if sources are unwilling to appear on screen:

> If they were not willing to appear on screen . . . then you wouldn't do the story . . . You can't do the 'sources told me' sort of line that you can do in the newspapers because you have to have someone on screen saying something or you have to

have a document on screen that shows something . . . if they don't put their faces to it, you don't do the story. (Science correspondent, TV news)

Market pressure was also seen as shaping TV reporting:

We are in the entertainment business ultimately and if you don't entertain people they are not going to watch. It doesn't matter what the hell is happening you have got to get them to watch first. (Science correspondent, TV news)

The entertainment value of television underpins the construction of AIDS stories and determines who appears on screen. Looking good and sounding good in television terms are as important as what is said.

The limitations of time, space and deadlines are often used by reporters to justify their decision not to explore other avenues of enquiry or consult other than the most predictable of sources of information. However, it is also the case that different news organisations have different working routines, practices and conventions which allow the specialist reporter more or less opportunity to examine an issue, consult a wider range of sources of information and explore alternative explanations for events. This does not mean that reporters always take advantage of these opportunities but they do help to explain why differences in coverage can occur.

News values

News values are often presented as the main criterion of journalistic action. If a story is 'newsworthy', it is argued, then a journalist is powerless to prevent him or herself writing it. Central to the culture of journalism is the obsession with the 'story'. This focus on the 'story' and its 'values' runs counter to definitions which stress 'education' or 'social responsibility'. Specialist reporters feel the pull of these opposing forces most acutely. One tabloid journalist explained how she conceived of the difference between being an 'educator' and a 'reporter':

Being a reporter doesn't always help other people. That's a terrible thing to say, isn't it? If something happens . . . there could be someone who the whole family has got AIDS or something. Well that is an amazing story. That wouldn't really educate people. But it is a good story that should be told. Or you could look at it with your halo on and say 'Oh yes it will because it can educate people that they are all at risk'. But you wouldn't really be telling 100% the truth. (Medical reporter, tabloid paper)

But what constitutes an 'amazing story' is a matter of disagreement between not only news organisations but journalists. News values are not 'universal'. Often they are a matter of negotiation and struggle inside the newsroom. The main keepers of 'newsworthiness' in most news organisations is the newsdesk. Most medical correspondents characterised their relationship with the newsdesk as one of negotiation and/or conflict. One medical correspondent on a tabloid newspaper described the relations with the newsdesk following the Kilbracken row:

> He [Kilbracken] did a lot of damage because a lot of people were only too willing to believe that man and you find yourself here saying 'It's garbage' – [and the news editor replies] 'ah yes but he's . . .' – you're trying to tone down the coverage and they say 'yes but it's a story' – well yes that's true so you have this, I won't say conflict, but differing interests.

A broadsheet medical editor articulated the same problem in more general terms:

> There are two conflicting things: there is the duty, and I think it is a duty to record movement in any given field so that people have information. Against that may be deeply unsatisfactory and frightening information to people who think they are doing the right thing for themselves. What do you do? Do you not report it? How much censorship should you impose? If it is stupid, I mean if you really think it is silly, you know it is a good line but it is silly, I won't do it, even if on occasions the newsdesk will argue that we should have done it, I will stick to my guns.

News values vary between countries and news outlets and are often the outcome of a struggle within organisations. Throughout the British press and television news, there is a distinctive hierarchy of story importance. At the apex is 'hard news': political news, centrally concerned with 'matters of state' which focus on Westminster and Whitehall. By contrast, health and illness are further down the hierarchy and are seen as relatively 'soft' in news terms. Amongst the political correspondents and other 'hard news' specialisms, there are very few women reporters. Hard news has been and remains a very male dominated and high status area of news reporting. Women reporters are more likely to cover 'softer' areas such as health and medicine. At the time of our research, eight national newspaper medical or health correspondents were women – two on quality newspapers, two on Sunday papers and four on tabloids. Part of the reason for the downgrading of health is that the distinction between 'hard' and 'soft' news is conceived of in gender terms. According to one medical editor:

> The reason why we haven't had health pages before is that newspapers are edited by men and health is seen in the female sphere and relegated to women's pages. (Medical editor, broadsheet press)

News values are also inflected with heterosexual assumptions, which makes it difficult to get news stories associated with homosexuality into the media (especially on to the news pages) unless they are packaged in a particular way (see Chapter 3). Part of the reason for this is the hierarchy of credibility which is applied to news sources. Given the marginal status of gay men and (especially) lesbian women in society, there is a temptation to go to an authoritative (i.e. non-gay identified) source rather than a gay organisation when covering gay issues. Alternatively journalists may disguise the source of a story to make it more 'credible'. This was the experience of Chris Woods, during his time as a journalist for *Capital Gay*, the London-based weekly gay paper:

> I've had a number of battles with publications to credit me for stories that they'd stolen wholesale from me and they don't want to be seen to be taking information

from a gay publication or if they do, they'll say that you're 'claiming that . . . ' or they'll distort the text to make it look as if you're coming from a non-factual point of view . . . For example, the *Independent on Sunday* opened up with the classic line 'Gay rights activists are complaining that' and completely trivialised what we were actually producing whilst at the same time making the claim for themselves to be objective.

Even though the strategies of gay organisations such as Stonewall and especially OutRage! have made gay politics and issues much more prominent in the British media, the very gayness of lesbians and gay men still sets them apart from the most credible i.e. 'expert' sources. According to Chris Woods:

There are often times when I know damn well there's a good story and I want that story to get wider appeal, but at the same time that story getting wider appeal serves a political purpose for me – it means . . . that I play advocate more and find myself acting as politician as much as journalist in certain situations . . . If you work for a gay paper you're being asked as a gay spokesperson rather than as a professional journalist so they exploit those contradictions as well.

While lesbian and gay issues have climbed the ladder of newsworthiness and gay organisations have risen in the hierarchy of credibility, hard news and the apparently neutral and non-gay identified 'experts' remain firmly ensconced at the top. However, during the development of the AIDS story news organisations increasingly used, indirectly and directly, gay sources in their reporting. This was a response to the efforts of organisations such as the THT to build their contacts and credibility with the news media as well as the increase in willingness of specialist reporters to use them and, in turn, to educate the newsdesk into accepting them.

Editorial process

A key feature of AIDS reporting was the negotiation between specialist reporters and the editorial hierarchy. There were struggles over the amount of time and space accorded to AIDS news, over who should cover the story, over the political line of the news organisation and the attitudes of the newsdesk. The outcome of these negotiations differed between news outlets but they were all shaped by a combination of the personality of the specialist correspondent, his or her position within the news organisation, the organisation's understanding of its audience, and the degree of editorial and proprietorial interest in the story.

The early association of AIDS with gay men made it more difficult for specialists to get interest from newsdesks. According to one medical correspondent, 'as it was nicknamed the gay plague the bosses weren't that interested'. Another reporter commented: 'Too much talk about gay sexual behaviour does not go down well in the *Telegraph*' (medical reporter, Sunday paper). Medical reporters often found it difficult to get stories into the paper: 'Even if the medical correspondent was interested, the newsdesk did not have much time for [AIDS]' (medical reporter, tabloid newspaper).

This reporter said that she first heard of AIDS from a friend who had picked up a gay newspaper on the tube. Her curiosity was aroused and she did some digging and started to come up with a number of stories about a strange illness killing gay men. She was, however, unable to get her reports into the paper; the newsdesk told her: 'who gives a toss about gays dying in America'. For Andrew Veitch, the *Guardian*'s medical correspondent, the poor performance of much of the press on AIDS was a product of the failure of specialists to reach the newsdesk and the sub-editors:

> I think that we . . . have failed to get through to the people who really make the papers – the editors, the sub-editors, the guys who decide what goes in the pages, the guys who write the headlines . . . Sometimes I wonder what we are up against . . . You have to be pretty queer to work on a newspaper, you have to be very queer to work on a newspaper at night and the result is that you end up with a lot of macho hairy-ass guys who are terrified to admit that one time in their dim and distant past they may have had a homosexual relationship. (Milbank Foundation, 1986: 128)

It is the job of sub-editors to write the headlines and to cut copy so that it fits in the space available in the paper. This can often result in headlines which are markedly different from the text beneath them and the reporter's copy can sometimes be radically changed to suit the needs of the paper and the understandings of the sub-editors. Medical correspondents are often aggrieved when this happens.

> I did a series . . . showing that these people [PWAs] were not freaks but that they are just like the rest of us, but even that was subbed. The title of the series was 'Sentence of Death' and that wasn't my doing. Though the positive pieces, the positive texts were featured, there was a negative message coming through at the beginning of it. (Health reporter, Scottish newspaper)

> You don't actually know what's really going into the paper until you actually open it the morning after. You might find they've [the newsdesk] added a lot. (Medical reporter, tabloid paper)

Such comments are often met with derision by news editors. Journalists are always concerned, said one tabloid news editor, about their 'precious prose' being 'hacked about'. The smaller amount of space devoted to news coverage meant that the subs on tabloid newspapers tended to make greater interventions in news stories. The interventions of the subs and newsdesk on AIDS was blamed for much of the more sensational and prurient reporting.

> A lot of the shit was fed in from the subs; from sub-editors who got the story and fed in the crap, fed in the gay plague, fed in the hatred, fed in the contempt. (Reporter, gay newspaper)

On midmarket tabloids like the *Mail* and the *Express* the tension between the efforts of the medical reporter and the editorial process was accentuated by the overt political line taken by the newspapers on AIDS. In response to a complaint made by a health educator about 'one of the worse pieces of gay bashing and junkie bashing that you can imagine', the medical reporter responded:

It was that or my mortgage because the editor . . . said, 'I am not having any more of your gay loving, junkie loving pieces. We are going to tell it like it is.'

Telling it like it isn't

Some medical reporters came under so much pressure from their editors that they had to suspend their professional judgement in the reporting of AIDS. However, others were able to resist the pressure. This was most apparent on broadsheet newspapers where specialist reporters have much more influence. They initiate many of their own stories. Yet there are still clear negotiations between journalists and news editors; one example of this concerned the use of language and imagery to discuss sexual practices. At a 1986 conference, Andrew Veitch of the *Guardian* said:

> I've been trying to use the words 'anal intercourse' for two years now and I can't get them into the newspaper. The usual reason I am given [is] it's too boring. So I try the words 'receptive anal intercourse' to get a bit of flavour into it and my editors say 'What's that?' I think next time we will try 'buggery' and see what happens. (Milbank Foundation, 1986: 128)

Whereas the *Guardian* could have a debate about the use of the word 'fuck', 'family' newspapers or TV news struggled over the use of less 'offensive' words. According to Andrew Veitch, it was easier to get the word 'fuck' into the *Guardian* on the arts page and in the theatre reviews where it is 'artistically justified' than on to the medical and health pages (Milbank Foundation, 1986: 128).

Battles over the representation of HIV/AIDS and sexuality in general are constantly in play. The particular taboo against describing sex (particularly what is assumed to be gay sex) was broken at least on broadsheet newspapers. However, as we saw in Chapter 4, explicit sexual terminology was exceptionally rare. Sex has always been a part of the output of the news media and questions of taste and what is suitable for a 'family audience' require certain kinds of sensitivity over what can be reported – even in the tabloid press.

> I have never been able to use explicit language. I never thought of it as a problem because I know I can't do it. Apart from not being able to use it I wonder whether our readers know what heterosexual is . . . You couldn't mention oral or anal sex. (Medical correspondent, tabloid paper)

Questions of taste and decency were at the fore in TV news coverage. As one TV medical reporter put it:

> AIDS is not a very clean disease and it is very difficult to explain it on television without people thinking you are causing offence – the real nature of the disease and how you catch it . . . You can't do things which the Independent Broadcasting Authority [IBA] considers offensive or you can't do things which your editor fears that the Independent Broadcasting Authority will find offensive. (Science correspondent, TV news)

The extent of broadcasting executives' sensitivity to what the regulatory bodies considered decent and in good taste and the lengths they go to meet these concerns were highlighted in another story covered by this correspondent. A story about the treatment of psychiatric hospital inmates on the Greek island of Leros was accompanied by footage of naked men and women in the hospital confines. This raised the problem of showing 'willies' before the 9p.m. watershed. To satisfy such concerns the news went to great lengths to cut out all shots of the male sexual organ:

> We had at one stage a person of great authority sitting there and watching frame by frame to see if you could see a willie and every willie was taken out. (Science correspondent, TV news)

Cutting out references to the penis occurred in the broadsheet press as well. A story on impotence for a major Sunday newspaper was a problem for one medical correspondent:

> The deputy editor got very worried because it was all about erections and he went through the copy and cut out in several places the words 'penis' and 'erection'. I was very angry. (Medical editor, broadsheet paper)

Taste and decency also affect the representation of drug use. Pictures of users shooting up caused problems and TV news executives insisted on carefully representing 'needles'.

> We have had drug addicts showing how they fill up, how they do everything but you can't actually show the needle going in. One excuse for that is that it might teach people how to inject. (Science correspondent, TV news)

The restrictions on what could and could not be shown on TV were a barrier to reporting AIDS in a comprehensible fashion:

> When you are talking about a disease like AIDS and you can't show actual injections and you can't show blood and you can't talk about anal intercourse, then it does cause problems. I am sure that is one of the reasons that it is very hard to convince people what the hell is happening with AIDS, because you couldn't use the terms, you couldn't use the words and you couldn't use the pictures. (Science correspondent, TV news)

Freelance reporters were most conscious of producing the stories that newspapers would buy and print, and taste and decency were important influences on copy.

> I did feel stuff was being censored on the *Sunday Times*. With the *Daily Telegraph* I was made aware that I had to be a bit cautious about what I said and certain parts of what I wrote were cut out, quite clearly for reasons of taste, as they wouldn't have been for the *Sunday Correspondent*. (Freelance medical reporter)

However, there is another source of influence on editorial judgements about language and representation. The law, libel suits and the strictures of various commissions such as the Press Complaints Commission (formerly the Press Council), the Broadcasting Complaints Commission and the Broadcasting Standards Council. The *Sun* and columnist Gary Bushell were censured by the Press Council in May 1990 for using anti-gay language.

Following this, previously unfamiliar terms such as 'gay community' started to appear in the *Sun* (see 'Bending truth', *Sun*, 17 October 1990; see also Sanderson, 1995, for an account of this). It may be that falling sales, expensive libel defeats, growing public disapproval of editorial excesses, the Calcutt Commission on press behaviour and the decline and fall of Mrs Thatcher all contributed to some change of direction at the *Sun* (see Chippindale and Horrie, 1990).

Commercial considerations

Concerns about taste and decency are partially informed by perceptions of the appropriate address for the audience. This, in turn, relates to commercial judgements about the sensitivities of the newspaper buying public. Some of the above points relate to the limits imposed on journalism by general editorial concerns with marketing and assumptions about the typical audience for the paper. But there are also moments when stories are chosen or news angles shaped very specifically to target new sections of the audience. This becomes most obvious when a newspaper is under pressure from falling sales or is attempting to break into a different market section. The *Sun*, for example, is well known for its Conservative political stance but in the 1990s featured columns by the MP Ken Livingstone, who as 'Red Ken' was a major bogeyman of the Right in the early 1980s.

The *Daily Sport* and *Sunday Sport* illustrate another variant in this process. In most areas they offer a similar populism to that of the *Sun*, with its mix of 'sex, sensation, scandal and sport'. Yet their attitude to gays was very different:

> Your broadminded *Sport* believes in sexual equality. That is why we launched a gay section in our lonely hearts column. For whether you are black or white, heterosexual or a homosexual, all need friends. And thanks to your *Sport*, thousands of gay guys and lesbians are no longer lonesome. (*Sunday Sport*, 26 June 1991)

And, of course, the revenue which 'classified' and other gay advertising attracts must also be a welcome addition to the paper's funding. This was an early recognition in the British press of the potential of the 'pink pound'. Around the same period both the *Guardian* and the *Independent* started increasing the profile of gay related stories in an attempt to tap the perceived new market. In the US the pulling power of gay readership had already been noted by the American Society of Newspaper Editors, who recommended more and better coverage of lesbian and gay issues as a result (Ghiglione et al., 1990).

The above examples show that changes in newspaper content in part reflect attempts to target new, or keep hold of current, readers. Much reporting is produced with audience response in mind. Indeed, according to advocates of the market as the best regulator of media content, it is precisely this relationship between producer and consumer which ensures that the public gets what it wants. However, it is not always clear how public demand is ascertained or assimilated by journalists. In practice judgements about what the public wants are regarded as part of the skill of being a journalist. For example many editors and news executives regarded news about an illness affecting gay men as irrelevant to their readers or viewers. According to a medical correspondent for a tabloid paper:

> The editors want stories in papers which have the widest readership and that will interest the most people. If they feel a certain subject, whatever it may be, people will say 'Oh that won't bother me' and turn it over, they don't want to run it.

In this way, media insititutions are able to shrug off difficult questions by reference to the audience, as in the circulation of anti-gay stories. A tabloid medical correspondent argues:

> you had that problem with readers . . . whose attitude – and unfortunately this is the attitude of people – was: 'well that is what they get for doing that sort of thing'.

The public were also held responsible by reporters across the press and in broadcasting for the decline in interest in AIDS, particularly after the period of 'emergency' in the late 1980s had passed:

> The public, the people out there, feel there is less of a risk. Heterosexual people feel less at risk. That has transferred to the newsdesk. (Medical reporter, broadsheet paper)

The means by which public preferences transfer to the newsdesk is, however, obscure. None of the journalists we spoke to claimed to have seen detailed opinion or attitude data. Almost universally, it was assumed that a good journalist simply 'knows' what the public wants without any formal means of finding out.

Proprietorial influence

The influence of the proprietor on the production process has been the subject of much discussion. Some proprietors, such as Robert Maxwell, were known to be very interventionist. Others were more willing to let the editorial staff run things, depending on the topic in question. Robert Maxwell, the proprietor of the *Daily Mirror*, had a public stance on the issue of AIDS and took an interest in its coverage in the newspaper. He became heavily involved in the founding of the National AIDS Trust. Maxwell's interest had a clear impact on the reporting environment and on the coverage of AIDS in the *Mirror*. As the paper's medical correspondent said: 'He got involved, so we got involved. It meant doing more stories about AIDS and what it was and more stories about the National AIDS Trust and things like that.' The *Daily Mirror* took a line firmly within the medical orthodoxy. The conflict between the specialist correspondent and the editorial hierarchy, which marked mid-range tabloids like the *Mail* and the *Express,* was replaced by an enthusiasm for stories on AIDS which fitted the orthodoxy.

In the Murdoch press (the *Sun, Today, The Times* and the *Sunday Times*) there have been areas of coverage where the views and interests of the proprietor are clearly reflected. For instance, both *The Times* and the *Sun* endorse Conservative political views on the economy although they sell to very different readerships. Both have been extremely critical of the BBC and advocate more open competition in broadcasting. Yet in the case of AIDS coverage there was no consensus amongst the Murdoch press. The respective editorial approaches of the *Sun* and *The Times* placed them on opposite sides in terms of the current political and medical orthodoxy. Where there is this latitude, the 'line' of the paper is more likely to be determined by its editorial staff. A number of variables will influence decisions made here. First, the sense of the paper's 'natural' audience and whether the paper will take a particular stance in relation to the supposed preferences of that audience. The *Daily Mail* and the *Daily Express,* for example, are both widely recognised as 'middle class' and conservative papers which have endorsed much of the 'Thatcherite' political agenda on declining moral standards, law and order, local government and trade union power. The *Sun* adds other 'populist' elements of xenophobia and anti-gay attitudes. It treads an uneasy line between its political agenda and the actual composition of its audience, which is substantially working class and Labour voting.

The second consideration is the need to follow 'good' story angles. This can be a source of potential contradictions in the tabloid press. For example, the 'Sun, sand, sea and sex at Club 18–30' type of story appeals to their most basic news values, and stories around these themes which stressed the dangers of heterosexual AIDS were reported despite the fact that their message about HIV transmission ran counter to the editorial line of 'no risk to heterosexuals'.

Covering dissident views on AIDS

In general, the British media followed the liberal/medical orthodoxy on AIDS. Television news exclusively so. However, there were spaces in the British media where the orthodox line on AIDS could be challenged, in particular (but not exclusively) from the right. We can distinguish two basic lines of argument which are sometimes but not always connected. First is the more widely featured line which suggests that the heterosexual epidemic has been exaggerated by an alliance, variously of liberals, Whitehall, the government, the nanny state, health educators, moral conservatives and the 'gay lobby'. Elements of this argument appeared in the press as early as 1987, reaching their peak in the *Daily Mail, Daily Express* and *Sun* in late 1989. Second is the argument at the level of science that HIV does not cause AIDS. This line is less associated with the political right and much of its argument originates with molecular biologist, Peter Duesberg. Its main media proponents have been independent television company Meditel (and those associated with it, such as Joan Shenton and Jad Adams: see Adams, 1989), *Sunday Telegraph* columnist and author of numerous articles for Social Affairs Unit pamphlets, Dr James Le Fanu, and latterly and most prominently the *Sunday Times*. The second line of argument is usually associated with the first, but it is quite common for adherents of the first not to promote the second.

We argued above that editorial priorities, news values and the anti-gay culture of many news rooms combined to allow the kind of commentary to be found in the *Mail*, the *Sun*, the *Express*, and the leader and features pages of *The Times* and the *Sunday Telegraph*. Not all of such writing came from staff writers, however. Much of the material in the midmarket tabloids and the broadsheets was written by outside columnists. These included a large number of people with connections to moralist or libertarian right wing organisations such as Family and Youth Concern, the Freedom Association, and the Social Affairs Unit. The bulk of such commentary centred on the first line of argument about the extent of heterosexual risk. Such views became popular in some papers even though many of the papers' own medical specialists took an opposing line wherever possible in their own writing.

The most prominent advocate of the second line of argument, at least from April 1992, was the *Sunday Times*. The prime mover behind the transition of the *Sunday Times* from follower of the medical orthodoxy to its most forceful critic was the paper's editor, Andrew Neil. In a memo in 1989 Andrew Neil asked science correspondent Neville Hodgkinson: 'Where is this threatened heterosexual spread? . . . Is it really happening' (cited in Garfield, 1994b: 344). At the time Hodgkinson wrote back reiterating the medical orthodoxy. According to Neil, at the end of the 1980s he began to feel that 'there was a kind of conspiracy beginning to develop – almost an unholy alliance among the government, the militant gay lobby and a sort of Christian moral majority Right' (cited in Garfield, 1994b: 346). Neil's views, then, were opposed to the moralism of organisations such as the Conservative Family Campaign and more in line with the coverage of newspapers, such as the *Sun*, which regularly criticised the AIDS campaign for its stigmatising of what one dissident has called the 'innocent pleasures of casual heterosexual intercourse' (James Le Fanu, *Sunday Telegraph* columnist in a letter to the *Independent*, 25 May 1993: 17).

In 1991, Neil ran excerpts from Michael Fumento's *The Myth of Heterosexual AIDS* which had caused controversy in the US and was not published in Britain. In late 1991 Hodgkinson returned to the paper, after a brief spell at the *Sunday Express*. Following a conversation with Joan Shenton at Meditel he says he became convinced that his previous rejection of the theories of Peter Duesberg was not sustainable. (The key piece of evidence he had used to dismiss Duesberg was an MRC report about a haemophiliac cohort in Scotland which showed that although all had been exposed to infected factor VIII at the same time only those who became infected with HIV showed a decline in health status. He says Shenton showed him evidence that the study did not compare like with like and that the HIV positive group was already more ill than the other group: Garfield, 1994b: 345–6.) In his first stint at the *Sunday Times* he had rejected Duesberg's theories in print. In early 1992, he spent 'about a month' studying Duesberg's claims: 'I checked out what people had written in response to what Duesberg had done and found that it was abusive, but it usually didn't answer his arguments' (Garfield, 1994b: 346).

> At first he couldn't stimulate any interest from his news desk. 'Challenging the HIV causation was too mind boggling. They didn't see how we could do it as a news story'. He then composed a 5,000 word memo to an assistant editor, setting out what he had discovered during his research. It was passed on to Neil, who said it should run almost in its entirety . . . In the next few months, Hodgkinson tried to place other doubting articles in the paper, with little success . . . The turnaround came in the spring of 1993. The preliminary Concorde results[1] appeared. If AIDS was not a viral disease, then the value of AZT was clearly also brought into question and Hodgkinson spared no opportunity in subsequent articles to stress its negative side. (Garfield, 1994b: 347)

We can discern in all this the influence of Hodgkinson and fundamentally the role of Andrew Neil as editor. Hodgkinson is one of a number of journalists (including James Le Fanu and Joan Shenton) who have contested the scientific orthodoxy on coronary heart disease as well as on AIDS, so doubting orthodox science was not a new experience. However, the line on AIDS also fits well with other elements of the *Sunday Times* editorial view in this period. As Neal Ascherson has put it:

> a *Sunday Times* speciality was the populist hymn of hate against an imaginary 'liberal intellectual Establishment' which lived in Hampstead, drank Montrachet at 'favourite watering-holes' and at 'the country's more fashionable dining-tables' plotted to promote 'ideals out of kilter with the aspirations of plain folk'. Those who dared to challenge this all-powerful Establishment were 'dissidents' whose opinions were censored off the BBC and blackballed from the Garrick club. Those who conspired against the 'aspirations of plain folk' formed cliques known as 'industries'. (Ascherson, 1993: 25)

Edwina Currie has claimed that Neil's motivation was also personal: 'Andrew Neil has a non-monogamous heterosexual lifestyle and it suits him fine that there should be no risk attached to that, and that's the argument he's making' (cited in Garfield, 1994b: 351). According to Garfield, Neil 'has insisted that his newspaper has never consciously run anti-gay articles and that its AIDS policy is not motivated by homophobia' (ibid.). However, some *Sunday Times* sources have reminded us of Neil's Scottish Protestant background, suggesting that this might be a relevant factor (interview with *Sunday Times* executive). Whatever the precise reasons for the *Sunday Times* perspective on AIDS, it is clear that the decision to criticise the orthodoxy was informed by particular political assumptions (as was the liberal approach) and was not simply about the pursuit of truth.

Conclusion

This chapter has outlined some of the factors that account for the differences in the coverage of AIDS in the British news media. While much of the reporting was framed within the confines of the liberal/medical approach to AIDS, other views have appeared which challenge or contradict the orthodoxy. The reporting has not been uniform or consistent. This reflects the nature of AIDS as an issue, but it also shows that there are openings for dissenting opinion in the edifice of the mass media. The ways in which these openings are used can account for changes in the coverage. In particular, the content of the media reflects the outcome of the interplay between sources of information, the commercial imperatives of the industry, what the government allows and struggles inside the production process over what is newsworthy.

Note

1. The Concorde trial appeared to show that AZT was less effective than had been hoped in combating HIV.

8

Media Impact on Public Beliefs about AIDS

Jenny Kitzinger

Exploring audience reception: questions and methods

Interest in the mass media, whether from politicians, gay activists or health educators, is premised on the belief that media representations have some influence. But can this be assumed? And, if press and television reports have 'impact', on whom do they impact and how?

Media coverage is crucial because, as we have already shown, it can influence policy and campaign strategy (see also Berridge, 1992). Many of those living with the virus have also written about the impact of media reporting on their sense of self-worth, hopes for the future, and indeed their own health (Dreuilhe, 1988; Moore, 1995; Rieder and Ruppelt, 1989). But what about its broader impact? Do the media help to shape knowledge and attitudes among the 'general public'?

At a basic level, it is possible to point to apparently straightforward examples of mass media impact; locating trends in public awareness which correlate with changes in coverage (GUMG, 1988). Certainly, survey respondents and our own research participants cite television and press reports about AIDS as their primary source of information. They also report a rapid learning curve during the late 1980s. Before 1986, very few people had even heard about the problem, but the intensive publicity that accompanied the first British government campaign led to widespread basic knowledge about AIDS. There was also an associated dramatic increase in condom sales. Particular media events can also be shown to mobilise direct audience responses. For example, the HIV diagnosis of a heterosexual central character (Mark Fowler) in the BBC soap opera *EastEnders* was followed by the highest ever number of calls to the National AIDS Helpline (PHLS, 1993).

Such examples should not be forgotten when discussing media power, although they are often ignored in the more 'sophisticated' media theories promoted in some of the specialist journals. (For discussion of such tendencies, see Barry, 1993; Corner, 1991; Curran, 1990; Robins, 1994.) However, on their own, the broad self-report data and basic correlations outlined above tell us very little about *how* media 'effects' might operate. In order to understand this, it is necessary to explore a series of supplementary questions such as: What factors influence the acceptance or rejection of a specific message? Why do some media messages mobilise public action and others do not? What do people bring to their understandings of AIDS? How are audience responses to AIDS media messages related to the broader cultural context and to people's socio-demographic positions and political identities?

The next two chapters address precisely these issues. This chapter introduces our research into audience reception and focuses on the features within the press and television coverage which helped to promote particular understandings. Chapter 9 then steps back to explore the boundaries of media influence; and examines both the potential, and the limits, of audience resistance to media messages.

Our research into audience understandings was based on focus group discussions with 52 different groups of people, involving 351 individuals. (For in-depth discussion of the focus group method see Kitzinger, 1994a.) The field work was conducted between 1989 and 1991. A variety of different groups were involved in the research including residents from different neighbourhoods, members of different clubs or organisations (e.g. the Round Table, or a group for retired people) and workers in various types of jobs (e.g. office cleaners and engineers). The groups were selected to cover a range of demographic characteristics such as age, class, ethnic and national identity. The sample was also structured to include those with some special social or occupational positions in relation to the epidemic, e.g. doctors, IV drug users, prison officers and male prostitutes (see Appendix for full list of groups).

In addition to engaging in general group discussion, each research participant completed three short questionnaires and was involved in a collective 'script-writing exercise'. The groups were presented with still photographs taken from television news reports, and asked to reproduce a TV news bulletin about AIDS. The stills represented a range of recurring media images, such as the image of a man in a white coat looking down a microscope, a picture of Norman Fowler (then Minister for Health), a typical street scene, a man sitting in bed and a woman holding a child (see Figure 8.1; for detailed discussion of this technique see Kitzinger, 1993a).

Media influence and public understandings of AIDS

Many media theorists emphasise the 'polysemy' (multiple meanings) of any 'text', be it a book, a newspaper report or television programme. Indeed, some argue that the media have little 'effect' because everyone brings their own interpretations to what they hear and see. There is, according to this argument, little consensus about the meaning of any media product; and therefore attempting to document the impact of any message is a fruitless

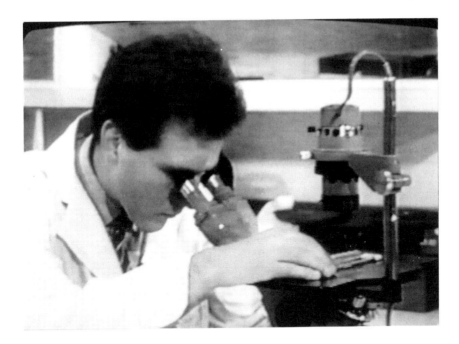

NORMAN FOWLER MP
Health Secretary

Figure 8.1 *The groups were presented with a set of stills taken from the TV coverage of AIDS and asked to reproduce a news report on this topic which was then discussed within the group*

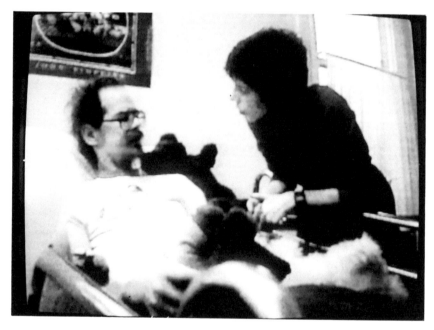

Figure 8.1   *(cont.)*

Figure 8.1 *(cont.)*

task. However, the research reported here found widespread similarities in how people understood the coverage of AIDS, and we identified systematic patterns in the information and impressions recalled by the research participants. It was also clear that aspects of the media coverage helped to inform, sustain and shape attitudes to the epidemic.

For a start, media coverage provided people with facts and figures, familiarised them with a vocabulary (such as 'safer sex', 'body fluids' or 'the heterosexual community') and introduced a new set of images (e.g. of death from immune deficiency related illness). Recurring sets of association (concepts, language and narrative structures) were triggered by each photograph used in the 'script-writing' exercise. For example, the picture of the scientist was routinely used to signal attempts to find a vaccine or a cure for AIDS; rather than other possible interpretations such as that the virus had been invented in a laboratory. The street scene was used to illustrate the threat to 'the general population' (in a way which excluded gay men and illegal IV drug users from being acknowledged as part of 'the community'). The picture of the man in bed was used to represent the 'despair' and 'horrific death' faced by those with AIDS; he was rarely given any voice in the news bulletins, and was routinely used as a gibbet display to warn others of the terrible fate awaiting them if they 'indulged' in unsafe sex. Research participants in this way demonstrated a common understanding and memory of 'typical' news reports.

However, such news reconstructions on their own do not tell us what people actually know or believe; or how they might react to any particular item of reporting. Did research participants only associate scientists with the search for a cure or did any actually believe that the virus could have been invented in a laboratory? Were they simply parodying the way the street scene is used in news bulletins? What were their attitudes toward people with the virus? Such questions can only be addressed through examining the surrounding group discussion. In other words, it is necessary not only to examine people's ability to reconstruct such media messages, but also to explore the extent to which they accepted or rejected them and negotiated their own beliefs in relation to such representations. Here we will illustrate these processes by looking closely at people's understanding of six issues:

1   HIV transmission and the role of saliva.
2   The origins and prevalence of AIDS in Africa.
3   AIDS as a disease of sinful or unnatural 'risk groups'.
4   The relationship between HIV and AIDS.
5   The 'vengeful AIDS carrier'.
6   'Safer sex' and 'the heterosexual threat'.

HIV transmission and the role of saliva

Our research demonstrates that mass media coverage and health education materials successfully conveyed basic official information about HIV trans-mission to the majority of research participants. Most people in our sample knew it could be transmitted through sharing needles and sexual intercourse. They also recognised that 'casual' contact was safe. A strong impression had been made by the behaviour of celebrities and royalty. At the time of our field work, Princess Diana was seen as part of the institution of the royal family. Her activities were assumed to be officially sanctioned. As one woman commented: 'They take Princess Diana into the AIDS hospitals so you can see her touching them . . . if Diana can go up and shake his hand then it must be all right.'[1]

However, there were some examples of unfounded fears (e.g. around donating blood) and the commonest area of uncertainty concerned the risk associated with saliva. Such uncertainty could be traced to the media coverage, in particular the use of vague terminology such as 'body fluids'. Throughout the late 1980s and early 1990s advertisements and mass media reports frequently asserted that 'mixing body fluids' or 'the exchange of body fluids' could result in HIV infection. Newspaper journalists sometimes wrote of 'body fluids' as a convenient euphemism for words like semen or vaginal secretions which might be judged too 'unpalatable' to present to readers over the breakfast table (Diamond and Bellitto, 1986; Edgar et al., 1989). Often the phrase was used without indicating that saliva is a very unlikely route of transmission (see Chapter 3). Research participants picked up on the ambiguous phrase 'body fluids' and, for some, it clearly contributed to their confusion. Asked *why* they thought saliva was dangerous, research participants repeatedly gave replies such as: 'because it's a body fluid' and 'it's a body fluid, is it not?'

People also recounted newspaper reports about shoplifters spitting on store detectives, suspects spitting on police officers, and prisoners biting warders. They recalled scare stories with headlines such as 'SPITTING AIDS WOMAN BAILED' (*Daily Record*, 20 January 1989) or 'AIDS FEAR OF BITTEN POLICEMAN' (*Sun*, 6 February 1990). Such stories featured in several newspapers and the irrationality of these fears was rarely highlighted. Given this coverage, perhaps it is not surprising that early surveys demonstrate that about a third of the population believed that HIV could be transmitted through kissing (Ford, 1991; McQueen et al., 1991).

Although the form and content of media messages clearly make a major contribution to public understandings, this is not to suggest that the messages operate in a purely instrumental and logical fashion. For example, if the generic use of the term 'body fluids' were alone responsible for the confusion surrounding the risks of saliva, one would expect similar concern to be expressed about another body fluid: tears. In fact, none of the research participants suggested that tears were dangerous. This may be partly because tears are not perceived as a potential weapon that may be ejected from one person's body on to another's. Tears also carry particular affective associations (joy/sorrow/regret), and are culturally defined as clean or pure; whereas saliva is already positioned as polluting. On a more practical level, saliva is implicated in the transmission of other types of disease. As one research participant commented: 'Anybody in the medical field will tell you that saliva or body fluids is the easiest way to catch *any* infection.'

However, most people in our sample accepted the current medical orthodoxy on saliva; and it is equally, if not *more*, important to look at the aspects of media coverage which encouraged people to accept this. Publicity about the safety of casual contact with those with the virus proved to be important, and the greatest impression was made by actual demonstrations. Just as Princess Diana's hugs conveyed that HIV could not be transmitted through touch, so actually seeing people kissing was a key influence. Some people, for example, took their cue from media presentations of AIDS buddies:

> These volunteers are on the spot, you see them [on television] kissing AIDS patients . . . and they don't seem frightened. So I don't think it could be passed on that way. (Women with children at a play group)

Other research participants used logic to explain why they believed saliva was safe. For example, one man said he did not believe media scare stories about casual transmission because if HIV was that infectious it would never have been concentrated in 'risk groups' in the first place:

> You can't get AIDS easily from a drinking glass . . . Saturday night, last orders has just been called, they're running out of glasses – wham – they don't wash them – if it's that easy to catch we'd all be dead. (Prisoners)

Debate within the groups also highlighted one particular piece of information which influenced audience belief in the *safety* of saliva. When some research participants declared that saliva was dangerous, others countered by declaring that one would need intimate contact with a great deal of saliva before transmission could occur. Someone would need, they said, to 'bathe in it, while covered in open sores'; or to drink 'one pint', 'two pints', 'five pints', 'six and a half pints', 'a litre', 'nineteen buckets', 'a gallon', 'ten gallons', or 'a thousand gallons'. Such quantities of saliva were unlikely to be absorbed even, as one young woman pointed out, if you spent 'all night snogging'.

The mass media were one direct source of this information. For example, the *Scotsman* reported that 'you'd have to drink saliva by the gallon to run any significant risk of acquiring the HIV virus' (*Scotsman*, 29 December 1989). However, such statements were rare; and research participants often identified their friends, rather than the mass media, as their source of information on this topic. Indeed, the animated discussion in the focus groups demonstrated such interpersonal communication in action. Discussions about body fluids caused a great deal of hilarity and were accompanied by jokes about pints of saliva being 'bottled just for your use', or remarks such as: 'You've got to have a mouth big enough to take one and a half litres in one go – they'd probably drown first anyway!' Information about the safety of saliva, presented in this way, has high 'social currency'. It would appear that such half-fascinating, half-repellent images are ensuring that this particular message enters everyday talk; it is recalled and repeated between friends, family and colleagues.

The precision (or lack of it) of media reports, the framing of particular information, and people's pre-existing knowledge about saliva all help to explain their reactions. It is also important to remember that although AIDS is a relatively new epidemic, the words, images, facts and figures surrounding it do not emerge out of a vacuum. Indeed, as will be shown, the power of specific messages often lay in their cultural resonance. In other words, some representations of AIDS were especially potent because of the way in which they tapped into images from history (e.g. around venereal diseases) or other cultural reference points (e.g. horror movies) or associations (such as the equation of homosexuality with death and disease). (For discussion of the cultural representation of gay men and lesbians see Armitage et al., 1987; Gibbs, 1994; Griffin, 1993; Russo, 1987; Sanderson, 1995.) The power of such broader cultural references is clearly illustrated by the following section which examines the racism that informed and reinforced constructions of 'African AIDS'.

'African AIDS'

During the late 1980s and early 1990s, press and television reports frequently stated that HIV had originated, and was widespread, in Africa. This image of Africa as both the cradle and hotbed of HIV infection was widely accepted by white research participants, and they explicitly identified the mass media as their source of information. There was little critical discussion of this 'fact'. Instead, many research participants unquestioningly reproduced images, statements and figures about Africa which closely echoed actual news bulletins. They presented dramatic statistics about the extent of the epidemic; tended to present the African continent as a single, undifferentiated socio-cultural block; and, just like some of the original reports, associated AIDS with 'blackness'. AIDS was said to be common in 'black countries' (Prison staff), 'black provinces' (Police staff), and 'black cities' (American student). Thus the advice from one young man that the way to protect yourself from HIV was: 'Don't go near the darkies.'

Why was there such ready acceptance of 'African AIDS' or 'black AIDS' among white participants? Further discussion with research participants revealed that such acceptance was encouraged by a broader context of reporting about Africa, whereby the idea that HIV came from 'over there' conformed to many white people's pre-existing images of 'the dark continent'. The apocalyptic African AIDS scenario is easily absorbed into existing images of Africa as a disaster zone; whereas such decimation would be, in the words of one research participant, 'unimaginable over here'. It also accords with images of Africa as a place of sickness and death. One young man commented that he was not surprised that AIDS originated in Africa because: 'Look at all the famine over there, all the disease coming off the dead cows and all that, they die and all that.'

More broadly, the idea that Africa was the source and hotbed of HIV infection conformed to some dominant assumptions about 'African culture'. African values were seen as militating against the practice of safer sex. According to one white civil engineer, for example: 'I'd heard that on a radio documentary . . . it's a macho thing, they [black men] won't use condoms.' AIDS was also sometimes associated with, and blamed on, African sexuality, which was presented as primitive, perverse and promiscuous. One police officer argued that it made sense that AIDS came from Africa because: 'there are some very primitive people in Africa . . . and [AIDS] is alleged to have originated from practices which were a bit extreme'. Another group of white police officers all agreed that AIDS is common in Africa because: 'They all go round doing it with one another, don't they? I mean it's accepted.' 'It's a cultural way of life.' When asked how they knew this, one officer replied: 'We've only got the media, haven't we? None of us have got personal experience from going over there'; and his colleague added: 'It's pretty well catalogued from Darwin onwards' (Police staff).

The idea of 'African AIDS' also fitted in with the idea of 'foreigners' and immigrants as carriers of infection. One woman explicitly drew links between black immigration to Britain and the advent of HIV. Others used it to justify racist immigration policy. As one white retired man commented, the association of AIDS with Africa is: 'A marvellous platform for Enoch Powell, actually. He was right, dead right. We should have kept them out.'

The racism in which images of 'black' or 'African' AIDS are embedded is not just about explicit National Front style politics, evident in some of the above quotes. It was also more subtle. In some cases, research participants unquestioningly accepted assumptions about the links between AIDS and Africa (or black people) in spite of their own expressed political views. One (all-white) group, for example, wrote a news script report which identified 'the Afro/Caribbean community' as 'responsible for the spread of the virus'. It was only after rereading the text that they expressed reservations about this statement, and one commented: 'We probably made a boob there.'

Another white research participant originally stated that AIDS was widespread throughout Africa, but reconsidered his position when challenged by black colleagues. He reflected that his ready acceptance did not accord with his critical political position but depended more on images of Africa from his schooldays:

> All I remember from my history about Africa is it's where slaves come from and people live in mud huts in tribes, you know. That's the sort of image you get of what African life is about. (NACRO workers' group)

There is no *necessary* link between racism, or anti-racism, and believing that Africa is, or is not, widely affected by AIDS; as we argued earlier, empirical facts can serve different political purposes. What is clear, however, is that the way in which 'African AIDS' is constructed, reported and accepted by many white audiences feeds on and into a racist agenda. Media coverage of 'African AIDS' was clearly influencing (white) public perceptions; and doing so because such reporting was plausible, acceptable and even useful within existing sets of images and beliefs. (For further discussion see Kitzinger and Miller, 1992.)

AIDS as a disease of sinful or unnatural 'risk groups'

In earlier chapters, we described how some media reports explicitly or implicitly linked AIDS with dirt, sin or deviation. Such themes were reiterated in the group discussions. The perception of HIV as a sexually transmitted disease (rather than say a blood-borne disease) in any case keyed into long-standing associations between sexually transmitted diseases and pollution (see also Brandt, 1987). One elderly man, for example, described how AIDS reminded him of 'the old days':

> They have always had that sexually transmitted diseases clinic, there was one in Black Street for years and people used to cross to the other side like this [holding nose]. That was for venereal disease and gonorrhoea but you don't know what else they were taking in there. (Retired people)

However, the existence of transmission via blood transfusion (or sex within marriage) allowed for the creation of some 'clean' or 'innocent victims'.

Research participants often made comments such as: 'I feel sorrier for the haemophiliacs because they never asked for it'; 'it's the innocent who suffer'; and 'the people I have sympathy for are the people that pick it up by accident. But when it comes down to the other ones, as far as I can see, it's self-inflicted.' Even when no such explicit statements were made, similar attitudes were often revealed by the way in which research groups related to one of the TV news stills – the photograph showing a woman and child. In their news bulletins, the groups used this photograph to accompany statements about the particular 'tragedy' and 'misfortune' of someone becoming infected in spite of, in the words of one research participant, having 'done nothing wrong'. Mothers and children were routinely referred to as 'innocent parties' or even, in one case, as 'innocent bystanders' (as if they had been caught up in someone else's war). Although some research participants did recognise and criticise such innocent/guilty divisions, others were unaware of their own discrimination between different categories of 'victim'; and some actively asserted the validity of such distinctions. For example, a group of retired people, commenting on their use of the picture of the woman and child, declared:

> *Resp. 1*: We are agreed that it [AIDS] was really started by irresponsible people, as far as we know. And it's been carried on, in most cases, by irresponsible people. But in some cases, [such as the] one lady there with her baby in her arms [*pointing to the photograph*], we assumed that this was a lady who had contracted the AIDS virus through a blood transfusion in the hospital and it has been passed on to her child, which is rather unfortunate . . . But the majority of cases we find that it is irresponsible people that's carrying it on.
> *JK*: What kind of irresponsible people?
> *Resp. 1*: Gays, lesbians.
> *Resp. 2*: Oh, and of course prisoners.

The first speaker's passing assumption that lesbians are a high risk group is particularly telling and by no means unique. Current scientific orthodoxy suggests that very few women have become infected as a result of sex with other women. (For debates about lesbians and HIV risk, see Richardson, 1994.) However, early surveys suggest that about two thirds of the public believe that lesbians are 'greatly' or 'quite a lot' at risk (Brook, 1988: 75).

Our work revealed that this is partly due to the way in which lesbians and gay men are linked in discussions of AIDS. The media often talk about them in the same breath, and use the term homosexual both in its accurate generic sense and in a male-specific way (see Hamilton, 1988). Thus some people deduced that lesbians must be at risk simply because they too are homosexual or, as one person put it, 'They are faggottesses.'

On one level, the misapprehension about lesbian risk status is unsurprising, given the media's failure to specify that lesbian sex might actually be *safer* than heterosexual intercourse. How people made sense of this absence of information and terminological vagueness is, however, not simply a question of linguistics. How people fill in gaps in texts reveals their reading of the underlying narrative. In the case of AIDS, this narrative links infection to perversity. Thus, when research participants were asked to explain why they thought lesbians were high risk, they often cast around for some memory of a media source for this information or tried to think of a biological justification. When they failed on both counts they resorted to explicit moral statements. Lesbians, they said, must have a high rate of HIV infection because, as one person stated, 'they are leading the same life as what two men are'; and this life was 'unnatural' or 'sinful'. A retired woman explained: 'The point is this: biologically your body is not made for either homosexuality or eh [*pause*] or eh [*pause*] lesbianism'. A young man in another group declared 'God made two kinds of sex, male and female. They go together. He didn't mean males to go with males and females to go with females. And that's how they got it [AIDS].'

Even some research participants who saw themselves as liberal or permissive echoed such associations. One man, for example, realised during the course of the research session that his perception of lesbian sex as high risk did not accord with his understanding of the biology of transmission. In spite of his 'better judgement' he had simply assumed they were high risk because he had a residual sense of lesbianism as 'abnormal'. 'It's just, I suppose, the way you've been brought up,' he commented; 'you think that a man and a woman is more normal than two women. I don't know whether, risk of infection-wise, whether that it's true or not; it's just the way that you were brought up.'

Public beliefs about lesbian risk status are thus formed at the intersection of four factors: media silence about lesbians; the ambiguity of the term 'homosexual'; the way in which AIDS was set up as a disease of deviation; and the cultural baggage that people bring to their understanding of the epidemic. The belief that lesbian sex is risky reveals presumptions about what is 'normal', 'natural' or 'godly'. It shows how public responses to media messages are not just based on specific terminology, but also relate to narrative structures and cultural contexts. People's beliefs are formed in response not just to stated fact, but to unstated assumptions too. However, it is not just language, silences, narrative structures and cultural baggage that are important; visual images are also crucial. The next section highlights how all these factors, but particularly the visual, can influence a fourth aspect of people's understandings: their perceptions of the relationship between HIV and AIDS.

The relationship between HIV and AIDS: audience understandings of asymptomatic HIV infection

Throughout the late 1980s and early 1990s medical orthodoxy has asserted that HIV is the primary and inevitable cause of AIDS. This assertion has been central to the health education campaigns and, indeed, the use of the term HIV was a specific site of struggle in the production of AIDS education and media messages (see Chapter 2). The use of terms such as 'AIDS virus' or 'AIDS' as a synonym for HIV has been criticised for, among other things, confusing people about the time-lag between becoming infected and becoming ill (Watney, 1989). Until 1988, official education material and the bulk of mass media accounts fell into this trap. However, the 1988–89 HEA campaign deliberately set out to promote public understanding of HIV; and some, but not all, journalists followed this lead. It is partly this history that is reflected in people's use and understanding of the term. A survey designed to evaluate the 1988–89 campaign found that around three quarters of the population agreed with the statement: 'You cannot tell who has HIV (the AIDS virus) by looking at them' (Wellings and McVey, 1990). However, this still left a significant proportion of people who were unclear on this point.

In our research, some people were unsure about the distinction between HIV and AIDS; and others, although acquainted with the term 'HIV', were unaware of its significance and were not prepared to use it in conversation with each other. Many people thought that HIV was just a 'posh' or 'technical' word for AIDS. This is not surprising given that the term was much more likely to be used by 'experts' and in health education materials than in the popular press.

We found that such lack of familiarity did not necessarily limit people's understanding of the distinction between the virus and the syndrome, but it could limit their ability to communicate this to others. This was illustrated during a dispute between two schoolboys; one of whom knew the difference between being a 'carrier' and 'actually having the disease', whereas the other one believed that anyone who was infected would show symptoms.

> *Resp. 1*: You can be a carrier *or* you can actually have the disease.
> *Resp. 2*: How can you carry something and not have it? Say you're carrying a shopping bag – you've got it.
> *Resp. 1*: It could be someone else's. You're just carrying it and you can pass it on to someone else . . . A picture that I saw on the TV, she was a carrier she gave it to her baby, she didn't actually have it.
> *Resp. 2*: How can you give somebody something that you've not got?
> *Resp. 1*: You're carrying a shopping bag, but it might not be actually your shopping bag.
> *Resp. 2*: How can you give somebody something if you've not got it? For God's sake man, wake up! Come off the mind-expanding drugs please!

A basic lack of familiarity with the meaning of HIV could also lead to straightforward misreading of health education advertisements. One of the HEA adverts, for example, stated that 'for this many people who have AIDS' (showing one face) 'this many people have HIV (the virus that leads to AIDS)'. The second statement appeared on a new page beneath a set of 30 faces. This advertisement was interpreted by one research participant to mean that only a very small proportion of those with HIV would go on to develop AIDS.

More common was the assumption that being infected with the virus was the same as having the syndrome; and this misinterpretation was more complex than any simple 'misreading'. It was partly related to the media's misuse of terminology, as noted above. However, the problem was compounded by the powerful visual images surrounding AIDS.

Television and press reports repeatedly displayed the figure of a haggard, painfully thin person dying of AIDS-related illnesses – young men with jutting bones, sunken eyes and listless expressions of despair. This death's-head image was used to introduce the issue in much of the early coverage. Indeed, such an image was explicitly identified as 'the face of AIDS' in ITN's 1986 review of the year on 30 December 1986. Throughout the 1980s some newspapers emphasised the physical degeneration of the body by displaying before-and-after portraits of people with the syndrome – photographs showing once handsome faces of gay men juxtaposed with those ravaged by disease (Wellings, 1988). The reporting of Rock Hudson's illness and death in 1985 was typical in this respect. The press contrasted the film star's original 'hunky' glamorous image with the 'frail skeleton' he had become (*Sun*, 18 June 1986). They highlighted his previous 'rugged good looks' as 'The Baron of Beefcake' versus the image of him 'As he is now . . . a haggard, tired Rock Hudson' (*Daily Express*, 25 July 1985).

Such representations made a powerful impression on the research participants. Asked what images came to mind when they thought about AIDS, participants responded with descriptions such as: 'someone white and skeletal'; 'images like Ethiopia'; 'disease-ridden, emaciated body sat in bed'; 'the image of a victim, forlorn and dying'; and 'someone fading away and dying – because that's what you see - they're more like a vegetable than a [human being]'. Such images formed a central part of many people's earliest memories about AIDS and were vividly recalled even five years later:

> These pictures of Rock Hudson at the end – they were really horrific . . . he looked really, really terrible . . . and when you remembered how he was in the films and that and saw . . . it was horrific. (Women with children at a play group)

Most people explicitly identified the media as the source of these impressions. As one man commented:

> I've never seen an AIDS victim, by the way. I've never seen one personally. I've read about it all the same. I've seen them looking all ghastly and I've seen how much weight they've lost. I've seen maybe photographs laid out. (Office janitor)

Such pictures are deeply shocking. They also tap into public fascination with horror-movie images; and for some, representations of the degenerating body of the gay man or junkie served to illustrate the ultimate 'wages of sin' (see Kitzinger, 1995). The classic Face-of-AIDS is also further impressed on people's memories by the way it is invoked in day-to-day interactions. Some research participants described speculating about people they saw in the street who looked very sick, or bullying classmates with 'disfigured' faces, accusing them of having AIDS. Indeed, the relish with which some participants sought to reproduce the Face-of-AIDS during the research session (contorting their faces, starting to squint or shake), also suggests that such images can exercise a voyeuristic fascination. The Face-of-AIDS has become absorbed into, and reiterated through, particular sub-cultures receiving an exposure over and above that actually given to it in the media.

The focus on such images has been widely criticised (e.g. Watney, 1987b). In our discussion groups, it was clearly frightening and offensive for those who saw themselves as at risk (or knew themselves to be HIV antibody positive). Such representations portray those with AIDS as without hope or dignity. They certainly offer no incentive for being tested, or trying to maintain one's health in the light of an HIV antibody-positive diagnosis. Given the lack of media discussion of treatment for (and the process of living with) HIV, these images can be totally devastating. They simply leave people with the impression that they will 'one day wake up looking just like the photographs that we had seen in the press of thin, gaunt and wasting bodies' (O'Sullivan and Thomson, 1992: 109). As one critic writes:

> they talk about people with AIDS as if we were already lost, already dead. And we all look alike to them too . . . all weigh the same, all wear the same AIDS mask and the same striped pyjamas. (Dreuilhe, 1988: 4)

Such images also proved alienating to those who viewed themselves as 'safe'. The Face-of-AIDS beloved by parts of the mainstream media distances the 'victims' from the viewer and renders them almost sub-human. The research participants' own descriptions of these images as showing 'vegetables', 'a body sat in bed' or 'living skeletons' demonstrate how these representations objectify and dehumanise the individual. The monopoly such images have over many people's associations with the word AIDS may also blot out alternative ways of seeing the issue. AIDS is equated with the death of isolated individuals rather than other possible equations such as, for example, the scandal of government inaction. People with AIDS are portrayed as 'united in facing an inevitable unpleasant death' (*Observer Magazine*, 22 July 1990), rather than as united by other forces such as anger, political activism or mutual support.

On a very immediate practical level these negative associations can also counteract crucial health education messages. The contrasting before-and-after images suggest rapid deterioration, and beg the question 'before' and 'after' what? Some of the pictures of people glowing with health may, in fact, be pictures taken while they were infected with HIV; but this is rarely pointed out. Instead we are repeatedly presented with photographs of 'AIDS carriers' who are visibly sick. This can undermine the message that 'you can't tell by looking who's got HIV'. This point was dramatically illustrated in some research participants' interpretations of one of the health education advertisements. The 1988–89 HEA campaign concentrated on informing the public that people with HIV can look and feel perfectly well. One advertisement showed a stereotypically attractive woman with the slogan: 'If this woman had the virus which leads to AIDS, in a few years she could look like

Figure 8.2
Source: Permission of the Health Education Authority

the person over the page' (see Figure 8.2). The next page reproduced an identical portrait with the caption, 'Worrying isn't it'.

A second advertisement simply bore the words 'Two eyes, nose, mouth' against a plain black background; and the main caption read: 'How to recognise someone with HIV'. The message was that anyone might be infected, they look just like anyone else (see Figure 8.3).

Although most research participants understood this message, a minority interpreted the advertisement to mean quite the opposite. Some male prostitutes, for example, declared that the advertisement meant that: 'Aye, their eyes are all black underneath', 'or red'; 'his face is all skinny'; or that people with HIV 'froth at the mouth'. Some members of a club for retired people thought that the advert was intended to convey the fact that 'their hair drops out'; and a group of young people in the care of social services declared:

> *Resp. 1*: Look at their eyes, look at their nose and look at their mouth and if they look queer you don't bother going near them.
> *Resp. 2*: If they are foaming at the mouth and blinking . . .
> *Resp. 1*: And if their nose is all running all the time . . . and they've got scabs round their nose. (Young people in intermediate treatment)

These people's pre-existing mental pictures of the Face-of-AIDS were superimposed on the abstract Face-of-HIV as presented in this advertisement. The vivid image of AIDS, the killer disease, swamped the supposedly neutral and less dramatic representation of the Face-of-HIV. Instead of representing a normal and healthy face, it became the physiognomy of devastating illness.[2]

It is clear that talking about an 'AIDS virus' rather than HIV, and the vague use of such terms (shifting over time and between different types of media and sources), played some part in obstructing public understanding of the differences between having the virus and having the syndrome. More important, however, are the mass media images used to represent AIDS. The photo-opportunities offered by AIDS (or, rather, created and sought out by journalists) emphasised images of degeneration, which made it difficult for some research participants to accept that those with the virus could look perfectly healthy. But people are not only influenced by words, narrative structures or visual images; specific stories can also make a great impression, and there was one particular tale which challenged the idea that people with HIV looked sick. This was the story of 'The vengeful AIDS carrier'.

The 'vengeful AIDS carrier'

The use of HIV as a weapon of intimidation or revenge was a recurring theme in the media coverage of HIV/AIDS during the late 1980s and early 1990s. Television and newspaper reports referred to people who 'may have been infected knowingly by sufferers seeking revenge', or warned of 'the avowed intention of some AIDS victims to deliberately infect as many other

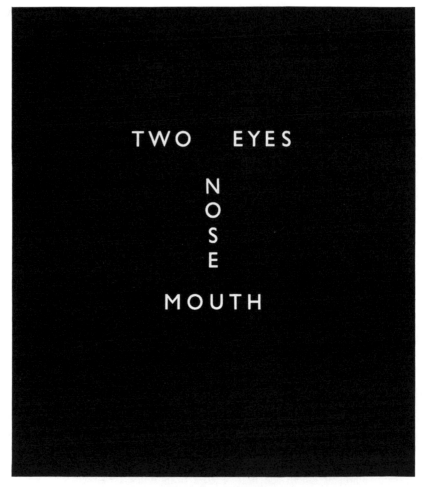

Figure 8.3
Source: Permission of the Health Education Authority

people as possible' (ITN, *News at 5.45* and BBC1, *Six O'Clock News*, 26 January 1988; *Glasgow Herald*, 17 February 1989). Such behaviour has also been dramatised, most notably in the American TV series *Midnight Caller*. Since field work was completed there have been two major cases reported in the British media. One of these involved a haemophiliac man in

Birmingham accused of having unsafe sex with a series of women (news-paper pictures showed him looking healthy and conventionally attractive); the other involved an 'AIDS vengeance girl' or 'Angel of death' in a small Irish town, who was alleged to be 'deliberately infecting scores of men' (e.g. *Express*, 14 September 1995; *Guardian*, 14 September 1995). As this book goes to press a third case, based in Finland, is attracting attention. The *Guardian* displays the man's mugshot on the cover of the tabloid section: 'STEVE THOMAS IS HIV POSITIVE' reads the headline in large red letters. 'He has had unprotected sex with more than 100 women' (*Guardian*, 17 April 1997).

Prior to these cases, the press had reported on incidents (trawled from all over the world) such as the man in the Soviet Union who, 'deciding he has only four or five years to live, announces he has left his wife and is going to sleep with every woman he can' (*Observer*, 1 October 1989); or the woman in Belgrade who 'owned up to bedding FIFTEEN of her colleagues. The pretty victim kept quiet about her illness as she moved from man to man' (*Sun*, 9 March 1989, emphasis in original).

Such stories were spontaneously raised in many of the audience group discussions:

> There was a girl, and she actually went out and pulled about half a dozen blokes in a day and just went to bed with them and afterwards said 'Guess what, you've got it'. (Prison staff)

> There was the incident in the Sunday papers a few months back about the girls . . . on holiday in Spain, and they had Spanish boyfriends and they got the present to take home in the aeroplane and when the girl opened it up it was a small replica of a coffin saying 'Welcome to the AIDS club'. (Nurses)

At times it was not just a case they had read about in the papers: people said that it had actually happened to 'a friend of a friend': 'That happened to my pal, by the way. He fucking ran right down to the doctors.' Often the discussion would lead to an exchange of such accounts:

> *Resp. 1*: I know of somebody who started having a little holiday affair and later got a card saying 'Welcome to the AIDS club'.
> *Resp. 2*: My friend's daughter at university had a relationship with somebody, and when she woke up there was a note on her door which said – exactly the same idea. (Nurses)

The frequent reference to such incidents partly reflects the ubiquity of these stories in a wide range of media (although they had nothing like the media prominence during the field work period as they have had since). But it should be noted that neither the reports in the media nor the experiences of 'friends of friends' carry any guarantee of veracity. Indeed, one newspaper account of 'Clive', who 'seemed to be developing a grudge' and had '[unsafe] sex with half a dozen men in one night' (*Independent*, 21 March 1989), was later exposed as a 'fiction' based on a 'composite character'

(*Sunday Telegraph*, 21 May 1989). Similarly, media reports about the number of men infected by the 'AIDS vengeance girl' in Ireland defy all statistical calculation. However, these stories are sought after by the media, and elaborated and incorporated into people's ways of thinking about AIDS, because they serve as cautionary tales which carry the attractive *frisson* of the thriller plot, and as articulations of different fears and moral positions (such as the dangers of anonymous sex).

In addition, these stories fit into, and perhaps epitomise, the logic of a primary theme in AIDS discourses, the theme of individual responsibility. This theme is particularly potent when combined with the assumption that 'deviants' are irresponsible and anti-social. Note, for example, how many of the quotations used already in this chapter slip between the idea of 'risk groups' and those 'responsible for the spread of AIDS': the potential 'victim' is simultaneously identified as a potential perpetrator. Indeed, the notion of deliberate infection is implicit in the way AIDS is often discussed, even when revenge is not explicitly mentioned. Health education advertisements which use *double entendre* slogans (such as the advertising slogan: 'It only takes one prick to give you AIDS') certainly suggest that 'AIDS' is something given to you by someone else; and a not very nice someone else at that.

Revenge tales also serve to justify draconian measures against 'risk groups'. Some research participants used such stories to justify calls for HIV identity cards, segregation or worse. For example, one participant, himself a prisoner, rounded off a lengthy exchange of various revenge tales in his group by declaring: 'Just get all these people, put them in a camp or something like that and protect all the future generations.' A young man in another group (of ex-prisoners) concluded the discussion of vengeful AIDS carriers with the statement: 'What they should do, man, is take everybody that's got AIDS and put them into one corner and just blow their heads off.'

The way in which such tales are told illustrates how fictional accounts may become accepted as real and how specific one-off events may become incorporated into generalised urban myths. The truth value of such tales is less significant than their social currency value. It also demonstrates how any one story may generate multiple reactions; the revenge tale may or may not have an educational interpretation (e.g. encouraging safer sex practices) but it certainly has an oppressive one.

Finally, we turn to people's understandings of safer sex. How did people define safer sex? Did they accept that heterosexual activity could transmit the virus? In particular, how did heterosexual participants relate to information about 'safer sex' and how did this influence their own behaviour? The final section demonstrates how both the form and the trajectory of a debate (the way in which it develops over time) can be crucial. It also explores the influence of the status of a source: for example is a newspaper quoting a doctor, an MP or a discredited expert? Finally it illustrates how facts and ideas promoted in the media relate to the broader cultural context and the ability of people to act on what they know.

'Safer sex' and 'the heterosexual threat'

Throughout the late 1980s and early 1990s the bulk of media reporting emphasised the existence of 'risk groups', but also stressed that AIDS was spreading to the 'general population' (see Chapter 2). A central tenet of the health education campaigns and much media reporting was that AIDS could affect anyone. However, during the course of our research there were several major attempts by newspapers to discredit the notion of 'the heterosexual threat' (e.g. by the *Sun*). These attempts were given a boost by Lord Kilbracken's intervention which led to the screening of a documentary about the debate (see Chapter 3).[3]

Such publicity did explicitly effect a minority of research participants. As one office janitor commented:

> That programme last week, right, you know what it says? There's only one heterosexual person, one heterosexual man has died of AIDS in Britain. The rest have all been homosexuals, drug addicts or people who have had sex with drug addicts . . . So, if you're a heterosexual, right . . . I think the chances of getting it are practically nil . . . if you're a plain-living man.

Nevertheless, most of the research participants at this time accepted that HIV could be transmitted via heterosexual sex. For example, of the 247 research participants who completed a questionnaire, all but seven indicated that HIV could be transmitted heterosexually. In addition to the steady stream of official information during the late 1980s and early 1990s, specific media events and health education advertisements had been particularly effective. One HEA advert (launched in January 1990) described a young woman who became infected after just one boyfriend. This startled some heterosexuals into perceiving themselves to be at risk. Others specified that they were influenced by TV dramas starring infected heterosexuals, or by reports about celebrities who contracted HIV.

The trajectory of the AIDS story as it emerged over time was also crucial in encouraging people to accept the 'heterosexual threat'. The original publicity identified risk groups, but then explicitly and increasingly talked about the heterosexual spread of the virus. This story trajectory made a return to the idea that HIV only affected 'risk groups' seem 'old-fashioned' and 'out of date'. In addition, sources promoting the idea that heterosexual AIDS was a myth were often seen to be unreliable.

> Let's just say I wouldn't take my information from doctor Vernon Coleman in the *Sun* . . . *still* saying things like: 'It's only a problem for drug users and gay people and we can just carry on the way we're doing already, don't worry about it.' (Market researchers)

Within this context most heterosexual research participants accepted the importance of safer sex. They usually defined this in terms of using a condom or monogamy, cutting down on the number of partners, or being careful who you 'slept with'. The notion of non-penetrative sex attracted little recognition, a gap in public perceptions which is also documented in survey data (see Johnson et al., 1994; Macintyre and West, 1993). This gap is not surprising given that such information was, in any case, rarely included in the publicity targeted at 'the general population'. Out of almost 2,000 press and TV news reports on AIDS in our sample period only two mentioned non-penetrative sex; and the message was only lately, and somewhat grudgingly, included in occasional health education materials. Many heterosexual research respondents were unfamiliar with the concept, and the act of penetration was often assumed to define 'real' sex.

Condom use can be problematic too. This was evident both in the focus groups conducted as part of this media study and during in-depth interviews with young women conducted at a later date (see Kitzinger, 1993b, 1995). For a start, using condoms runs counter to dominant media constructions of sexuality. Sex is meant to be spontaneous, romantic and uncontrollable (Jackson, 1978; Lees, 1986). It is this discourse which informs the bulk of media representation of sexuality in drama and in many commercial advertisements. It is no coincidence that some commercial advertisers (who often use sex appeal to sell products) threatened to withdraw their advertising from slots sandwiched between AIDS programmes (*Sunday Telegraph*, 14 December 1986; *Independent*, 17 December 1986).

In the focus group discussions, research participants referred to dominant constructions of sexuality to explain their resistance to, or the impracticality of, safer sex advice. Some participants, particularly heterosexual men, thought that all safer sex messages were unrealistic because of what one man called 'the uncontrollable male urge'. 'I think the man in the street realises [the facts about AIDS],' said another, 'but his sex urge overcomes it. He just goes into town and does the necessary.' Others made remarks such as: 'Your willie takes charge doesn't it?' or 'a standing penis has no conscience'. Three groups also mentioned a cartoon characterisation which presents dialogue between a man and his independent penis.

> It's like the wee book *Willie* – you see the guy talking to the wee thingamy, it's got a voice and all that, it's got a mind of its own. If that reacts you do something about it, don't you? (Prisoners)

There were, then, obvious tensions between AIDS advertisements and broader media/cultural messages. There were also contradictions *within* the health education campaigns themselves.

One of these tensions is between the advice 'You can't tell who is infected just by looking', and the assertion that HIV infection is most common among certain risk groups. Some of our research participants did not use condoms; instead they relied on avoiding certain types of partner, based on their appearance or their 'outsider' status. Ideas about who to avoid were tied in with notions about gender, class, race and sexuality. Many middle-class research participants assumed that illegal IV drug users or prostitutes could not possibly be part of their social circle. At the same time, some heterosexual women spoke of being suspicious of men who 'look effeminate' or were known to be 'a bit of a lad'; and heterosexual men talked about the need to avoid 'tarts', 'slags', 'gang-bang Joans', 'dirty nails', 'mattress-backs', 'bits of fluff' and 'girls with a reputation'. Some of the white men also made explicit reference to the dangers of 'dusky maidens' or 'darkies'. Ideas about drug use were also important within this schema. People 'carrying the AIDS virus' would, according to some research participants, 'look like junkies' – a look of degeneration and ill health which has been actively promoted by certain government anti-heroin advertisements (e.g. in the Department of Health advert showing a pale, sick-looking individual with the caption 'skin care by heroin': see Kitzinger, 1991).

A second major tension within different health education messages is crystallised in the strap line: 'If you're not 100% sure about your partner, use a condom'. Such advice was used in advertisements and complemented by statements in the press emphasising a sort of 'stranger-danger' concept of HIV infection. For example, the government's Chief Medical Officer, Sir Donald Acheson, was reported as saying that his advice 'to anyone who has vaginal intercourse with someone they do not know well is that they wear a condom or ensure one is worn . . . I am not aware of any better advice other than they do not have sex with someone they do not know' (*Daily Telegraph*, 16 October 1990; cited in Ingham et al., 1991). Some people interpret such advice to mean that as long as they 'know' their partner, condoms are unnecessary and (as research by Ingham et al. has shown) 'knowing' one's partner can be a very variable term, including having talked to them for a few hours or knowing them to be the friend of a friend (Ingham et al., 1991).

In sum, any mass media or advertisement message enters a pre-existing universe of complementary or contradictory messages. Straightforward exhortations to use condoms conflicts with complex discourses (often promoted by other elements of the media) about gender and sexuality, definitions of 'real sex', ideas about pleasure, stereotypes about 'risk groups' and stigma surrounding HIV. It also conflicts with implicit messages from other health education material (including other AIDS adverts or anti-drug campaigns).

One of the ironic consequences of such complexity is that the very success of health education messages, associating condom use with protection against HIV, may sometimes actually inhibit their use. Certainly, some research participants expressed hesitation about condom use within a stable relationship, fearing that it would signal a lack of trust and introduce suspicion. Others spoke of abandoning condom use as a relationship became 'serious', in order to signal commitment. (For more detailed studies of heterosexual responses to safer sex advice see Holland et al., 1990, 1991, 1992a, 1992b, 1994; Wight, 1993, 1994.) Some research participants said that if a 'casual' partner suggested condom use they would be suspicious that he or she might be infected. One man stated that if women requested safer sex then: 'I'd want to see them in the light'. As a parallel to this some would not suggest condom use themselves in case they were suspected of having the virus. The message that condoms protect against HIV may make it more difficult for some people to initiate or maintain condom use because of the associated stigma. An individual message may thus have unintended meanings, once it is taken in conjunction with other messages (and in Britain, of course, there has never been an anti-discrimination campaign to challenge such stigma).

Concluding remarks

This chapter has highlighted some of the patterns that occurred in the group discussions and shown how people draw on the language, phrases, images, and stories about AIDS promoted in the media and in health education messages. Media scare stories, negative images, the nature of the AIDS story trajectory, the silences and the narrative logic of reporting have all helped to frame how people understand and react to the AIDS epidemic. The details of media reporting are vital; struggles around the words, images and stories used to represent AIDS are a crucial part of attempts to live with and challenge the epidemic.[4]

The examples discussed above also illustrate how public confusion or 'failure' to respond to education campaigns can *not* be assumed to be a problem with the audience (using explanations relating to their 'psychological resistance', 'locus of control' or 'ignorance'). Rather public reactions reflect confusion *within message content* and *conflict at the level of production* both of health education messages and within the mass media.

Our research also demonstrates that the 'power' of any media report or advertisement is not embedded solely in the individual message itself. Each image or item of information enters a world already populated by a multitude of other sources of influence. It is this that can lead to 'misunderstandings'; such as the selective interpretation of safer sex messages, or thinking the Eye-Nose-Mouth advert means that people with HIV look odd and lose their hair. Mass media messages intersect with moral judgements and broader cultural assumptions and compete with, or reinforce, messages from other non-media sources, such as the attitudes and behaviour of friends, pervasive sexism, racism or heterosexism, and the practicalities of their day-to-day lives. Each message thus interacts with people's personal experiences and structural positions; and it is this which will be examined in more detail in the next chapter, which focuses on the audience diversity only hinted at so far.

Notes

1. All quotes come from the focus groups' discussions, unless otherwise specified. For ease of reading we have not identified which type of group individual short quotes come from. However, longer and interactive sections of transcript are accompanied by an ID label, referring to the nature of the group within which the discussion took place.

2. Some of the HEA adverts themselves might reinforce the idea that, at the very least, the period between becoming infected and becoming ill would be very short. As one man commented, the television advertisement showed how 'You start off healthy and finish up

broken. It was a deterioration . . . it was very quick. At first it appears to be OK and then you deteriorate slightly and then all of a sudden it's just, you know, from one minute feeling not too good and within a couple of months that's you' (Prison staff).

3. More recently, in the mid-1990s, the general emphasis shifted again as the heterosexual epidemic apparently failed to emerge and pressure to 're-gay' AIDS increased. However this development occurred after field work with audience groups had been completed.

4. Different ways of researching audience reception processes will identify different types of findings and facilitate different levels of analysis. One method of choice is to interview people about their viewing of a particular 'genre' such as soaps or to observe their consumption habits (e.g. Collett and Lamb, 1986). The other main method of choice for many media researchers is to actually show people video tapes of specific programmes. By contrast, our own approach was 'audience-led', in starting from people's own memories and understandings and then working backward to locate sources of information and influence. Although this makes some questions less accessible, it has advantages. For example, facilitating the exploration of *cumulative* effects and the impact of story trajectory: the reiteration of themes or images (e.g. the Face-of-AIDS) and shifts in reporting over time (e.g. in relation to 'the heterosexual threat'). It is worth noting that what people say when invited to comment on a particular programme may differ from the impressions they are left with long after the event, and the cumulative effect of different media messages is not simply a sum of the parts. Memories of a programme or media event may also change over time as they are 'reframed' by contemporary events and 'frameworks' of understandings (see Kitzinger, in press).

9

Resisting the Message: The Extent and Limits of Media Influence

Jenny Kitzinger

The previous chapter focused on the nature of the media coverage and the social context which supported particular media constructions of AIDS. This chapter shifts the focus on to the factors helping people to challenge or resist media influence. It also highlights the diversity of audience responses. It addresses questions such as: When and why do some people distrust the media, the government and the scientists? Why did some members of the public resist clear media messages? How are different understandings of AIDS related to age, gender, class, sexual, national or ethnic identities? Through addressing such questions it is possible, on the one hand, to explore the implications for developing AIDS prevention strategies and, on the other, to consider the implications of our research for theories about media power.

Access, attention and identification

Although there was a broad consensus among our research participants concerning the basic facts about AIDS, not everyone agreed; and there were varying levels of knowledge. One simple explanation for the diversity of research participants' understandings of AIDS lies in the extent of their exposure to different media messages. For example, although massive publicity and the delivery of English-language leaflets to every household meant that most people were aware of basic information, this was not true for everyone. Clearly this initial strategy was not designed for the homeless and depended on the recipient's ability to read English. Our own research was limited by only including research participants who spoke English (for discussion see Frayne et al., 1996). However, even among these people, a few individuals lacked basic information. For example, a young male prostitute with limited reading skills commented that it was only as a result of participating in the study that he realised that condoms should be used for anal sex.

Research participants also differed in what they chose to read, the degree of attention they gave reports about AIDS and their access to alternative sources of information. Being part of the gay community was one obvious key difference, mediated by whether or not the individual lived in a large city with access to gay literature and community organisations (for discussion of the importance of community see Kippax et al., 1992; Watney, 1990). Here it is crucial to note that engaging in gay sex does not mean an individual is part of a gay community or even gay-identified – see, for example, the young male prostitute quoted above. However, our research groups included a group of gay men living in a major Scottish city. These research participants had closely followed the issue since it first appeared in the mass media. Most of them had watched 'Killer in the village' (*Horizon*, BBC2, 25 April 1983). They had also read about AIDS in the gay press. One had a lover who worked on an AIDS helpline and several had friends who were HIV antibody positive (none chose to discuss their own sero-status). For them, as one explained, AIDS meant:

> You've got to change your whole life . . . There was a time when AIDS always happened to someone else; it can't actually happen to you, and you may have a cavalier attitude to start with. But you actually knew it was getting nearer and nearer to people you knew . . . Your views on AIDS became more toned and more sensitive, and now you have to face the fact that people you know may actually be carrying HIV. You know people who have HIV or actually are dying.

By contrast with these men's experiences of being 'inside' the epidemic, other research participants had a very different sense of self and community. Some saw AIDS as totally irrelevant to their own lives, a perspective summed up by one individual who commented: 'I'm a clean living man, it's not my problem'. This is confirmed by surveys which show that those with negative attitudes toward homosexuality are less likely to pay attention to news about AIDS (Kennamer and Honnold, 1995). At the other extreme, several participants deliberately avoided publicity about AIDS because it was too close to home and they lacked community support. One woman, who was worried she might be infected with HIV after being raped by several men, explained that she would switch off anything about AIDS to avoid thinking about it.[1]

Access, identity and experience all influence what people read or watch. However, even if people read the same newspaper article or view the same programme, they may take away very different messages. Media theory has become very engaged with this issue and a great deal of academic effort focuses on exploring the 'active audience' and documenting 'deviant readings' (for discussion see Eldridge et al., 1997). How did people 'negotiate readings' of AIDS coverage? Were there different interpretations of the same programme? When were people able to 'resist', or simply disagree with, prevalent media messages? These are the questions now explored.

'Negotiated readings', interpretations, reactions and 'resistance'

As one might expect, some of the strongest evidence of 'negotiated readings' were displayed during discussion of the more 'open' media formats of drama and discussion programmes rather than news reports. For example, in 1987 the BBC screened *Intimate Contact*, a drama about a heterosexual businessman infected with HIV after sex with a prostitute (see Chapter 5). Some research participants said that this film had challenged their attitudes and beliefs. For example, one woman (in a group of residents on a Glasgow housing estate) explained that watching this had made her reconsider her judgemental approach to AIDS: 'It taught me not to turn my back on people.' In a group of retired people, however, the impression left by the drama had been rather different: 'It made a great impression on me: it made an impression on me of the horror of pursuing sexual relationships outside marriage.'

Research participants also had very different reactions to another commonly mentioned programme: a televised debate about a man whose son had committed suicide because he was gay. The father now gives 'Christian guidance' to people wishing to resist homosexuality. A group of school students thought that the programme exposed the father's hypocrisy and conveyed the importance of tolerance. A group of retired people (which included several committed Christians) described their reactions differently:

> *Resp. 1*: This was a man and a woman whose boy had taken his life at 21 or 22 and he had left a note. And he had said because he realised that his parents could never condone his way of homosexuality that he would prefer not to live. [There was a young man in the audience] he was glorifying in it. He says to this man: 'That could have been my father, do you not think that you could have accepted his way?' . . .
> *JK*: Can I just ask how that programme affected you?
> *Resp. 1*: I tell you how it affected me . . . the people who got up were shouting and bawling about the gay fraternity and all this carry on, that man was made to look like dirt . . . They were made to sit there and they were ridiculed and I thought it was really disgraceful . . . [I remember] the week when homosexuality was made legal . . . and this country has gone down the drain since then, since the homosexuality got made legal. And they are everywhere, they are creeping into churches . . .
> *Resp. 2*: I think it's dreadful . . . it's unnatural, it's a sickness, an illness.

This group talked at length about the 'bad manners and lack of respect' of the 'homosexuals' in the studio audience and argued that the programme 'was a disgraceful ridiculing of a man's Christian values'. The statement by the dead man's mother that she would rather have her son 'a happy homosexual than an unhappy not-homosexual' was simply seen, by this group, to demonstrate the extremes of mother-love. This perspective was echoed in another group, which clearly saw a mother's support for her own flesh and blood as an indiscriminate maternal duty without general moral or political content:

> You would support them, no matter what. Just like they [mothers] believe a rapist or something, they are still yours. You may not like what they have done or whatever, but I think you have still got that support for them – a *mother* does anyway. (Office cleaners)

A woman's change of heart, because of her son's homosexuality or sero-positive status, was not then recognised as offering a wider example to the 'general population'; and homosexuals in general could still be identified as deviant and unworthy people.

Such diverse responses to the same programme demonstrate that reactions are not purely determined by the words, images or narrative structures of the 'text' (TV programme or newspaper report). Such data is often used within media studies as evidence of the different ways in which people may 'read' a programme and proof that the message that people take away is influenced by what they bring to their encounter with the media. However, it is important to distinguish between people's interpretations and their reactions. In our discussion groups people often shared a common *interpretation* of an article or TV programme, but differed in the meanings they took away with them. Research participants across a wide range of groups usually shared a common understanding of the broad intended or 'dominant' meaning of the programme – even a programme as 'open' as a discussion involving a studio audience. The students who felt the programme exposed the father's hypocrisy thought the programme was 'good'; the group of retired people saw it as 'biased' and 'unbalanced' and felt that the father was 'set up'. The groups thus agreed about the 'preferred' meaning of the programme. The point is that different people may recognise the efforts of the programme makers to convey a liberal (or reactionary, or critical) perspective, but identify with the 'wrong' individual (such as the reactionary father) and reject the message; selectively gleaning from a programme to reinforce their own perspective.

In addition, sometimes people may accept the particular message, but refuse to generalise from that message or fundamentally change their perspective. Stuart Hall suggested that a 'negotiated reading' could involve accepting the generalisability of a message, while rejecting its particular applicability (Hall, 1980). We found examples where the mirror-image of this process occurred. This is implicit in some of the quotations presented above, for example where people commented that films showing a mother's support for her son did not modify their underlying value systems (a mother would support her son whether he was gay or a rapist). It was also evident in the way in which research participants discussed films, such as *Intimate Contact* and *Sweet as You Are* (see Chapter 5) as 'family dramas', 'a tale of everyday folk' and 'showing family situations with real people'. As one social worker commented:

> I remember that coming home to me . . . I suppose it was very much the human element, sort of families, you know, children and . . . it could be anyone . . . it suddenly comes home that, you know, it is not just gay people, it's not just coloured people, but it's actually anybody in this room that could be infected.

The irony of using a white, middle-class woman to 'bring home' such messages is that it exploits and reinforces dominant understandings about whose life 'counts' and does not reflect the real demographic distribution of

HIV infection. These dramas often do not seem to challenge underlying views about what constitutes 'the human element' or who can represent 'anyone'. Nor do they counteract assumptions about who counts as 'real people' or 'everyday folk'. Audiences' responses to the heterosexual AIDS dramas suggested that people were able to 'enjoy' and be 'moved' by the stories but maintain their assumptions about the (lack of) integration between communities (as if gay men are not part of 'ordinary families') and still neglect to question their definition of 'us' and 'them'. The social worker's last sentence revealed her own, incorrect, assumption that 'anybody in this room' did not include gay people – at least one lesbian (the researcher) was present at the time.

Of course it could be argued that, in spite of the best intentions of the producers, these limitations actually lie in the film content. At the very least, such films are open to such limited interpretations. Certainly, those writing from a critical perspective have highlighted limitations of 'family drama' representations of AIDS and, as discussed in Chapter 5, the producer of *Intimate Contact* now acknowledges some problems with his work. Such reservations were borne out by our empirical work, which highlights the way in which reactionary politics can be supported by liberal representations. Indeed, the division between 'us' and 'them', 'worthy' and 'unworthy victims' or 'good gays' and 'bad gays' was a recurring theme in discussion. Such divisions were not challenged by liberal programmes trying to appeal for empathy or to represent 'them' as 'just like us'. Thus one community group sympathetically discussed a programme which showed 'nice lesbians': 'Authors . . . painters . . . people of good intelligence living very quietly and modestly in their lesbian existence'. However they still complained vehemently about encountering 14 lesbians in their local community centre: 'sitting smoking in this room discussing lesbianism'. These women were, they said, blatant examples of 'a lesbian movement that eats up grants of thousands of what used to be my ratepayer's money, but you never hear of the youngsters who are contaminated by these people'.

People do not just select, 'negotiate' or 'particularise' in response to media representations. They may also explicitly reject some messages. In a very straightforward way audiences quite simply do not believe everything that they are told. This can be illustrated in more depth by examining the factors which undermined the 'authority of the text' and by identifying the other factors impacting upon research participants' beliefs. In particular, we will examine distrust of the media, government information and scientific knowledge, and how people's opinions changed in the light of personal experience.

Distrust of the media, the government or the 'experts'

For many research participants, AIDS media information (particularly news reports and education messages) carried great weight because of the saturation coverage, the broad consistency of the main messages and the status of the sources (e.g. government ministers, scientists and medical experts). However, some people started from a position of scepticism. The perception that the media sensationalise issues, distort the facts and mislead the public is widespread. Although participants usually distinguished between different parts of the media (e.g. TV news is seen as more authoritative than the *Sun*), they sometimes expressed a generalised mistrust. Such misgivings were increased by personal experience of events that received media coverage. One research participant, for example, commented that she no longer believed anything in the press because:

> I've a wee boy with a heart condition and there was a report put into the paper about . . . this great operation he's had and how great he's going to be. [But] some days I have to carry him to school. All [the coverage was] 'this is wonderful' and I felt like an idiot . . . So I don't believe anything that goes in black and white . . . I thought, if they can do that with him – what can they do with other things? (Women with children at a play group)

Another participant described his growing cynicism after witnessing a picket during the 1984–85 miners' strike:

> Like the miners' strike, we saw a lot of things on the television about the brutality of the miners and yet actually being there, seeing the police causing a lot of the problems, it was a bit of an eye-opener . . . You suddenly realised that what we're actually being told and what was happening in reality was a different thing . . . All of a sudden you realise that no longer is there the written word that we can depend on any more. (Prison staff)

(This man is not alone in his reactions to the media coverage of the miners' strike – see Philo, 1990.)

Those with jobs routinely attracting media attention were particularly vocal about their reservations. Police officers became cynical due to media distortion of events of which they had personal knowledge, such as civil disturbances and rape trials. Similarly, prison officers complained of media misrepresentation of their profession. As one protested: 'Prison officers are portrayed as either apathetic spineless weaklings with no mind of their own, or they're Neanderthal Nazis.'

Suspicion about media reporting was also related to a very different sort of scepticism: scepticism about the (Conservative) government and its control over the media. A group of school pupils, for example, agreed that newscasters 'wouldn't be slagging off the government in any way because they'd be taken off the air'; while a prisoner commented: 'the media's controlled to a degree by the politicians . . . let's face it, if the government don't want to frighten the people they're not going to put the message over.' Not surprisingly, such mistrust was often related to political affiliation and sexual and ethnic identity. For example, some black and/or gay and lesbian participants felt disenfranchised by the government and alienated by media representation (or non-representation) of their communities. They were also sceptical of government responses in the light of legislation on immigration, race relations and homosexuality.

Because our field work included research participants from both England and Scotland, we were also able to address the impact of this aspect of national identity. Many of the research participants in Scotland talked about their resentment of Westminster's treatment of Scotland to explain their suspicions of 'Fleet Street' reporting. For example, a group of Glasgow women (Labour and Scottish National Party voters) described why they were suspicious of the 'official line' on AIDS by referring to central government policy on the Chernobyl disaster, and soon broadened their criticism to include references to salmonella and nuclear power:

> *Resp. 1*: They've got some farms that still can't sell their things. They're still killing their cattle, their sheep, you name it. The grass – the radiation affects the grass, the earth, we're eating potatoes and carrots and whatnot.
> *Resp. 2*: They said it was all right and then later they said it could have been in the rain, it could have been carried.
> *Resp. 1*: They tell you a lot of rubbish.
> *Resp. 2*: Even salmonella in the eggs, that's another theory – how they covered that up.
> *Resp. 1*: Also, how many of you would let your children go in the water on a beach near a nuclear power station? I mean I wouldn't . . . The government tell too many lies and you can't trust them for nothing.
> *Resp. 2*: They tell you what they want to tell you. (Women with children at a play group)

Others referred to government mismanagement and secrecy. In 1990, for example, when much of the field work was conducted, there was extensive media discussion of BSE (see Kitzinger and Reilly, 1997). This contributed to public scepticism about government information:

> *Resp. 1*: You're scared to come out the house! This BSE . . .
> *Resp. 2*: You can't even eat your mince now.
> *Resp. 1*: Who in their right mind feeds cattle with infected meat, infected sheep?
> *Resp. 3*: Unemployment's down as well, according to statistics. I think it's got to the stage now you're terrified to trust anybody or anything. (Prison staff)

This scepticism about official information was reinforced by the perceived uncertainty of expert knowledge. Much of this mistrust was rooted in the contradictory or changing reports of expert opinion and the perceived helplessness of science in the face of the AIDS epidemic. As one prison officer commented: 'I had a training video that said we're not at risk. Full stop. We're not at risk because the experts, who *still* haven't found a cure and don't know why, and don't know what it is, are saying it's OK.' A remark to which his colleague added: 'The stock answer for that is: "There has been no recorded case of catching it this way." I wouldn't want to be the one that's been recorded!'

But scepticism is not uniformly applied, nor does it predict people's reactions to any particular item of information. For example, scepticism about the government could lead some people to reject the idea that there was a risk to heterosexuals: 'They're just trying to make people behave themselves.' However, it made others accept the idea because that would explain why MPs appeared so concerned. Several groups made reference to the (heterosexual) 'sex scandals' surrounding Members of Parliament. As one woman commented:

> None of those health ministers were going to bother their backsides [about AIDS] as I see it . . . unless they could be going to get it. Everybody does it. Business-men, the lowest, the highest, the lot, go to prostitutes. They could be catching it now, so they're getting their knickers into a pickle! (Women with children at a play group)

Reactions to different media messages are thus influenced (but not totally determined) by scepticism or trust towards the media, the government and the experts. Nobody actually maintained either a uniformly sceptical or uniformly accepting stance in relation to all AIDS messages. Scepticism did not operate in isolation as an explanation for people's responses. Other factors came into play; factors such as their personal 'stake' in the message, socio-demographic and structural position, political perspective, personal experience and their access to other sources of information.

The influence of personal experience

Personal experience is a key source of influence. Research participants often themselves identified particular events and encounters which had changed their attitudes and beliefs. For example, one research participant's attitudes had been transformed over the last few years after a close relative came out as gay: 'At one time I could have dismissed the whole group as poofs . . . but there's no way you could do that now. We know quite a few gays now.' For another individual, it was her professional experience, as a doctor, which made her reassess her stereotypes about the physical appearance of 'risk groups': 'Before I worked here I always thought I'd know a prostitute on sight, but I don't. No way, and that surprised me . . . They don't all have dyed blonde hair and short skirts.' Another woman reassessed her under-standing of HIV transmission after she contracted herpes: 'That's how I can really understand the advert saying "You can't tell by looking at someone." Well, you can't . . . there was nothing there . . . He looked so healthy!'[2]

It was this type of experience which accounted for many of the marked differences between research participants in otherwise apparently homo-geneous groups. For example, a group of white, working-class women whose children attended the same play group had all seen *The Ryan White Story* (a made for television film first screened in the US in 1996 and shown in Britain on ITV on 1 December 1992 for World AIDS Day). This was a dramatisation of a true account of a young boy with HIV who was excluded from school. All the women thought it was a powerful and moving story. They all agreed that what they called the 'persecution' of Ryan White has been horrendous and unacceptable. However, most of them still insisted that they would want to know if a child in their play group was HIV positive and might discriminate against such a child in the way illustrated in the film. As one commented:

How would you feel if . . . two kids fell and the two of them cut themselves at the same time and your kid, God forbid, got AIDS through that? You wouldn't be worrying about persecuting them then – you think of your own first. (Women with children at a play group)

Only two members of the group supported an infected child's right to privacy and full social participation. They both had quite distinct experiences. One was a child-care worker and referred to routine safety practices and her professional training to explain her point of view. The other revealed that her daughter had received several blood transfusions as a baby: 'She's only four now and I don't know whether she's got it or not, I just presume she hasn't.'

Similarly, in a group concerned about casual transmission from 'junkies', only one woman expressed whole-hearted confidence that casual contact was safe. She explained her confidence by talking about her brother, who injected illegal drugs. She had no worries, she said, about sharing cups with him or leaving him in charge of her children. Her personal experience had led her to inform herself about HIV. This information worked in *combination* with her everyday experience of interacting with her brother. This, in turn, had led to a generalised sense of confidence in the safety of casual contact and the possibility of taking basic precautions.

Often a constellation of factors come into operation to influence reactions to any particular media message. This can best be demonstrated by looking at examples where people rejected prevalent media discourses or questioned official information. This is the focus for the following section, which highlights the range of influences that can come to bear in relation to any particular message and explores the clash between individual media messages and the broader cultural, political and personal context.

Constellations of influence: four examples

Although the diversity of the media coverage of AIDS makes it difficult to identify 'dominant' message, there were some consistent assertions that were very prevalent. This section explores audience responses to four such assertions. First, we will examine rejection of a prevalent item of information: that casual contact is safe. Secondly, we will look at people's 'failure' to adopt widely publicised safer sexual practices. Thirdly we will examine audience criticism of the routine media construction of 'African AIDS'. Finally, we will discuss resistance to the campaign slogan, 'AIDS, You're As Safe As You Want To Be'. Through this discussion we can show how a constellation of influences can undermine health education messages or enable people to challenge mass media constructions. We can also explore how people related to different forms of communication, including factual information, advice, broad constructions and ideological premises.

Fear of casual contact

The previous chapter emphasised how particular phrases and stories encouraged people to believe that casual contact, such as kissing or sharing a drink, was dangerous – or not. A key additional factor, which had nothing to do with the media, was the perceived behaviour of professionals. The television pictures of celebrities or activists (such as Princess Diana or buddies) hugging and kissing people with AIDS count for very little if the audience are surrounded by professionals behaving in a very different way. One prison officer, for example, described how his faith in official information was undermined by the behaviour of medical staff:

> If we take somebody to hospital you go like this [handcuffed]. You're attached to the guy if you like, and all of a sudden the people that are dealing with them . . . come in with masks, the works, and you're just standing looking at it. So there's *something* you know, they're medical people . . . If it's so safe, why are these experts taking so many extra precautions?

Another research participant, in a club for retired people, declared that she had been told by a police sergeant that: 'If a policeman is spat on . . . he is actually watched for the AIDS virus.' She concluded: 'If they don't think this can be transmitted through saliva they wouldn't watch that policeman.' Another woman in the same group argued that saliva must be dangerous as this would explain the popularity of throw-away utensils: 'I think that's why McDonald's and people like that give us cardboard cups. It's not so much the economics of a dishwasher, it's the fact that they're absolving themselves' (Retired people).

Even if people accepted the factual veracity of information about what is 'risky' and what is 'safe', this did not predict risk-taking behaviour. Reactions to official advice were influenced by what precautions people considered acceptable and possible. For example, one woman described how she had instructed her daughter never to share a can of drink with a girl at school whose parents were 'known' to inject illegal IV drugs. This was in spite of her knowledge that HIV is *not* spread via saliva:

> *Resp. 1*: I had warned her [my daughter] – 'No, don't take anything off of her' [the 'suspect' child]. But again that is ignorance . . .
> *Resp. 2*: Aye.
> *Resp. 3*: Of course it is!
> *JK*: And yet, you've also said to your daughter that she shouldn't take anything off this girl?
> *Resp. 1*: Aye, don't drink [*pause*] Aye. Because I just [*pause*] I don't know [*pause*] I don't know what [*pause*] I mean, I'm not saying [*pause*]. They've not got AIDS, but . . .
> *Resp. 2*: It's just to be on the safe side. It's just that you don't know. You're just making sure till they find out what they can get it from.
> *Resp. 1*: Aye, this is it! (Women living on the same Glasgow estate)

This final point was greeted with assent by other members of the group. The experts, they said, may underestimate the virulence of the virus: 'A lot of them don't know what they are talking about'; 'there's too many mistakes';

'too many ifs and buts'. Another member of the group then confided that she always pulls her sleeve down over her hand before pressing the button at a pedestrian crossing – in case she cuts her finger and the button is already contaminated with infected blood; 'and if [my son] says: "Can I press it?", I make him put his gloves on before I let him'.

Such attempts to avoid the risk of casual transmission were not matched by equally careful responses to the potential risks associated with hetero-sexual sex. None of the women suggested that it was 'better to be safe than sorry', and therefore always use a condom during sexual intercourse with their husbands. This was in spite of making remarks about never knowing if your partner is faithful and professing to believe in heterosexual trans-mission. Clearly people's risk-taking behaviour is not just based on their understanding of 'the facts'. It also depends on the perceived social/moral/personal acceptability of the evasive actions concerned. It also depends on people's power to effect change and actually adopt the relevant safer practice. This was even clearer in discussions of safer sex advice.

Barriers to safer sex

The previous chapter explored the conflicting messages about safer sex within health education messages, within the media, and within the broader culture. However, resistance to safer sex goes beyond 'representation' and understanding of 'the facts' into the depths of people's social exchanges, their experiences of their sexuality, sense of agency and actual power. For a start, people could clearly understand an intended message, but still consider it irrelevant. In fact, commenting on a television health education advertisement featuring a beautiful woman (with, it was implied, HIV), one participant rhetorically asked his colleagues: 'I mean the way that girl looked, who was going to say: "Sorry darling but I'm not coming back to your place tonight?"'.

Even if such statements serve more as declarations of red-blooded masculinity than as actual descriptions of intended behaviour, the senti-ments illustrate the cultural context of heterosexuality. It was also clear that some men assumed that it was the woman's role to take responsibility for any form of contraception. As one man, complained: 'I went to the dancing and I had a bird, she never produced a condom to me'. When asked if he had thought of using one, he simply replied: 'No, it wasn't on my mind, know what I mean? Think about it yourself, you go to the dancing with a couple of pints in you, that's the last thing on your mind.' At the same time, some men would clearly resent a woman suggesting safer sex. One stated that a woman would not present a man with a condom or help him to put it on, 'unless she was a dirty nymphy [nymphomaniac] or something'.

Negotiating condom use was also seen to involve making a clear state-ment about sexual intentions. Women worried that this would make them appear to be 'slags' and expose them to abuse (see Kitzinger, 1993b). Both men and women also expressed concern that condom use destroys the ambiguity of a sexual encounter, by specifying in advance that penile penetration is expected. This was seen to raise the possibility of rejection and maximise anxiety about performance (see also Wight, 1993). Some men felt condoms interfered with pleasure ('like eating a bar of chocolate with the wrapper on'). Others were worried about the actual practicalities of rolling them on. As one man commented: 'We take too many chances, but a condom, who is going to wear one of them, to be honest, here?' A comment to which his friend responded with the question: 'How do you put one on?' For some female research participants, condoms could also endanger their 'right to say no'. As one young woman explained: 'If a girl goes back with a guy with condoms in her bag, and he sees them, he'll think "Oh well, she's got them, she must want sex", and she might not want to.'

Some of the HEA advertisements explicitly attempted to grapple with such problems. Adverts such as 'And she's too embarrassed to ask him to use a condom' or 'It's the little things that show he cares' (see Figures 9.1 and 9.2) did provide a rationale and vocabulary for negotiating condom use in some cases. However, transforming sexual attitudes is an uphill battle, and education or information alone is not enough. The advertisement: 'I didn't want to carry condoms because I'd look easy – that's her excuse, what will yours be?' accurately identifies the problem that a woman who carries condoms may be labelled as a 'slag'. However, it dismisses this as 'just an excuse', without acknowledging the costs of 'getting a reputation' (see Holland et al., 1992b; Kitzinger, 1993b). The risks of safer sex are not simply suspended in 'discourses' or images unconnected with reality: the fundamental problem is that 'safer sex' is actually risky.

Deconstructing 'African AIDS'

The previous chapter showed how the construction of 'African AIDS' was widely accepted because it conformed to many white research participants' existing ideas about Africa. However, in some groups, participants who asserted the African origins theory were quickly challenged by friends or colleagues:

> *Resp. 1*: I think somebody brought it over from Africa, you get it there.
> *Resp. 2*: Shut up you!
> *Resp. 1*: What?
> *Resp. 2*: Blame the Africans!
> *Resp. 3*: Racism straight away! (Young people in intermediate treatment)

Several participants also reported incidents prior to their participation in the research which had caused them to alter their opinion. One man said he used to think HIV came from Africa but had changed his mind at a conference where the Terrence Higgins Trust leaflets were criticised for promoting this idea. The THT, he said, 'admitted that they threw that in without actually knowing. They're not awfully sure where it came from.' The fact that people he trusted (the THT workers) accepted the criticism

Figure 9.1
Source: Permission of the Health Education Authority

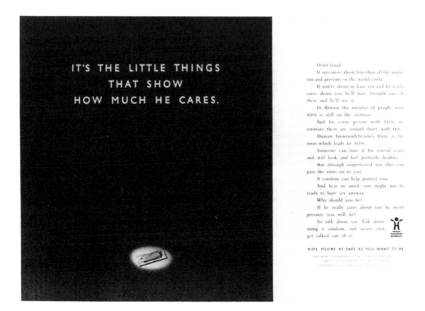

Figure 9.2
Source: Permission of the Health Education Authority

influenced this him accepting this challenge to the African origin theory. In addition, he could readily comprehend how this theory could feed into racism. He linked his understanding of this directly to his own experience of oppression as a white gay man:

> [It's] the same with that AIDS being spread into the heterosexual population as though it's sort of 'sewer of homosexuals' who are starting this disease and now are infecting the general population and it's our fault, or blacks, or whoever you can blame, prostitutes' fault.

Another form of more direct experience was related by a Tanzanian research participant. He did not accept the Western media's cataclysmic scenarios about AIDS in Africa because he knew the places they were talking about. 'The Western press focuses on AIDS in Africa, as if you'd just visited Dar es Salaam or Nairobi you'd find bodies, people dying in the streets – which is not the case.'

Many of the research participants who most assertively rejected the association of AIDS with Africa were black. The importance of this factor was most clearly demonstrated in our work with two groups of ex-prisoners in resettlement schemes – one in Glasgow, the other in London. Both groups were predominantly male and working class. However, the Glasgow group was all white and the London one mostly black. Comments such as '[It was] they black bastards that brought AIDS over here' were common in the Glasgow group. In contrast, some of the London group produced a tongue-in-cheek news bulletin which gave quite a different message. This bulletin suggested that AIDS had been deliberately introduced into Africa by the Pentagon as a means to control world population. Although not entirely serious in this suggestion, the group were quite sure that AIDS had not originated in Africa. When asked why, one man replied: 'I am biased on the subject, right, because I'm a black man.'

We can thus see how a complex set of factors operate to encourage some people to resist the dominant media coverage of 'African AIDS'. These factors included conversations with friends, personal experience, knowledge of African countries, political consciousness and socio-demographic position and these often related to whether people defined themselves as black or white.

Criticising 'You're as safe as you want to be'

Similar complexity is evident in reactions to a single slogan from the AIDS campaign: 'You're as safe as you want to be' – a theme which also implicitly ran through much of the mass media coverage. Most people accepted this slogan as if it were entirely unproblematic. However, some resisted this message. They objected to its individualistic and potential victim-blaming sentiment. Some Scottish participants commented that they were all too familiar with being the targets of such victim-blaming from English politicians. As one young, white, Scottish professional man commented:

It's like Edwina Currie saying that people in Scotland and the North of England have high rates of heart disease because they eat the wrong food so they are to blame . . . To an extent you are, yeah, but you don't go up to someone with heart coronary [disease] and say: 'You're to blame'. (Market researchers)

Others drew on their own experience of illegal drug use or prostitution. A prisoner, for example, challenged the slogan with the comment: 'Nobody wants to use dirty needles unless they're desperate.' Another commented:

It's all right for them to say that, but if they're on the other side of the city and they don't have a set of tools with them . . . you can't play safe because you're that strung out withdrawing from drugs or whatever. (Prisoners)

The men in this group also protested that they knew women who were forced into prostitution to pay for drugs. They argued that the solution to the AIDS crisis lay in social/policy change, as well as 'personal responsibility'. For example, several believed that needles and prescription drugs should be provided to users:

Resp. 1: That would save half the birds going out on the game to fucking earn money to get the junk and it would save us going out [doing] whatever to get the drugs.
Resp. 2: A lot of lassies that's on the game, they're into it for one thing . . . they're not getting enough readies [cash]. If a lassie is a prostitute and she's got the virus and she's got two kids, how can there not be a special fund put by to give her a few quid a week plus regular checks? And if she's still at it, then she just gets the money took off her.

The slogan 'You're as safe as you want to be' was also challenged for assuming people had information that may not, in fact, have been available to them at the time. As one man commented:

I'd heard of it [AIDS], but not over here. I'd heard of it like from America and Africa and things like that. Like at the time when I caught it, and most of my mates caught it, nothing had been said about it being over here. (Prisoners)

The slogan, 'You're as safe as you want to be', caused some resentment. This was particularly evident among those who stated that they were, or could be, HIV antibody positive and among the prisoners, who were acutely aware of their limited choices. In addition, there appeared to be a specific gender dimension to reactions to this slogan. Some women talked about the possibilities of their husbands being unfaithful with prostitutes (a fear not shared by heterosexual men): 'There's always a risk . . . I mean my husband could go out and go with a prostitute and give it to me.' Others spoke about feeling vulnerable to sexual trickery or attack. 'No, that [slogan] doesn't hit home . . . you could go out and get raped.'

Patterns of resistance, 'interpretive communities' and the extent and limits of media influence

The above discussion demonstrates the importance of what people bring to the media and how this influences what they take away from the coverage.

It shows that people do not indiscriminately absorb every message. This signals some of the boundaries of media power. Media audiences interpret what they hear and see in the context of what they already know and what they learn from other sources. They selectively highlight, oppose or reconstruct statements. They are often able to analyse and deconstruct dominant themes, drawing on personal experience, political belief or a general critique of media or government sources.

The experiences and perspectives which people bring to the media can be distinctly individual or even idiosyncratic. However, personal experience is socially patterned and acceptance or rejection of messages about AIDS is related to gender, class, ethnic identity and 'risk status', to name just a few key elements. It was also clear that participants in the research groups often supported one another in developing a collective resistance to certain messages. This resistance was based on their shared socio-cultural position or experiences (but often only developed through participation in the group discussion).[3] It is this observation that has led some media sociologists to underline the importance of 'interpretive communities' and to emphasise the fact that there is no uniform predictable reaction to media messages but that these are patterned by people's position within society (Morley, 1980). This led to a blossoming of studies which highlight the different ways in which class, gender and national and ethnic identity may influence viewers' responses (e.g. Katz and Liebes, 1987; Liebes and Katz, 1990; for discussion see also Eldridge et al., 1997).

Such studies bring important insights to media sociology. However, the 'discovery' of 'interpretive communities', audience activity and the extent of diversity has led some media sociologists away from recognising any media 'effect' at all. Our work shows that recognising such issues should not preclude acknowledging the power of the media. Logic, scepticism, personal experience and critical thinking can enable people to resist media messages. But such resistance cannot be guaranteed.

The limits of logic and scepticism

Our research identified many examples of impressions, gained from the media, overriding logic. This was evident in some research participants' assumptions that lesbians must be intrinsically 'high risk'. Some people made such assumptions in spite of their knowledge of the biological facts and safer sex guidelines which suggest that semen, and penile penetration, can be particularly risky.

The research also demonstrated that cynicism does not necessarily immunise one against media influence – especially if there is no alternative source of information. For example, a group of white Scottish men expressed cynicism about the media portrayal of Edinburgh as an epicentre of HIV infection:

That's people just starting to label. That's like us saying 'Oh no, it's all that Edinburgh mob that's got it', if you're from Glasgow, or 'all that Perth mob' or 'all that Dundee mob' . . . They're all riddled *there*, but nobody in here is riddled with it. (Prisoners)

However, they did not extend their understandings of the labelling process to assumptions about Africa. They simply unquestioningly accepted the idea that AIDS was common, and originated, in Africa. Even those who expressed total cynicism either displayed, or admitted, that they relied on the media for some information. One prison officer commented:

> Since I was involved in one sort of article and it was totally misrepresented, I said: 'Good God! . . . the way they portrayed it was totally inaccurate.' And from then on I said: 'Well, that is it, I'll never believe another thing in the paper.'

Yet he added, quite unselfconsciously: 'I still read them [newspapers], simply because you do get an idea of what's going on in the world.' Evidence of people's use of logic or scepticism to challenge some media messages cannot be assumed completely to undermine media influence. The media still provide people with, at the very least, 'an idea of what's going on in the world'.

The limits of personal experience and critical thinking

The research also demonstrated that people were not necessarily able to resist all messages that they would consciously wish to reject. For example, many of the gay men who participated in the research had the strong foundations of a political gay identity. They were part of an 'alternative community' or 'counter-culture' and had a critical perspective on the mass media coverage of gay issues in general and AIDS in particular. However, several of the gay men involved in our research identified limits to their ability to consciously pick and choose among media messages. They, like many others in the study, found that during the course of the research discussion they were producing statements and images that, at least on reflection, did not accord with their preferred political position. One (middle-class) gay man, for example, commented that intellectually he knew that people with the virus did not look different from anyone else but he still had a residual mental picture of the typical HIV positive person as 'scruffy, with rips in their jeans, not fashionable rips made deliberately, but rips in old and unwashed clothing!'

Indeed, participants were often surprised by the ease with which words and whole phrases came to mind. They made comments such as: 'It's uncanny how much I've absorbed'. They were also sometimes disturbed by the assumptions that they made. It was this that led one man to conclude:

> You find that you look at pictures and automatically you are conditioned by the news media. Phrases automatically come to mind . . . That is the thing about the media – no matter what they report on, you are conditioned by it to a certain extent. (Gay men's group)

Although personal experience can provide a foundation for challenging media messages, personal experience is not necessarily a media-free zone.

Collective or politically analysed experiences can provide a basis for questioning pervasive media messages. However, there are many *common* experiences which are not *shared* and 'raw', isolated, individual experience provides only shaky and preliminary ground for challenging prevalent cultural definitions (see also Kielwasser and Wolf, 1992).[4] Indeed, personal experience may be shaped by, and reinforce, media constructions of reality.[5]

Television and newspaper texts are still, for many people, the lens through which they view AIDS. It is this lens which shapes how they perceive events and interpret personal encounters. For example, scare stories in the media about casual transmission framed the woman's perception of fast food outlets' practices ('that's why McDonald's . . . give us cardboard cups'). Similarly, press and television images of the visible ravages of disease formed the template for many people's perceptions of 'the look' of those with HIV/AIDS. They may have friends or acquaintances who are seropositive, but be unaware of this because the person 'looks OK'. At the same time, they may meet people who look very ill and then assume that they have AIDS. This sort of process was evident in the course of some of the focus group discussions. For example, one of the male prostitutes (the only one out of six to do so) protested that he had seen information stating that people with the virus might look perfectly well. However, another young man in the group countered by declaring: 'A guy came up last night, his eyes were all black under there, his face all stinging, his face was all red there, wee scabs, his lips were all scabby . . . they *do* look different!' Because this client's face apparently resembled a photomontage of the press and television images of AIDS, the research participant assumed that he must have the virus. Here we can see how a media representation came to define 'real-life encounters' which, in turn, carry more credibility than might be credited to media images on their own.

Chapters 8 and 9 have examined the operation of both the media and the audiences as they construct the meaning of AIDS. We have demonstrated the importance of the details of media content as well as showing how these details interact with other sources of influence and experience. Together the two chapters point to the need for close attention to the language, images, assumptions, stories and narrative structures and trajectories of AIDS publicity. They also draw attention to the need to consider audience diversity. Our findings support the argument that health promotion strategies should reach beyond straight educational advertisements and explicitly address the racism, sexism and heterosexism within which much of the discussion is embedded. More broadly, the research highlights the potential of complementary strategies (such as peer education and community development) and the necessity for social, legal and political change.

The two chapters also chart some of the potential and the limits of media power. We believe this work challenges some existing media studies theory. In particular, it suggests a need to rethink concepts such as 'reading', 'polysemy' and audience 'resistance'. We conclude with a closer look at these concepts from media theory.

Rethinking 'reading', 'polysemy' and audience resistance

In rethinking terms such as 'reading', 'polysemy' and audience resistance we wish to emphasise four key concerns. First, the term 'reading' needs to be unpacked. This term is commonly used in a way which does not distinguish between interpretation and reaction; yet our research demonstrates that audiences frequently share a common interpretation of the intended meaning of a TV programme or news report, while differing in their reactions. In Hall's work on encoding/decoding he argued: 'It is possible for the reader to decode the message of the photo in a wholly contrary way, either because he does not know the sender's code or because he recognises the code in use but *chooses to employ a different code*' (Hall, 1980, emphasis in original; cited in Corner, 1986: 55). Much work on decoding or 'reading' fails to disentangle different levels of reading – yet such distinctions are crucial both in terms of the meaning of the text and in terms of strategies of resistance. Ignorance of the sender's code is different from the choice to employ a different code. More fundamentally, sometimes people quite simply disbelieve the facts or disagree with the media's interpretation. An intertwined issue is that the polysemy of texts has been exaggerated. Our research shows that diversity in responses cannot be equated with diversity of 'meaning' and, by demonstrating media 'effects', our research challenges the extent of the 'semiotic democracy' celebrated by Fiske (Fiske, 1991; for discussion see also Curran, 1990).

Secondly, it is important to recognise that 'deviant readings' may be as much influenced by *other* media messages to which the individual has been exposed as by some kind of counter-cultural reservoir of alternative perspectives. Observing that people 'resist' or read against the grain of any individual media product does not mean that the media lack power. In any case it is misleading to play off textual power against reader 'freedom' as if the reader came to the text with an independent view. Identity and personal experience are not media-free zones and, as Corner points out: 'Cultural power and ideological reproduction operate as much, if not more, through the social factors bearing upon interpretive action as they do through that "inscribed" in media texts themselves' (Corner, 1991: 271).

Thirdly, our work suggests that the ability to deconstruct media messages and develop a critical reading in a research setting is not necessarily the same as being able to reject the message conveyed via the media on a day-to-day level. Within the focus group discussion there was more frequent evidence of the former than the latter. It was sometimes only within the research setting that people challenged attitudes or facts conveyed by the media which they had previously accepted without question. A key research question is to identify the circumstances which facilitate such challenges but also to examine the extent and limits of these challenges.

This leads us to our final point, which is that a 'resisting' reading is not necessarily the same as a 'progressive' or 'liberated reading'. Audiences may resist or quite simply misunderstand a 'progressive' or 'accurate' message in ways that preserve prejudice and may endanger themselves or others. Audience resistance and 'critical readings' are not something automatically to celebrate (Roscoe et al., 1995). Some audience resistance to AIDS media messages is literally fatal and some 'resistance' involves retaining reactionary stances in the face of the liberal/medical orthodoxy. For all these reasons, evidence that audiences can criticise and deconstruct programmes in research sessions should not be used uncritically as positive evidence of audience 'freedom', 'power' and 'democracy'.

In conclusion, the focus group work reported here took into account what people brought to their understandings of TV and press reporting. It recognised the pleasure people gain from the media, the social currency of different phrases and stories and the way in which media messages are incorporated into day-to-day talk and interact with broader cultural values. It also demonstrated audience diversity and the influence of individuals' own social and political position. The complexity of the reception process means that some messages are interpreted in entirely unexpected ways or rejected altogether, while other messages may be embraced and take on a life of their own (even becoming urban myths). Acknowledging these levels of complexity does not mean we have to desert attempts to theorise about media influence. Media power is certainly not absolute, nor does it exist in a vacuum, and audience reception is not an isolated encounter between an individual and a message. The media do not operate as a single force in a hermetically sealed ideological conspiracy. However, there can be a powerful interaction between media messages and broader contextual assumptions and the media still influence the way we think.

Notes

1. Media studies involve considerable debate about *how* people watch television (see Moores, 1993). Research which focuses on television viewing within the home shows that TV viewers are often not 'viewing' the television at all and that 'watching telly' is combined with a whole range of other activities (Collett and Lamb, 1986; McQuail, 1972). This is often used to signal audience freedom from media domination and control (Fiske, 1991: 73). However, the 'inattentive' viewer may be more rather than less vulnerable to absorbing dominant reiterated themes (headlines, basic themes and repeated concepts). The casual (or evasive) viewer may miss the more subtle or alternative accounts that are inserted into a text.

2. This quote is taken from interviews conducted with young women during 1992. See Kitzinger, 1993b, 1995.

3. The unique strength of the focus group method is the way in which the interaction of research participants both generates, and should be considered as part of, the data (see Kitzinger, 1994a). It was only through close attention to group interaction, dialogue and dynamics that we could identify the importance of 'social currency' (e.g. in jokes about saliva) and peer communication (e.g. around the language of HIV). The group process also allowed observation of the development of collective analysis of shared experience and the impact of certain types of argument (as evident when people changed their minds during the groups). It is important here to be sensitive to the ways in which the 'collective interview' method helps to '*construct* the culture it seeks to describe and understand' (Ang, 1996: 101, emphasis in original).

4. Indeed, the attempt to translate from one to the other has been central to many liberation movements. The women's liberation movement, for example, included the private experience of sexual abuse within the home being transformed through feminist analysis and survivors speaking out (Armstrong, 1994). It also involved the transformation of housewives' common, but isolated, experiences into the shared analysis presented in Betty Friedan's book *The Feminine Mystique* (1963) (see also Bland et al., 1978; Hobson, 1978).

5. The gay or lesbian viewer is often ignored in media theory and cultural studies (for example many studies of 'youth culture' ignore the position of the young gay man or lesbian). However, there are specific issues around sexuality and identity that influence audience reception. On the one hand, as Watney points out, media silence and distortion may be particularly evident to lesbians and gay men because media power and prejudice is 'baldly exposed in the space between our lived experience, and the representations made of us in the media' (Watney, 1987b: 125). On the other hand: 'Because, as gays, we grew up isolated not only from our heterosexual peers but also from each other, we turned to the mass media for information and ideas about ourselves' (Dyer, 1984: 1). The image (and self-image) of gays and lesbians may be particularly vulnerable to the mass media because of certain features of this minority status e.g. routinely growing up within heterosexual families without access to an obvious geographical community or visible way of identifying each other (Gross, 1991).

10

AIDS, the Policy Process and Moral Panics

David Miller and Jenny Kitzinger

In this book we have pointed towards new ways of examining the relationship between promotional strategies, the media, the state and the public. The most developed writing about such relationships has tended to draw on liberal or critical perspectives. The former emphasises the complexity of the bureaucratic process and attempts to achieve official 'balance'; the latter often presents AIDS as a 'moral panic'. It is our view that both approaches have severe limitations. In the next section we will examine each approach in turn.

The liberal approach emphasises the complexities of policy formation in 'pluralist' societies. Writers such as Fox, Day and Klein, for example, see AIDS as simply another unproblematic or positive example of the dominance of medical professionals in policy making around health:

> In each country, some people emphasised moral and emotional issues in the epidemic. But even in the United States, where these groups have been loudest and occasionally effective, policies have been made mainly in response to the opinions of the customary actors in health affairs. (Fox et al., 1989: 93–4)

These authors assume that both moralism and emotion are absent from the main policy-making activities of governments and the opinons of the 'customary actors in health affairs'. We are told that policy response to AIDS in the US, Britain and Sweden has offered many examples of the 'triumph of the ethic of professionalism over the confused and conflicting claims of morality and ideology. Given uncertainty, it has suited everyone to leave AIDS, like most areas of policy, to the professionals' (Fox et al., 1989: 110–11). In a later article, Day and Klein argue, specifically in relation to Britain, that: 'The groping, incremental policy response of the British government was not only a predictable but also entirely rational way of handling the issue' (Day and Klein, 1990: 351). This rational response was to treat AIDS as a 'technical' problem. The technical approaches of the government are seen as simply enlightened, not ideological. Given this, it is not difficult for Day and Klein to recommend the exclusion of popular voices from policy making. According to them AIDS 'provided another illustration perhaps of the fact that liberal public policies on certain emotion laden subjects, like homosexuality and capital punishment, can only be implemented if signals from the public are ignored' (Day and Klein, 1990: 351). Day and Klein provide no evidence on public opinion, simply deducing it from media coverage which, according to them, was of little consequence except as an indication for policy makers and politicians of a potential witch hunt. This, in turn, confirms them in their preference for technical responses.

We reject this analysis. First, policy making is never free of ideology and value commitments; and as we have shown (Chapters 2 and 6), this was definitely not the case with AIDS. Secondly, we agree with Berridge and Strong (1990) that Day and Klein's argument is ahistorical. Berridge and Strong identify a number of phases during which AIDS policy evolved. In particular, they describe a move from a period of official ignorance ('no one knew anything') through a period of relatively open ('bottom up') policy approach to the more usual 'top down' policy process (Berridge and Strong, 1990). Paying attention to these historical shifts is very important, and fits with our third point, which is that the formation of policy on AIDS was a much more dynamic process than Day and Klein allow. The outcome of policy struggles was not determined beforehand, but was the result of negotiation and contest. Day and Klein underestimate the extent to which the values of the liberal/medical policy community were vulnerable to challenge. Our research demonstrates that the activities of gay and AIDS activists, and the media reporting, were important elements in the construction of agendas on policy formation; and in promoting some forms of action and marginalising others. We also found many examples of moral absolutist interventions in the public education campaign (see Chapter 2), the 'main theme' of policy (Day and Klein, 1990: 348).

Day and Klein, and indeed some other writers including Berridge and Strong, underestimate the influence of homophobia. For example, Berridge and Strong challenge the suggestion that the government was slow to respond to the AIDS crisis; and argue that the response to AIDS was, if anything, 'remarkably swift' (1991a: 129). They quote Roy Porter's 'perceptive' comment that 'had AIDS struck middle class heterosexual whites first, it is by no means obvious that the extraordinary hodge-podge of agencies would have dealt with it any better' (Porter, 1988, cited in Berridge and Strong, 1991a: 134). Porter was writing of the US, but Berridge and Strong apply his argument to Britain (Berridge and Strong, 1991b). While agreeing that routine bureaucratic and organisational issues are significant factors, we saw in Chapter 2 that advertising and education campaigns were delayed precisely because of the people who were mostly affected, namely gay men.

Analyses emphasising 'technical' responses neglect contestation and the role of ideology in policy making. Very different analyses come from critical perspectives. These perspectives have tended to stress the concept of 'moral panic'. This concept has been widely used by a variety of authors, and is the main alternative approach in the literature. It gives prominence to 'ideology', but it also neglects contest. Although AIDS activists are involved in the day-to-day practice of identifying points at which they can effectively intervene, this experience seems to be written out of much academic theorising. We argue that reliance on 'moral panic' allows slippage over important theoretical and strategic questions.

A critique of moral panic theory

The term 'moral panic' was coined by Stan Cohen in his influential book *Folk Devils and Moral Panics*, first published in 1972. Cohen argued that inegalitarian social orders created problems for powerless and marginalised sections of society, and then used their rebellion to reinforce the social order via the mechanism of 'moral panic'. He defined a 'moral panic' as follows:

> A condition, episode, person or group of persons emerges to become defined as a threat to societal values and interests: its nature is presented in a stylised and stereotypical fashion by the mass media; the moral barricades are manned by editors, bishops, politicians and other right-thinking people; socially accredited experts pronounce their diagnoses and solutions; ways of coping are evolved or (more often) resorted to. (Cohen, 1972: 9)

Panics are held to function as a mechanism of control by the 'control culture' in which the mass media act as a means of deviancy 'amplification'. This analysis was developed further, and 'politicised' (Harris, 1992) by Stuart Hall and his colleagues in their widely influential book *Policing the Crisis* (Hall et al., 1978; see also Hall, 1988). According to this development the 'moral panic' is

> one of the principal forms of ideological consciousness by means of which a 'silent majority' is won over to the support of increasingly coercive measures on the part of the state, and lends its legitimacy to a 'more than usual' exercise of control. (Hall et al., 1978: 221)

Not all of those who have used the concept of moral panic have done so uncritically. In relation to AIDS, Simon Watney has noted two limitations of the model. The first is that

> the very longevity and continuity of AIDS commentary already presents a problem for 'moral panic' theory, in so far as it is evidently a panic which refuses to go away – a permanent panic, as it were. (Watney, 1994: 8; cf. Rocheron and Linné, 1989: 411–12)

The concept, according to Watney, 'obscures the endless "overhead" narrative of such phenomena as one panic gives way to another, and different panics overlap and reinforce one another' (1994: 9). Furthermore 'classical' moral panic theory

> interprets representations of specific 'scandals' as events which appear and then disappear, having run their ideological course. Such a view makes it difficult to

theorise representation as a site of *permanent* ideological struggle and contestation between rival pictures of the world. (1994: 10)

A second and related problem is that viewing AIDS as a discrete moral panic invites us to ignore the historical processes which have constituted contemporary dominant notions of homosexuality. As Watney puts it: 'it is thus particularly unhelpful to think of AIDS commentary as a moral panic which somehow makes gay men into monsters, since that is an intrinsic effect of the medicalisation of morality which accompanied the emergence of the modern categories of sexuality in the course of the last 200 years' (Watney, 1994: 12). However, Watney did argue that the concept had descriptive usefulness, as have other theorists including Weeks (1993), Altman (1986), and even Rocheron and Linné (1989: 430) and Dickinson (1989) who are more critical of moral panic theory than the rest.

A further, and widely noted, limitation of the concept of moral panic is that, as Cohen himself observed, it becomes difficult to explain how panics subside. Within the sequence of events said to define a moral panic 'no readily available explanation exists as to how and why the sequence ever ends' (Cohen, 1972: 198). Cohen's own answer was that there was 'a lack of interest' from the public and the mass media. Interest would wane once it was felt that 'something is being done about it' (1972: 200). In the variant elaborated by Hall and his colleagues, this problem is compounded by their notion of a 'more than usual' exercise of control. When *Policing the Crisis* was being written there was abundant evidence of the drift to a 'law and order' society (under, it should be remembered, a Labour government). However, the problem with the theorising in *Policing the Crisis* is the lack of any indication of a mechanism by which the degree of control could be lessened. If the state was able to secure a 'more than usual' level of control in the 1970s, then are we now in a period where it is able to secure 'much more than usual' control? If not, the question is how did we get back to 'usual' or 'normal'? Asking this question raises further questions such as: What is the usual level of control in advanced capitalist societies? How do panics decline, and how were the coercive measures rolled back?

In fact the key problem is the lack of a theory about the mechanisms by which society changes at all, except as dictated by the state, or the more nebulous 'structure' of society. The most serious flaw of the concept of moral panic, especially in the variant developed by Hall, is its lack of agency. It is never very clear who is doing the panicking. Is it the media, the government, the public, or who? (cf. Barker, 1992). One reason for this lack of clarity is that distinctions between the media and the state, between the media and public belief, and between the state and other social institutions and groups are dissolved into Cohen's notion of the 'control culture'.

We can examine these limitations specifically in relation to AIDS. If there was a 'moral panic' about AIDS then we would expect to find all the following four processes in operation. First, AIDS is presented in a 'stylised and stereotypical fashion by the mass media'. Secondly, 'the moral barricades are manned by editors, bishops, politicians and other right thinking people'. Thirdly, a 'silent majority' of public opinion is won over (Hall et al.). Fourthly, 'ways of coping are evolved or resorted to' (Cohen), or 'increasingly coercive measures on the part of the state' are legitimised (Hall et al.).

Our research suggests that none of these four processes can be said to have occurred straightforwardly in response to AIDS. There is also no necessary causal connection between the four in the process of a 'moral panic'. Let us examine each of these components of 'moral panic' theory in turn.

Stylised and stereotypical coverage in the mass media

The predominant view in social science and media studies on the media response to AIDS has been that the media have stigmatised people with HIV, distinguished between innocent and guilty victims, promoted homophobia, and/or been dependent on official medical and political sources. Coverage of HIV/AIDS is characterised by many authors as almost universally limited and distorted. Some see this as emerging from media values that promote sensationalism or irresponsibility (e.g. Albert, 1986; Wellings, 1988). Other authors view the problem as a more all-embracing 'homophobia', in which gay men and people with HIV or AIDS get nothing but negative coverage.

There have certainly been many examples of stylised and sterotypical media reporting; and we would agree that much coverage has been characterised by sensationalism, inaccuracy and homophobia. However, critiques of such reporting have tended to collapse distinctions between views which emanate from distinct political pedigrees (cf. Hallett and Cannella, 1994), overemphasise the frequency of negative coverage, overlook possibilities of 'positive' coverage, and ignore variation in reporting. For example, there were many stories in the broadsheet press, discussions on documentary programmes and even reports in the tabloids, in 1986–87 in which the government was urged into action (see Chapters 3, 4 and 5). This strand of coverage is missing from the analysis of most writing in the area, and many writers ignore (or explicitly deny) distinctions between different media. Simon Watney, for example, argued that the first five years of reporting on the AIDS epidemic showed that:

> British TV and press coverage is locked into an agenda which blocks out any approach to the subject which does not conform in advance to the values and language of a profoundly homophobic culture – a culture, that is, which does not regard gay men as fully or properly human. No distinction obtains for this agenda between 'quality' and 'tabloid' newspapers, or between 'popular' and 'serious' television. (Watney, 1988a: 52)[1]

Such analyses obscure the achievements of gay men, for example, working both within and outside the media. They also disregard differences between reports (and among diverse media outlets) which it is strategically important to understand.

Moral barricades – sources of AIDS news

It is certainly true that the moral barricades have been manned (and 'womanned') by 'right-thinking people'. Yet, such explicitly 'moral' activists did not have a monopoly on the media. Indeed, as we argued in Chapters 3 and 4, moral absolutist voices in the media were not usually privileged, even in the tabloid press, although they did excite considerable comment across the media. Furthermore, the sources routinely used by journalists working for national newspapers or television news were predominantly scientists and doctors, government ministers, or AIDS charities such as the Terrence Higgins Trust. This suggests that the promotional activities of groups such as the Conservative Family Campaign were less than straightforwardly successful in gaining media attention or sympathetic coverage.

The power and influence of the moral right has been exaggerated by some commentators.[2] Weeks and others have asserted that 'a moral counter-revolution has always been close to the heart of Thatcherism' (Weeks, 1988); and that moral concerns represent part of the Thatcher government's 'ideological commitments' (Weeks, 1989b: 129). However, such arguments fail to recognise the 'vast gap between rhetoric and reality' (Durham, 1989: 70). As Martin Durham has argued:

> The Thatcher government has moved only partially in a 'moral Right' direction. On many issues that concern organisations such as the Conservative Family Campaign, the government has been reticent or even antagonistic, and its taking up of Clause 28 (and other initiatives) falls far short of what 'the moral Right' desire. (Durham, 1989: 70–1)

On AIDS this has meant that: 'Despite what we might expect [the government] has not used AIDS in order to enforce a traditionalist moral stance' (Durham, 1991: 130). In general: 'Where medical health or scientific research was involved, then the Thatcher government was likely to harken to the advice of its civil servants, the British Medical Association or scientific bodies' (Durham, 1991: 140).

Clearly, the moral right have had some sympathy at the very highest levels of government, and have had an impact on particular policy decisions or advertising campaigns (as we saw in Chapter 2). Nevertheless, we should be clear about the differences between such perspectives and both government policy and medical responses to AIDS. As Durham writes:

> It is vital to disentangle the New Right and Thatcherism. Thatcherism as a particular combination of neo-conservative and neo-liberal themes was only one (albeit the major) element in the New Right. In addition, Thatcherism, whether in opposition or, even more, in power, operated under circumstances that make the consistent pursuit of an ideological project impossible. The government included

non-Thatcherites, it had to negotiate its way through both the Civil Service and civil society, it was buffeted by public opinion, economic shifts, international tensions. It is distinctly unhelpful to amalgamate the New Right, Thatcherism and the Thatcher government into one identical object (let alone combine them with moral crusades as well). (Durham, 1991: 139–40; for more on this see Durham, 1991: especially 140–2 and Chapters 8 and 9)

Is the public reactionary?

The 'silent majority', which is supposedly won over to consent for increased repression during a moral panic, is also problematic. The assumption of moral panic theorists such as Cohen and Hall is that the public endorses reactionary social change as a result of the manipulation of the media by the state. Yet in the case of AIDS it is not at all clear that public opinion in general was in favour of some of the more draconian suggestions made by Conservative backbenchers, police officers or other moral absolutist activists (such as Green, 1992). Nor was it clear in the case of mugging in the 1970s or beach battles in the 1960s. Similarly the extent to which public opinion simply reflects the content of media reporting is nowhere directly examined. Instead, public beliefs are simply 'read off' from an analysis of news coverage. Public opinion may or may not follow the lines suggested (Chapters 8 and 9). In the case of AIDS our work *does* provide evidence of some causal links. It does this through thorough empirical exploration. The point is that moral panic theory as a *model* actually disregards and inhibits empirical investigation of the impact of the media on public belief and opinions.

There is a further problem in that the legitimation of reactionary social or legislative change by the 'control culture', the state or the moral right is assumed necessarily to include winning over at least some elements of popular opinion. Certainly Hall and his colleagues in their interpretation of Gramsci, and their theorising about hegemony, place a great deal of importance on the winning of the consent of the governed for reactionary policies. Yet we would question the extent to which reactionary (or indeed progressive) social, political or legislative social change does in fact rely on popular support, consent or even indifference. State actions can *sometimes* be constrained by lack of consent *when opposition is mobilised*, as the case of the poll tax shows (Deacon and Golding, 1993). However, if the state always relied on public legitimation before acting, there would be precious little legislation in an average year.[3] Conversely, there are examples where overwhelming popular support for particular measures exists but is not transformed into legislative or other changes. There is then no straightforward relationship between public opinion and social control. Instead of assuming such a relationship, the task of social science should be to examine influences on public opinion and belief and, in turn, to investigate the influence of public opinion (or indeed *representations* of public opinion) on policy formulation and the wider structures of society.

There is one further adaptation of the concept which is worth noting here. Jeffery Weeks was one of the first social scientists to apply moral panic theory to the AIDS crisis in his 1985 book *Sexuality and its Discontents*. Although this was written before the major governmental response to AIDS in Britain, and before Watney's critique of moral panic (Watney, 1987b, 1988a), subsequent events have not led him to abandon the concept. Thus, in an essay, published in 1993, Weeks argues that although there are some problems, the concept still retains a certain descriptive usefulness 'as a helpful heuristic device' (Weeks, 1993: 25). In particular, after noting some limitations, he describes the societal reaction to AIDS between 1983 and 1986 as a period of moral panic 'not least because a perception of how the public was reacting determined the responses both of the community most affected, and of the government' (Weeks, 1993: 27). Our analysis certainly confirms this. However, the key caveat in Weeks's statement is that it was *perceptions* of public reaction rather than systematic information about actual public responses that guided policy responses. If it is only perceptions of public opinion which might be important, then this is a radical problem for the concept of moral panic.

The state and the legitimisation of repression

Next we turn to the question of results of the panic. Has the advent of the AIDS crisis and the accompanying media coverage resulted in a 'more than usual' exercise of control by the state? It is clear that there were some increases in state control in this area between 1980 and 1995, such as Clause 28 (although some commentators have concluded that Clause 28 did not have the extensive impact feared by many: Evans, 1989). However, there have also been changes which appear to be in the opposite direction, such as the lowering of the age of consent for gay men to the (albeit still discriminatory) age of 18. Similarly, there were, especially in the pre-1987 period, many examples of what might be described as panic reactions to HIV and AIDS; and there is ample evidence that gay men in general (and sometimes lesbians too) suffered discrimination, hostility, stigmatisation and violence which can be attributed to, or were legitimised by, public debates on AIDS. Attacks on gay men increased in this period, and violence and discrimination against drug users and sex workers also rose (Social Services Committee, 1987a, 1987b, 1987c).

However, it is an oversimplification to suggest that such responses were carried out (or deliberately inspired by) the state, or even the 'control culture', although it can be argued that it was the absence of state action which allowed the phase of 'panic' to continue. Furthermore, it is not at all clear that the status of gay men (or even injecting users of illegal drugs) in society has declined as a result. Indeed, Denis Altman (1988) has argued that the impact of AIDS on gay men as a social constituency amounted to 'legitimation through disaster'. In the US, as Altman has noted, 'the conservative Reagan administration has had more contacts with organised gay groups than any of its predecessors, largely because of AIDS' (Altman, 1988: 302). Similarly in Britain, AIDS and gay organisations have been consulted and funded by central government; also a first. The evolution of AIDS policy in Britain has been slow, painful and in many respects problematic. Nevertheless, the state, rather than successfully legitimising repression, has largely moved in the opposite direction; albeit hedging such changes with all sorts of conditions, reversals and contradictions.

Finally, on panics

The term 'moral panic' has sprung from the pages of social scientific texts and become a buzzword for the media. It is used to describe a whole range of controversies, depending on the writer's desire to validate or dismiss the apparent threat. One hears the concept applied to anything from single mothers to working mothers, from guns to Ecstasy, and from pornography on the Internet to the dangers of state censorship. Part of its attraction for some media is that it explains away the reporting of tabloid papers and 'right thinking people' as irrational, not the sort of thing that could fool educated liberals and the readers of the *Guardian* or *Independent*. To be sure, the popular use of the term in the media involves something of a simplification and distortion of its usage in the original sociological studies. Especially in the work of Hall et al. (1978), there is an implication that such panics are in fact in the interests of the panickers, or at least of those who whip up the panics. Nevertheless, there is a sense in which the term moral panic, in its proper usage, necessarily conjures up the irrational: it is as if the panic (of the tabloid papers, conservative backbenchers or the public) was an involuntary 'moral frisson' (Mort, 1987: 214) over which conscious control was difficult. The subject of the panic is also seen as non-existent, or at least as exaggerated. It might be objected that the term is not meant to refer to individual states of consciousness or panic, but is intended as a collective term to describe a kind of societal psychology. However, this interpretation would also be vulnerable to the charge of labelling processes of social control as irrational.

Part of the original impulse behind the work of Cohen and his followers was a desire to portray the behaviour and culture of stigmatised and powerless groups as rational responses to inequality in contemporary capitalism. Mods and Rockers were not 'mindless hooligans', but engaged in ritual or stylistic rebellions. It is ironic, then, that the term is now often used in ways which implicitly present the process by which powerless groups become stigmatised (and further marginalised) as irrational and closed to serious sociological study.

The moral panic model assumes a straightforward relationship between state interests, media content and public opinion, in which the media circulate reactionary social wisdom, the public believe it, and the state is then able to secure consent for its actions. This is, despite the protestations of some moral panic theorists, a very instrumental model of the role of the media in supporting a dominant ideology and securing hegemony. It leaves out a series of important possibilities for investigating, theorising and intervening in the process of 'panic'. If reaction to AIDS is or was a 'moral panic', then it was a moral panic *manqué*; and the reasons behind the failure of the moral panic or the success of resistance need to be examined. It is this which our study has attempted to achieve.

Notes

1. Five years later Watney had slightly modified his argument:

For the better part of a decade, AIDS coverage across the mass media has consistently positioned readers and viewers alike in contradictory ways, implying that they both *are* and *are not* at risk. This is the context in which gay men appear as threatening rather than threatened, and in need of punitive control rather than support. However, this agenda has not been established without some resistance, and several attempts have been made over the years to 'de-sensationalise' the coverage of the epidemic, both in the press and on network TV. Nonetheless, most coverage continues to regard gay men as if they were members of a uniform culture, with a shared 'gay lifestyle' and identical sexual needs. We appear simultaneously as villains and as victims, but never as a social constituency facing the worst natural disaster in the history of any minority group within many Western societies. (Watney, 1992: 153–4)

2. Neil Small has explicitly counselled us to recognise 'the power of the "moral right". Harsher forms of control have not been far from achieving support that would ensure their implementation. When one has to rely on the "balance" of the Secretary of State to hold back absolutist explanations and remedies suggested by his back benchers then no one can feel secure' (Small, 1988: 27). As well as being an extraordinarily individualistic model of politics (policies decided on the whim of the Secretary of State), this underestimates both the monolith of the British civil service and policy-making machinery and overestimates the power of backbench Conservative moralists. The reason that successive Conservative secretaries of state for health, whatever their own views, have not taken the road suggested by moral conservative groups, has little to do with them possessing a high degree of 'balance' and more to do with the atmosphere and ethos of the policy community surrounding them. This confusion about the relationship in New Right thinking between the free market and morality runs through much of the debate on Thatcherism (see Hall and Jacques, 1983; Hall, 1988).

3. Here we agree with Abercrombie et al. in *The Dominant Ideology Thesis* (1980) and in *Dominant Ideologies* (1990), that there has been a tendency to overemphasise the role of ideology in assuring the reproduction of capitalism. However, governments and others do expend considerable ideological labour in legitimising particular policies and actions. This does not mean that they are always successful, or that success requires that the entire working class believes the latest piece of propaganda. But there are times when significant numbers of people do believe information which has originated with one section or another of dominant groups, which is intended to support the interests of those groups and which is misleading, ideological or simply false. Sometimes this is important in legitimising particular actions and at other times the belief of the public will be simply irrelevant to the state's ability to carry out a particular act. Either way, there is a clear case for the empirical examination of the circulation of information in society and an assessment of its consequences. (For a longer critique of *The Dominant Ideology Thesis* see Miller, 1997.)

11

Conclusion

Jenny Kitzinger and David Miller

The mass media play a central role in the reproduction and transformation of contemporary society. The study of the media ought, therefore, to be central to the study of society. Yet, the role of the media is neglected or oversimplified in mainstream sociology. At the same time, the disciplines of media and cultural studies often discuss cultural products without much attention to broader configurations of power in society as a whole. Contemporary media/cultural studies has increasingly concentrated on the 'politics of consumption' or the power of 'discourses' while sidelining questions about media impact and ignoring the political movements and pressure groups which seek to influence public debate and representations.

The research findings reported in this book place the media back at the centre of debate about the reproduction and transformation of societies. Our work highlights the *limitations* of viewing the media as a discrete topic of enquiry and the *importance* of examining how the media are fundamentally enmeshed in the societies in which they operate. At one end of the process we have the priorities of interest groups, corporate capital and government which centrally involve public relations and promotional struggle. At the other end we have questions of public belief and opinion and their impact (and that of the media) on public behaviour, policy decisions, culture and society. In the middle, of course, are the interests and strategies of media corporations and their own processes of production. It is our view that all of these processes and their interactions need to be examined together if the role of the media is to be properly understood. This means examining promotional politics, information campaigns, mass media production, content, audience responses and policy impacts.

Promotional politics

Our research on HIV/AIDS demonstrates the increased centrality of promotional politics and public relations strategies to interest groups and other organisations. It emphasises the centrality of the institutions of the state both in terms of their superior promotional resources and in their ability to manage media agendas. But it also demonstrates that definitions of social issues do not simply emerge from the centres of political power. Campaigners did manage to influence the production and circulation of definitions around AIDS. In addition, the media can themselves contribute to modifying the definitions of the powerful. Most importantly, we have suggested that the construction of 'primary' definitions in the media may not necessarily set the terms for policy decisions. As we saw in the discussion of the health education campaign (Chapter 2), the ability of ministers or others to intervene in the production process was sometimes quite independent of the dominant definitions carried in the media. Nevertheless, promotional strategies do routinely incorporate attempts to manage the media and the media remain important in the policy process.

Information campaigns

The AIDS public education campaign was itself a promotional strategy. But it was one in which media products were also created (advertising, leaflets, etc.). The literature on information campaigns tends to concentrate on analysis of content or on evaluation of success in persuasive aims. Our work also examined the campaign from the point of view of those involved with it. It seems to us that this gives a better picture of the aims, intentions and strategies of the producers than reliance on analysing content or evaluating impact alone. Our own study emphasised the fraught process which spawned the AIDS public education campaign rather than the technical models which are prevalent in the literature.

Media production

Struggle and dissent within media hierarchies around the representation of AIDS replicated the struggle in the wider public sphere. The struggles within the media were not random or individual, but were socially structured according to the constraints of differing media formats, development and variations in specialist beats within journalism, editorial priorities and power. There is a continuing need for studies of media production, not simply because of changes in the media environment, but because it varies according to the subject matter, the sources and journalists involved. What is important is not the generalities of media production (although these exist) but the specifics which explain the different profiles, trajectories and evaluations of specific social issues in their political and social context.

Representation

There are two identifiable approaches which are often taken to be mutually inconsistent in the analysis of media content. The first of these might be described as 'ideological analysis', which attempts to demonstrate the relative closure of media texts, or, at least, to provide a critique of problematic media reporting. The second type of approach looks for variation in media coverage and attempts to explain this. These approaches can be interpreted as demonstrations of the relative closure or openness of media texts and are not necessarily opposed to each other. Resolving the apparent differences depends on some sophistication in the analysis of meaning (the sort of analysis of AIDS representation often evident among those coming from a critical perspective). However, it also requires some element of quantification which can identify dominant trends. Our analysis suggests that many of the negative features identified by critical analysis were widely available, but were not necessarily dominant. Our own conclusion was that, notwithstanding the variation between and within media, the predominant approach of the news and entertainment media was to promote the liberal/ medical orthodoxy.

Audience reception

Our research has also attempted to reopen debate about media 'effects'. In the last ten years audience research has increasingly focused on exploring why people watch what they do (choices in consumption and sources of pleasure) and how they actually consume (e.g. how they incorporate television viewing into daily lives). It has also increasingly concentrated on the different 'readings' diverse audiences may take from the same programme or newspaper article. These 'new' questions are often set up in opposition to 'old-fashioned' effects research which concentrated on how the media impacts upon audiences (how it influences their attitudes and beliefs). This shift of emphasis has produced a problem within contemporary media studies. We agree with John Corner (1991: 267) that the question of media power as a political issue has slipped almost entirely off the main research agenda: 'so much effort has been centred on audiences' interpretative activity that even the preliminary theorization of influence has become awkward'.

We argue that it is possible to consider audience pleasure, and to examine audiences' identities and 'active' processing of media messages while also empirically exploring media 'effects'. This is what we attempted to do in the focus group discussions about AIDS. In the light of our research it would seem that some of the most common terms used within contemporary media theory blur crucial reception processes and overemphasise audience autonomy. In particular we think that terms such as 'reading', 'active consumption' and 'polysemy' need to be clarified or challenged and there is an urgent need to reconsider the implications of audience 'resistance' (see Chapter 9).

Media impacts on policy

Finally, media impacts on public attitudes and on culture more generally are also complemented by impacts on policy makers. Our research supports the argument that the media played a 'critical role both in generating a growing sense of crisis and in focusing on issues with which the government and their advisors had to deal' (Berridge and Strong, 1990: 247). Furthermore we agree that 'the net effect of press and TV attention was to establish a climate of opinion which required government action or gestures of action' (Greenaway et al., 1992: 87). However, we have also argued that the media had a reactionary impact on some elements of public opinion in some periods, increasing homophobia for example. Furthermore, seemingly contradictory effects such as these are in fact simply an index of the complexity of struggles in contemporary society.

The making of policy can be conceived as the end of the process in which the media plays a part. But it is necessary to remember that new decisions alter the political landscape and so alter the planning of promotional strategies, media coverage and public opinion. It is this never ceasing spiral of promotional politics which helps to constitute and reproduce contemporary power relations. If we are to understand them, and to intervene in them, it is necessary constantly to be open to changes in promotional culture and anchor our understanding of such changes in specific cases.

We wish to conclude by drawing attention to the implications of our research for health promotion strategies. The work reported here highlights the need for holistic approaches which combines imaginative development of advertisements with a broader mass media strategy and engagement with the production of health promotion strategies as well as the socio-political and economic context of health and illness.

Health promotion strategies

Although public 'misunderstanding' or 'failure to respond' are often seen as the core challenge for health educators our research suggests that this places the emphasis in the wrong place. Not only are such concepts misleading but it is evident that at least equal attention should be given to problems at the level of production. Compromise and tensions during the development of AIDS campaigns resulted in contradictory, confusing, incomplete and vague health education messages. In particular, AIDS campaigns were undermined by ministerial intervention and, on occasion, the (presumed) implications of laws against the 'promotion' of homosexuality. Section 28 urgently needs to be abolished and, more broadly, we believe that ministerial intervention should be institutionally distanced from the production of public information materials.

More generally, the history of AIDS health education draws attention to the importance of continuing to develop alternative ways of pre-testing and designing advertisements. These alternative approaches need actively to challenge (rather than simply reflect) existing cultural attitudes and move beyond the traditional models used for marketing consumer products (e.g. depending on 'impact', fear arousal or traditional notions of feminine and masculine 'sexiness'). It is also important to continue to be aware of the wider mass media context which may overwhelm or subvert the messages (see Chapter 9). In addition, attention to a *range* of potential audiences (not just the target audience) is crucial. In the case of AIDS, for example, health education campaigns often disregarded (and negatively portrayed) the HIV positive audience and the 'liberal' approach failed to challenge the divide between the 'general population' and 'risk groups'. Our research confirms the importance of outreach work, multi-media approaches, 'narrowcasting' (as well as broadcasting) and strategies which recognise the role played by identity and community as well as peer communication.

However, information alone is not enough: the practical as well as ideological limitations on people's ability to act must be considered. The provision of services (from needle-exchanges to community centres) is crucial. Health promotion can also only have limited success without parallel anti-discrimination strategies and attempts to address the broader socio-political and legal context.

The power and persistence of particular images and misunderstandings in the public imagination (such as the Face-of-AIDS discussed in Chapter 8) and their ability to undermine health education messages lie not only in the media representation. They are also rooted in the social structure of personal experience – and specifically in the segregation and closeting of people with HIV infection and AIDS. This means that attempts to transform public understandings need to include measures to protect the human rights of people with the virus (and those in traditional 'high risk' groups). Stigma, discrimination and legal sanctions against minority groups have aided and abetted the spread of HIV. The ongoing struggle against AIDS requires resources and political will. It also requires a vision that encompasses the politics of AIDS as a medically defined syndrome, a media event, a site of political, medical and scientific conflict, an international crisis and a personal and community experience.

Appendix: A Note on Method and Sample

Promotional strategies and media production

Our analysis of the production of the government campaign on AIDS, of promotional strategies, of journalistic and fiction production is based on 106 interviews and many more conversations and exchanges. Our interviewees were chosen to reflect the wide range of occupational, professional and political groupings involved in constructing health education materials, factual and fictional coverage (some interviewees were involved in more than one area). These comprised administrative civil servants, medical officials and information officers from the Department of Health and Social Security/Department of Health, Central Office of Information and the Northern Ireland Department of Health and Social Services; health education personnel (including public relations and advertising professionals) in the Health Education Authority, Health Promotion Authority of Wales and Health Education Board for Scotland. We also spoke to advertisers and market researchers (from companies involved in the campaign); members of non-government organisations and pressure groups (including moral right groups, professional groups such as the BMA, voluntary organisations such as Terrence Higgins Trust, and activist groups such as OutRage!) as well as clinicians dealing with AIDS. Finally, the study included interviews with a wide range of journalists and television personnel (concentrating on the specialist journalists who cover AIDS as part of their brief, but also examining the perspectives of news editors, sub-editors, script editors, TV producers, directors and executives). Only two of the people we approached refused to be interviewed. We also obtained press releases together with internal, unpublished and confidential documentation from some of these organisations and a variety of other sources.

Media content

The sample of press and television coverage on which Chapters 3 and 4 are based was composed of two samples of all press coverage of HIV and AIDS in British national daily and Sunday newspapers between 1 November 1986 and 31 March 1987, a total of 17 months including 1,736 items and between 1 November 1988 and 31 August 1991, a total of 34 months including 4,147 items. We also examined Scottish press reporting (in the *Scotsman*, the *Glasgow Herald*, the *Daily Record* and the Glasgow *Evening Times*) between 1 November 1988 and 30 April 1990.

We examined television news coverage (the early evening and main nightly news programmes on each of the four channels) from 1 October 1986 to 30 April 1990, a period totalling 3 years 7 months including 317 bulletins. Our sample includes the early evening and main nightly news programmes on each of the four channels (ITN *News at 5.45*, BBC1 *Six O'Clock News*, *Channel Four News*, BBC1 *Nine O'Clock News*, ITN *News at Ten* and BBC2 *Newsnight*).

The analysis of non-news programmes in Chapter 5 was based on the archival records of the broadcasters, from which we calculated the number and form of non-news programmes on AIDS between 1983 and 1990. We then built up an archive of more than 70% of these programmes from which we chose a small representative sample of programme forms for more detailed analysis.

Audience reception analysis

The aim of our audience research was to explore what people bring to their understandings of mass media messages and how social interaction may mediate such understandings. We therefore elected to study pre-existing groups (those who already lived, worked or socialised together) rather than drawing individuals together for the purposes of the research. We used the technique of focus group discussion. We conducted discussions with 52 groups (351 individuals).

Table A.1   *The range of people who participated in the study*

Group	No. of groups of this type	Total no. of participants in these groups
I. People with some occupational interest, involvement or responsibility		
Doctors	1	4
Nurses/health visitors	1	6
Social workers	1	4
Drug workers	1	5
SACRO* workers	1	3
Police staff	2	16
Prison staff	5	32
Teachers	1	5
African journalists	1	4
Community council workers	1	3
II. People targeted as 'high risk groups' by the media or with some special knowledge of, or political involvement in, the issue		
Male prostitutes	2	6
Gay men	2	9
Lesbians	2	6
Family of a gay man	1	4
Prisoners	5	28
Clients of NACRO† and SACRO	4	27
Clients in drug rehabilitation centre	1	7
Young people in intermediate treatment	1	5
III. People who, as a group, had no obvious special interest or involvement in the issue		
Retired people	3	25
Women living on the same Glasgow estate	1	4
School students	3	26
Women with children attending play group	2	14
Engineers	2	18
Round Table group	1	14
American students	1	25
Office janitors	1	7
Market researchers	1	3
Office cleaners	1	4
British college students (England, Scotland and Wales)	3	37
Total no. of all groups	52	
Total no. of participants in all groups		351

* Scottish Association for the Care and Resettlement of Offenders.
† National Association for the Care and Resettlement of Offenders.

Since we wished to explore the diversity of possible audience understandings of AIDS media messages, we selected a range of audience 'types'. Some groups were chosen because they might be expected to have particular perspectives on AIDS (e.g. doctors, male prostitutes, lesbians); others because, as a group, they were not necessarily expected to have any particular interest in AIDS (e.g. women living on a Scottish housing estate, civil engineers working in a London office and people attending a club for retired people). See Table A.1 for a description of the groups.

Research participants were requested to join in a tape-recorded focused discussion, to fill in three separate questionnaires, and to complete a series of group exercises. The main exercise was 'the script writing exercise', a technique in which group members used a set of photographs to construct a TV news bulletin about AIDS (see Kitzinger, 1993a). Most of the groups also played 'the card game', during which they debated a set of statements about 'who is at risk from HIV', taken from the British Social Attitudes Survey (Brook, 1988). Half the groups also completed 'the advertisement exercise', in which they were presented with an advertisement in a step-by-step manner, and asked to reconstruct and comment on the message.

References

Abercrombie, Nicholas, Hill, Stephen and Turner, Bryan S. (1980) *The Dominant Ideology Thesis*. London: George Allen and Unwin.

Abercrombie, Nicholas, Hill, Stephen and Turner, Bryan S. (eds) (1990) *Dominant Ideologies*. London: Unwin Hyman.

Acheson, Donald (1992) 'Behold a pale horse: a view from Whitehall', *PHLS Microbiology Digest*, 10(3): 133–40.

Acheson, Donald (1994) 'Foreword', in Wellings, Kaye, Field, Julia, Johnson, Anne M. and Wadsworth, Jane *Sexual Behaviour in Britain*. Harmondsworth: Penguin.

ACT UP/NY Women and AIDS Book Group (1990) *Women, AIDS and Activism*. Boston: South End Press.

Adams, Jad (1989) *AIDS: The HIV Myth*. London: Macmillan.

Albert, Edward (1986) 'Acquired Immune Deficiency Syndrome: the victim and the press', *Studies in Communications*, 3: 135–58.

Alcorn, Keith (1989) 'AIDS in the public sphere: how a broadcasting system in crisis dealt with an epidemic', in Carter, Erica and Watney, Simon (eds) *Taking Liberties: AIDS and Cultural Politics*. London: Serpents Tail, in association with the ICA.

Alexander, Priscilla (1988) 'Prostitutes are being scapegoated for heterosexual AIDS', in Delacoste, Frederique and Alexander, Priscilla (eds) *Sex Work*. London: Virago. pp. 248–63.

Altman, Denis (1986) *AIDS and the New Puritanism*. London: Pluto.

Altman, Denis (1988) 'Legitimation through disaster', in Fee, E. and Fox, D. (eds) *AIDS: The Burdens of History*. Berkeley: University of California Press.

Altman, Lawrence K. (1988) 'The press and AIDS', *Bulletin of the New York Academy of Medicine*, 64(6) July–August: 520–8.

Amis, Martin (1987) 'Double jeopardy: making sense of AIDS', in *The Moronic Inferno*. Harmondsworth: Penguin.

Ang, Ien (1996) *Living Room Wars: Rethinking Media Audiences for a Postmodern World*. London: Routledge.

Armitage, Gary, Dickey, Julienne and Sharples, Sue (1987) *Out of the Gutter: A Survey of the Treatment of Homosexuality by the Press*. London: Campaign for Press and Broadcasting Freedom.

Armstrong, Louise (1994) *Rocking the Cradle of Sexual Politics: What Happened when Women Said Incest*. New York: Addison-Wesley.

Ascherson, Neal (1993) 'Wilful ignorance on AIDS is a relic of Thatcherism', *Independent on Sunday*, 23 May: 25.

Baker, Andrea J. (1986) 'The portrayal of AIDS in the media: an analysis of articles in the *New York Times*', in Feldman, D.A. and Johnson, T.M. (eds) *Social Dimensions of AIDS – Method and Theory*. New York: Praeger.

Baker, K. (1993) *The Turbulent Years: My Life in Politics*. London: Faber and Faber.

Barker, Martin (1992) 'Stuart Hall, *Policing the Crisis*', in Barker, M. and Beezer, A. (eds) *Reading into Cultural Studies*. London: Routledge. pp. 81–100.

Barry, Andrew (1993) 'Television, truth and democracy', *Media, Culture and Society*, 15: 487–96.

Beharrell, Peter (1993) 'AIDS and the British press', in Eldridge, John (ed.) *Getting the Message*. London: Routledge. pp. 210–49.

Berridge, Virginia (1992) 'AIDS, the media and health policy', in Aggleton, P., Davies, P. and Hart, G. (eds) *AIDS: Rights, Risk and Reason*. London: Falmer. pp. 13–27.

Berridge, Virginia (1996) *AIDS in the UK: The Making of Policy, 1981–1994*. Oxford: Oxford University Press.

Berridge, Virginia and Strong, Philip (1990) 'No one knew anything: some issues in British AIDS policy', in Aggleton, P., Davies, P. and Hart, G. (eds) *AIDS: Individual, Cultural and Policy Dimensions*. London: Falmer. pp. 233–52.

Berridge, Virginia and Strong, Philip (1991a) 'AIDS and the relevance of history', *Social History of Medicine*, 4(1): 129–38.

Berridge, Virginia and Strong, Philip (1991b) 'AIDS in the UK: contemporary history and the study of policy', *Twentieth Century British History*, 2(2): 150–74.

Berridge, Virginia and Strong, Philip (eds) (1993) *AIDS and Contemporary History*. Cambridge: Cambridge University Press.

Bland, Lucy, Brunsdon, Charlotte, Hobson, Dorothy and Winship, Janice (1978) 'Women "inside and outside" the relations of production', in Women's Studies Group Centre for Contemporary Cultural Studies, *Women Take Issue: Aspects of Women's Subordination*. London: Hutchinson University Library. pp. 35–78.

Boase, Massimi, Pollit (1988) *BMP/HEA Total Communication Package*, 25 August.

Boffin, Tessa and Gupta, Sunil (eds) (1990) *Ecstatic Antibodies: Resisting the AIDS Mythology*. London: Rivers Oram Press.

Brandt, Allan (1987) *No Magic Bullet: A Social History of Venereal Disease in the United States since 1880*, expanded edn. New York: Oxford University Press.

Brindle, David (1989a) 'Community health projects become a bone of contention', *Guardian*, 16 May.

Brindle, David (1989b) 'Controversy clouds future', *Guardian*, 6 December: 25.

Brook, L. (1988) 'The public's response to AIDS', in Jowell, R., Witherspoon, S. and Brook, L. (eds) *British Social Attitudes, the 5th Report*. Aldershot: Gower. pp. 71–91.

Bruck, Peter (1989) 'Strategies for peace, strategies for news research', *Journal of Communication*, 39(1) Winter: 108–29.

Bruck, Peter and Raboy, Marc (1989) 'The challenge of democratic communication', in Raboy, M. and Bruck, P. (eds) *Communication For and Against Democracy*. Montreal: Black Rose Books.

Buckingham, David (1987) *Public Secrets: 'EastEnders' and its Audience*. London: BFI Books.

Carter, Erica and Watney, Simon (eds) (1989) *Taking Liberties: AIDS and Cultural Politics*. London: Serpents Tail.

Carter, George (1992) *ACT UP, the AIDS War and Activism*, Open Magazine Pamphlet Series. Westfield, NJ: Open Media, No. 15, January.

Check, William (1987) 'Beyond the political model of reporting: non-specific symptoms in media communication about AIDS', *Reviews of Infectious Diseases*, 9(5), September–October: 987–1000.

Chibnall, S. (1980) 'Chronicles of the gallows: the social history of crime reporting', in Christian, H. (ed.) *Sociology of Journalism and the Press*, Sociological Review Monograph 29. Keele: University of Keele.

Chippindale, Peter and Horrie, Chris (1990) *Stick it up Your Punter! The Rise and Fall of the 'Sun'*. London: Heinemann.

Chirimuuta, Richard and Chirimuuta, Rosalind (1989) *AIDS, Africa and Racism*. London: Free Association Books.

Cohen, Stan (1972) *Folk Devils and Moral Panics: the Creation of the Mods and Rockers*. London: McGibbon and Kee.

COI (Central Office of Information) (1986) 'AIDS campaign creative development research', *COI Management Summary*, RS 2054, COI Research Unit, January.

COI (Central Office of Information) (1987) 'DHSS: AIDS youth campaign development', *COI Management Summary*, December 1986, RS 2160, March.

Colby, David C. and Cook, Tim (1991) 'Epidemics and agendas: the politics of nightly news coverage of AIDS', *Journal of Health Politics, Policy and Law*, 16(2): 215–49.

Collett, P. and Lamb, R. (1986) *Watching People Watching Television*. London: IBA.

Collins, H.M. (1987) 'Certainty and the public understanding of science: science on television', *Social Studies of Science*, 17: 689–713.

Cook, Tim (1989) 'Setting the record straight: the construction of homosexuality on television news'. Paper prepared for the Inside/Outside Conference of the Lesbian and Gay Studies Center. Yale University, New Haven, Connecticut, October.

Cook, Tim and Colby, David (1992) 'The mass mediated epidemic: the politics of AIDS on the nightly network news', in Fee, E. and Fox, D. (eds) *AIDS: The Making of a Chronic Disease*. Berkeley: University of California Press. pp. 84–125.

Corner, J. (1986) 'Codes and cultural analysis', in Collins, R., Curran, J., Garham, N., Scannell, P., Schlesinger, P. and Sparks, C. (eds) *Media, Culture and Society: a Critical Reader*. London: Sage. pp. 49–62.

Corner, John (1991) 'Meaning, genre and context', in Curran, J. and Gurevitch, M. (eds) *Mass Media and Society*. London: Edward Arnold. pp. 267–84.

Curran, James (1990) 'The new revisionism in mass communication research: a reappraisal', *European Journal of Communication*, 5: 135–64.

Currie, Candace (1985) *Press Coverage of Health-Related Topics with Special Reference to AIDS*, Working Paper No. 12, Research Unit in Health and Behavioural Change, Edinburgh: RUHBC.

Dada, Mehboob (1990) 'Race and the AIDS agenda', in Boffin, Tessa and Gupta, Sunil (eds) *Ecstatic Antibodies: Resisting the AIDS Mythology*. London: Rivers Oram Press. pp. 85–95.

Day, N., Anderson, R., Daykin, C., Gore, S., Gill, O., Greenberg, G., Hillier, H., Isham, V., Johnson, A., McCormick, A., Medley, G., Tillett, H. and Wilkie, A. (1990) 'Acquired Immune Deficiency Syndrome in England and Wales to end 1993: projections using data to end September 1989: report of a working group convened by the Director of the Public Health Laboratory Service (The Day Report)', *Communicable Disease Report*. London: Public Health Laboratory Service, January.

Day, Patricia and Klein, Rudolf (1990) 'Interpreting the unexpected: the case of AIDS policy making in Britain', *Journal of Public Policy*, 9(3): 337–53.

Daykin, Norma and Naidoo, Jennie (1995) 'Feminist critiques of health promotion', in Bunton, R., Nettleton, S. and Burrows, R. (eds) *The Sociology of Health Promotion*. London: Routledge.

Deacon, David and Golding, Peter (1993) *Taxation and Representation: the Media, Political Communications and the Poll Tax*. London: John Libbey.

Dearing, James W. and Rogers, Everett M. (1992) 'AIDS and the media agenda', in Edgar, T., Fitzpatrick, M.A. and Freimuth, V. (eds) *AIDS: a Communication Perspective*. Hillsdale, NJ: Lawrence Erlbaum.

Department of Health and Social Security (1990) *Private Office Guide*, March. London: DHSS.

Diamond, E. and Bellitto, C. (1986) 'The great verbal cover-up: prudish editing blurs the facts of AIDS', *Washington Journalism Review*, 3 March: 38–42.

Dickinson, Roger (1989) 'Beyond the moral panic: Aids, the mass media and mass communication research', *Communications*, 15(1/2): 21–36.

DoH/HEA (Department of Health/Health Education Authority) (1990) *Memorandum of Understanding*, June. London: DoH.

Dreuilhe, Emmanuel (1988) *Mortal Embrace: Living with AIDS*. New York: Hill and Wang.

Durham, Martin (1989) 'The Thatcher government and "the Moral Right"', *Parliamentary Affairs*, 40: 58–71.

Durham, Martin (1991) *Sex and Politics: The Family and Morality in the Thatcher Years*. Basingstoke: Macmillan.

Dyer, R. (ed.) (1984) *Gays and Film*. New York: New York Zoetrope.

Eckstein, Harry (1960) *Pressure Group Politics: The Case of the British Medical Association*. London: George Allen and Unwin.

Edgar, T., Hammond, S. and Freimuth, V. (1989) 'The role of the mass media and inter-personal communication in promoting AIDS-related behavioural change', *AIDS and Public Policy Journal*, 4(1): 3–9.

Eldridge, John, Kitzinger, Jenny and Williams, Kevin (1997) *The Mass Media and Power in Modern Britain.* Oxford: Oxford University Press.

Entwistle, V. and Beaulieu-Hancock, M. (1992) 'Health and medical coverage in the UK national press', *Public Understanding of Science*, 1: 367–82.

Ericson, R., Baranek, P. and Chan, J. (1987) *Visualizing Deviance.* Milton Keynes: Open University Press.

Ericson, R., Baranek, P. and Chan, J. (1989) *Negotiating Control: a Study of News Sources.* Milton Keynes: Open University Press.

Evans, David (1989) 'Section 28: law, myth and paradox', *Critical Social Policy*, 9(3): 73–95.

Ferriman, Annabel (1988) 'AIDS guide for schools pulped in morals row', *Observer* 19 June.

Fiske, John (1991) *Television Culture.* London: Routledge.

Fitzpatrick, M. and Milligan, D. (1987) *The Truth about the AIDS Panic.* London: Junius Publications.

Ford, N. (1991) *The Socio-sexual Lifestyles of Young People in the South West of England.* Exeter South Western Regional Health Authority/Institute of Population Studies, University of Exeter.

Fowler, Norman (1991) *Ministers Decide.* London: Chapman.

Fox, Daniel, Day, Patricia and Klein, Rudolf (1989) 'The power of professionalism: policies for AIDS in Britain, Sweden and the United States', *Daedulus*, Spring: 93–112.

Franklin, Bob (1994) *Packaging Politics.* London: Edward Arnold.

Frayne, S., Burns, R., Hardt, E., Rosen, A. and Moskowitz, M. (1996) 'The exclusion of non-English speaking persons from research', *Journal of General Internal Medicine*, 11(1): 39–43.

Fumento, Michael (1991) *The Myth of Heterosexual AIDS.* New York: Basic Books.

Gans, H. (1981) *Deciding What's News.* London: Constable.

Garfield, Simon (1991) 'The age of consent', *Independent on Sunday Review*, 10 November: 2–6.

Garfield, Simon (1994a) 'High-risk activity', *Esquire*, 4(10), December: 62–72.

Garfield, Simon (1994b) *The End of Innocence: Britain in the Time of AIDS.* London: Faber and Faber.

Geraghty, Christine (1991) *Women and Soap Opera: A Study of Prime Time Soaps.* Cambridge: Polity.

Geraghty, Christine (1992) 'British soaps in the 1980s', in Strinati, D. and Wagg, S. (eds) *Come On Down: Popular Media Culture in Post-war Britain.* London: Routledge.

Ghiglione, L., MacCluggage, R., Aarons, L. and Stinnett, L. (eds) (1990) *Alternatives: Gays and Lesbians in the Newsroom.* Washington, DC: American Society of Newspaper Editors.

Gibbs, L. (ed.) (1994) *Daring to Dissent: Lesbian Culture from Margin to Mainstream.* London: Cassell.

Gilbert, Gerard (1992) 'Heterosexual doubt on homosexual credibility', *Scotland on Sunday*, 9 February.

Gitlin, Todd (1980) *The Whole World is Watching.* Berkeley: University of California Press.

Goldenberg, E. (1976) *Making the Papers.* Lexington, MA: D.C. Heath.

Green, Stephen (1992) *The Sexual Dead-End.* London: Broadview Books.

Greenaway, John, Smith, Steve and Street, John (1992) *Deciding Factors in British Politics: a Case Studies Approach.* London: Routledge.

Griffin, G. (ed.) (1993) *Outwrite: Lesbianism and Popular Culture.* London: Pluto Press.

Gross, Larry (1991) 'Out of the mainstream: sexual minorities and the mass media' in Wolf, M. and Kielwasser, A. (eds) *Gay People, Sex and the Media.* London: Haworth Press. pp. 19–46.

GUMG (1988) *AIDS: Monitoring response to the Public Education Campaign, Feb. 1986–Feb. 1987*, report for the DHSS. London: COI.

Hall, Celia (1989) 'Health education body "loses independence"', *Independent*, 16 May: 2.

Hall, Stuart (1980) 'Encoding/decoding', in Hall, S., Hobson, D., Lowe, A. and Willis, P. (eds) *Culture, Media, Language*. London: Hutchinson. pp. 128–38.

Hall, Stuart (1988) *The Hard Road to Renewal: Thatcherism and the Crisis of the New Left*. London: Verso.

Hall, Stuart and Jacques, Martin (eds) (1983) *The Politics of Thatcherism*. London: Lawrence and Wishart.

Hall, Stuart, Critcher, Chas, Jefferson, Tony, Clarke, John and Roberts, Brian (1978) *Policing the Crisis: Mugging, the State and Law and Order*. London: Macmillan.

Hallett, Michael and Cannella, David (1994) 'Gatekeeping through media format: strategies of voice for the HIV-positive via human interest news formats and organizations', *Journal of Homosexuality*, 26(4): 111–34.

Hamilton, M. (1988) 'Masculine generic terms and misperception of AIDS risk', *Journal of Applied Social Psychology*, 18(14): 1222–40.

Harris, D. (1992) *From Class Struggle to the Politics of Pleasure*. London: Routledge.

Harris, Myles (1994) 'Why this sickly, useless quango deserves to die', *Daily Mail*, 4 July.

Hart, Graham (1993) 'Review of the HEA communications strategy for HIV/AIDS and sexual health among men who have sex with men – Part I'. Unpublished report for the Health Education Authority.

Health Education Authority (1992) *The Health Education Authority Annual Report 1991/92*. London: HEA.

Health Information Trust (1987) *AIDS: Beyond the Adverts*. London: Health Information Trust.

Heaton, Louis (1988) 'When does information become propaganda?', *The Listener*, 10 March: 8–9.

Hickson, Ford (1993) 'Getting the best of both worlds', *Gay Times*, October: 21–2.

Hobson, Dorothy (1978) 'Housewives: isolation and oppression', in Women's Studies Group Centre for Contemporary Cultural Studies, *Women Take Issue: Aspects of Women's Subordination*. London: Hutchinson University Library. pp. 79–95.

Holland, J., Ramazanoglu, C., Scott, S., Sharpe, S. and Thomson, R. (1990) 'Sex, gender and power: young women's sexuality in the showdown of AIDS', *Sociology of Health and Illness*, 12(3): 336–50.

Holland, J., Ramazanoglu, C., Scott, S., Sharpe, S. and Thomson, R. (1991) 'Between embarrassment and trust: young women and diversity in condom use', in Aggleton, P., Davies, P. and Hart, G. (eds) *AIDS: Responses, Inventions and Care*. London: Falmer Press. pp. 127–48.

Holland, J., Ramazanoglu, C., Scott, S., Sharpe, S. and Thomson, R. (1992a) 'Pressure, resistance, empowerment: young women and the negotiation of safer sex', in Aggleton, P., Davies, P. and Hart, G. (eds) *AIDS: Rights, Risk and Reason*. London: Falmer Press. pp. 142–62.

Holland, J., Ramazanoglu, C., Sharpe, S. and Thomson, R. (1992b) 'Pleasure, pressure and power: some contradictions of gendered sexuality', *Sociological Review*, 40(4): 645–73.

Holland, J., Ramazanoglu, C., Sharpe, S. and Thomson, R. (1994) 'Achieving masculine sexuality: young men's strategies for managing vulnerability', in Doyal, L., Naidoo, J. and Wilton, T. (eds) *AIDS: Setting a Feminist Agenda*. London: Taylor and Francis. pp. 122–50.

Holmes, P. (1985) 'How health hit the headlines', *Nursing Times*, 10 April: 18–19.

Hornig, Susanna (1990) 'Television's *NOVA* and the construction of scientific truth', *Critical Studies in Mass Communication*, 7: 11–23.

Howes, Keith (1993) *Broadcasting It: An Encyclopaedia of Homosexuality on Film, Radio and TV in the UK 1923–1993*. London: Cassell.

Husband, Charles (ed.) (1975) *White Media and Black Britain*. London: Arrow Books.

Ingham, Roger, Woodcock, Alison and Stenner, Karen (1991) 'Getting to know you . . . young people's knowledge of their partners at first intercourse', *Journal of Community and Applied Psychology*, (1): 117–32.

Jackson, S. (1978) *On the Social Construction of Female Sexuality: Explorations in Feminism, No. 4*. London: Women's Research and Resource Centre.

Johnson, Anne, Wadsworth, Jane, Wellings, Kaye and Field, Julia (1994) *Sexual Attitudes and Lifestyles.* Oxford: Blackwell Scientific.

Karpf, Anne (1988) *Doctoring the Media: The Reporting of Health and Medicine.* London: Routledge.

Katz, Elihu and Liebes, Tamar (1987) 'Decoding *Dallas*: notes from a cross-cultural study', in Newcomb, Horace (ed.) *Television, the Critical View.* Oxford: Oxford University Press. pp. 419–32.

Kennamer, J. and Honnold, J. (1995) 'Attitude toward homosexuality and attention to news about AIDS', *Journalism and Mass Communication Quarterly,* 72(2): 322–35.

Kerr, P. (1990) 'F for fake? Friction over faction', in Whannel, G. and Goodwin, A. (eds) *Understanding Television.* London: Routledge.

Kielwasser, A. and Wolf, M. (1992) 'Mainstream television, adolescent homosexuality and significant silence', *Critical Studies in Mass Communication,* 9(4): 350–73.

Kilborn, Richard (1994) '*Drama over Lockerbie*: a new look at television drama-documentaries', *Historical Journal of Film, Television and Radio,* 14(1): 59–76.

King, D. (1990) '"Prostitutes as pariah in the age of AIDS": a content analysis of coverage of women prostitutes in the *New York Times* and the *Washington Post*, September 1985–April 1988', *Women and Health,* 16(3/4): 155–76.

King, Edward (1993) *Safety in Numbers: Safer Sex and Gay Men.* London: Cassell.

Kinsella, J. (1989) *Covering the Plague: AIDS in the American News Media.* New Brunswick, NJ: Rutgers University Press.

Kippax, Susan, Crawford, June, Connell, Bob, Dowsett, Larry, Rodden, Pam, Baxter, Don and Bertg, Rigmor (1992) 'The importance of gay community in the prevention of HIV transmission: a study of Australian men who have sex with men', in Aggleton, P., Davies, P. and Hart, G. (eds) *AIDS: Rights, Risk and Reason.* London: Falmer Press. pp. 102–18.

Kitzinger, Jenny (1990) 'Audience understandings of AIDS media messages: a discussion of methods', *Sociology of Health and Illness,* 12(3): 319–35.

Kitzinger, Jenny (1991) 'Judging by appearances: audience understandings of the look of someone with HIV', *Journal of Community and Applied Social Psychology,* 1(2): 155–63.

Kitzinger, Jenny (1993a) 'Understanding AIDS – media messages and what people know about Acquired Immune Deficiency Syndrome', in Eldridge, J. (ed.) *Getting the Message.* London: Routledge. pp. 271–304.

Kitzinger, Jenny (1993b) *Safer Sex and Dangerous Reputations: Contradictions for Young Women Negotiating Condom Use.* MRC working paper, 6 Lilybank Gardens, Glasgow G12 8QQ.

Kitzinger, Jenny (1994a) 'The methodology of focus groups: the importance of interactions between research participants', *Sociology of Health and Illness,* 16(1): 103–21.

Kitzinger, Jenny (1994b) 'Visible and invisible women in AIDS discourses', in Doyal, Lesley, Naidoo, Jennie and Wilton, Tamsin (eds) *AIDS: Setting a Feminist Agenda.* London: Taylor and Francis. pp. 95–112.

Kitzinger, Jenny (1995) 'I'm sexually attractive but I'm powerful: young women negotiating sexual reputation', *Women's Studies International Forum,* 18(2): 187–96.

Kitzinger, Jenny (in press) 'Media templates', in Philo, G. (ed.) *Message Received.* London: Longman.

Kitzinger, Jenny and Kitzinger, Celia (1993) 'Doing it: representations of lesbian sex', in Griffin, G. (ed.) *Outwrite: Lesbianism and Popular Culture.* London: Pluto. pp. 9–25.

Kitzinger, Jenny and Miller, David (1992) '"African AIDS": the media and audience beliefs', in Aggleton, P., Davies, P. and Hart, G. (eds) *AIDS: Rights, Risk and Reason.* London: Falmer Press. pp. 28–52.

Kitzinger, Jenny and Reilly, Jacquie (1997) 'The rise and fall of risk reporting', *European Journal of Communication,* 12(3): 319–50.

Kristiansen, C. and Harding, C. (1984) 'The mobilization of health behavior by the press in Britain', *Journalism Quarterly,* 61(2): 364.

Laishley, Jenny (1975) 'The images of blacks and whites in the children's media', in Husband, Charles (ed.) *White Media and Black Britain*. London: Arrow Books.

Lees, Sue (1986) *Losing Out: Sexuality and Adolescent Girls*. London: Hutchinson.

Lesti, Elli (1992) 'The AIDS story and moral panic: how the Euro-African press constructs AIDS', *The Howard Journal of Communications*, 2(3 and 4) Winter–Spring: 230–41.

Liebes, T. and Katz, E. (1990) *The Effort of Meaning: Cross-Cultural Readings of 'Dallas'*. Oxford: Oxford University Press.

Ling, J. (1986) 'Media and health must forge a partnership', *Hygiene*, 5(1): 23–6.

Livingstone, S. and Lunt, P. (1993) *Talk on Television: Audience Participation and Public Debate*. London: Routledge.

Loshak, D. (1986) 'Medical journalists in society', *THS Health Summary*, February.

Lupton, Deborah (1994) *Moral Threats and Dangerous Desires: AIDS in the News Media*. London: Taylor and Francis.

Macintyre, Sally and West, Patrick (1993) 'What does the phrase safer sex mean to you? Understandings among Glaswegian 18 year-olds in 1990', *AIDS*, 7(1): 121–5.

McGrath, Roberta (1990) 'Dangerous liaisons: health, disease and representation', in Boffin, T. and Gupta, S. (eds) *Ecstatic Antibodies: Resisting the AIDS Mythology*. London: Rivers Oram Press. pp. 142–55.

McKeone, Dermot (1993) *Impact: Impact Media Analysis Trend Report for the Health Education Authority (AIDS and HIV Coverage) April 1993–July 1993*. London: Infopress, 17 September.

McKie, Robin (1986) 'Ministers vetoed AIDS risk ads', *Observer*, 30 March: 2.

McNeill, William (1977) *Plagues and Peoples*. Oxford: Basil Blackwell.

McQuail, D. (ed.) (1972) *Sociology of Mass Communication*. Harmondsworth: Penguin.

McQueen, D., Robertson, B. and Nisbet, L. (1991) *AIDS-Related Behaviours. Provisional Data from the RUHBC CATI Survey. No 26. Nov/Dec 1990*. Edinburgh: Research Unit in Health and Behavioural Change, University of Edinburgh.

Mann, Jonathon, Tarantola, Daniel J. M. and Netter, Thomas W. (eds) (1992) *AIDS in the World: A Global Report*. Cambridge, MA: Harvard University Press.

Meldrum, J. (1990) 'The role of the media in the reporting of AIDS', in Almond, B. (ed.) *AIDS – A Moral Issue: The Ethical, Legal and Social Aspects*. Basingstoke: Macmillan.

Mihill, Chris (1992) '"Sensitive" Thatcher kept out of drive against AIDS', *The Guardian*, 27 August: 6.

Milbank Foundation (1986) *AIDS: Impact on Public Policy: Proceedings of a Conference 28–30 May*. New York: New York State Department of Health and the Milbank Foundation.

Miller, Carl (1993) 'A leap of faith', *Gay Times*, October: 21–2.

Miller, David (1993) 'Official sources and primary definition: the case of Northern Ireland', *Media, Culture and Society*, 15(3), July: 385–406.

Miller, David (1994) *Don't Mention the War: Northern Ireland, Propaganda and the Media*. London: Pluto Press.

Miller, David (1997) 'Dominant ideologies and media power: the case of Northern Ireland', in Kelly, M. and O'Connor, B. (eds) *Media Audiences and Cultural Identity in Ireland*. Dublin: UCD Press.

Miller, D. and Reilly, J. (1995) 'Making an issue of food safety', in Maurer, D. and Sobal, J. (eds) *Eating Agendas: Food and Nutrition as Social Problems*. New York: Aldine de Gruyter.

Miller, David and Williams, Kevin (1993) 'Negotiating HIV/AIDS information: agendas, media strategies and the news', in Eldridge, J. (ed.) *Getting the Message*. London: Routledge. pp. 126–42.

Miller, J. (ed.) (1990) *AIDS: Crisis and Criticism*. Toronto: University of Toronto Press.

Moore, Oscar (1995) 'AIDS: redrawing the battle line', *The Guardian*, 27 September: 7.

Moores, Shaun (1993) *Interpreting Audiences*. London: Sage.

Morley, David (1980) *The 'Nationwide' Audience: Structure and Decoding*. London: BFI Books.

Mort, Frank (1987) *Dangerous Sexualities: Medico-Moral Politics in England since 1830*. London: Routledge.

Murphy, S. (1987) 'A content analysis of AIDS week'. Unpublished dissertation for MSc in Social Research Methods, University of Surrey.

Murray, John (1991) 'Bad press: representation of AIDS in the media', *Cultural Studies Birmingham*, 1(1): 29–51.

Murrell, Rachel Kerys (1987) 'Telling it like it isn't: representations of science in *Tomorrow's World*', *Theory, Culture and Society*, 4: 89–106.

Naylor, William (1985) 'Walking time bombs; AIDS and the press', *Medicine in Society*, 2(3): 5–11.

Nelkin, Dorothy (1991) 'AIDS and the news media', *Milbank Quarterly*, 69(2): 293–307.

O'Sullivan, Sue and Thomson, K. (eds) (1992) *Positively Women: Living with AIDS*. London: Sheba Feminist Press.

Patton, Cindy (1985) *Sex and Germs: The Politics of AIDS*. Boston: South End Press.

Patton, Cindy (1990) *Inventing AIDS*. London: Routledge.

Perl, Susan (1991) *Reflections on Using the Mass Media for AIDS Public Education*, HIV/AIDS and Sexual Health Programme Paper, No. 13. London: Health Education Authority.

Philo, G. (1990) *Seeing and Believing*. London: Routledge.

Philo, G. (1993) 'From Buerk to Band Aid: the media and the 1984 Ethiopian famine', in Eldridge, J. (ed.) *Getting the Message*. London: Routledge. pp. 104–25.

Philo, G. (1995) 'Television, politics and the rise of the New Right', in Philo, G. (ed.) *The Glasgow Media Group Reader Vol. II*. London: Routledge. pp. 198–233.

PHLS AIDS Centre (HIV, STD Division, Communicable Disease Surveillance Centre) and the Communicable Disease (Scotland) Unit (1993) *AIDS/HIV Quarterly Surveillance Tables*, No. 18: Data to end December 1992. London.

Prentice, Thomson (1987) 'I was signing my death warrant, says health chief', *The Times*, 28 March: 1.

Prentice, Thomson (1988) 'Health agency in rift with Whitehall over use of TV', *The Times*, 28 October: 5.

Redmond, Phil (1987) *Phil Redmond's 'Brookside': The Official Companion*. London: Weidenfield and Nicholson.

Reflexions (1986) *AIDS: Reactions to Advertising Concepts and a Candidate Advertising Campaign*. Full report, prepared for COI, RS 2054, January. London.

Reflexions (1988) *AIDS: Notes from the Presentation of Results of a Qualitative Survey to Aid Creative Development*. Prepared for the Health Education Authority and their advertising agency TBWA, February. London.

Rhodes, Tim and Shaughnessy, R. (1989a) 'Selling safer sex: AIDS education and advertising', *Health Promotion*, 4(1): 27–30.

Rhodes, Tim and Shaughnessy, R. (1989b) 'Condom commercial', *New Socialist*, 61, June/July: 34–5.

Rhodes, Tim and Shaughnessy, R. (1990) 'Compulsory screening: advertising AIDS in Britain', *Policy and Politics*, 18(1): 55–61.

Richardson, Diane (1994) 'Inclusions and exclusions: lesbians, HIV and AIDS', in Doyal, Lesley, Naidoo, Jennie and Wilton, Tamsin (eds) *AIDS: Setting a Feminist Agenda*. London: Taylor and Francis. pp. 159–70.

Rieder, Ines and Ruppelt, Patricia (1989) *Matters of Life and Death: Women Speak about AIDS*. London: Virago.

Robins, Kevin (1994) 'Forces of consumption: from the symbolic to the psychotic', *Media, Culture and Society*, 16(3): 449–68.

Rocheron, Yvette and Linné, Olga (1989) 'Aids, moral panic and opinion polls', *European Journal of Communication*, 4: 409–34.

Rogers, Everett M., Dearing, James W. and Chang, Soonbum (1991) *AIDS in the 1980s: The Agenda-Setting Process for a Public Issue*, Journalism Monographs, No. 126.

Roscoe, Jane, Marshall, Harriet and Gleeson, Kate (1995) 'The television audience: a reconsideration of the taken-for-granted terms active, social and critical', *European Journal of Communication*, 10(1): 87–108.

Russo, Vito (1987) *The Celluloid Closet: Homosexuality in the Movies*, revised edn. New York: Harper and Row.

Sabatier, René (1988) *Blaming Others: Prejudice, Race and World-wide AIDS*. London: Panos.

Sanderson, Terry (1995) *Mediawatch: The Treatment of Male and Female Homosexuality in the British Media*. London: Cassell.

Schlesinger, Philip (1990) 'Rethinking the sociology of journalism; source strategies and the limits of media centrism', in Ferguson, M. (ed.) *Public Communication; the New Imperatives*. London: Sage.

Schlesinger, P. and Tumber, H. (1994) *Reporting Crime: The Media Politics of Criminal Justice*. Oxford: Clarendon.

Schramm-Evans, Zoe (1990) 'Responses to AIDS, 1986–1987', in Aggleton, P., Davies, P. and Hart, G. (eds) *AIDS: Individual, Cultural and Policy Dimensions*. London: Falmer Press. pp. 221–32.

Segal, Lynn (1989) 'Lessons from the past: feminism, sexual politics and the challenge of AIDS', in Carter, E. and Watney, S. (eds) *Taking Liberties: AIDS and Cultural Politics*. London: Serpents Tail.

Shilts, Randy (1987) *And the Band Played On: Politics, People and the AIDS Epidemic*. New York: St Martin's Press.

Siddall, John, Stride, Chris, and Sargent, John (1987) 'Are you homosexual, heterosexual or bisexual? If so you could develop AIDS', in *The Market Research Society, 30th Annual Conference*. Metropole Hotel Brighton. London: Market Research Society. pp. 37–56.

Singer, Linda (1993) *Erotic Welfare: Sexual Theory and Politics in the Age of Epidemic*. London: Routledge.

Small, Neil (1988) 'Aids and social policy', *Critical Social Policy*, 21 (Spring): 9–29.

Social Services Committee (1987a) *Problems Associated with AIDS*. Third report from the Social Services Committee, Session 1986–87, Volume I Report together with the Proceedings of the Committee, HC 182–I. London: HMSO.

Social Services Committee (1987b) *Problems Associated with AIDS*. Third Report from the Social Services Committee, Session 1986–87, Volume II Minutes of Evidence (4 February–25 March 1987), HC 182–II. London: HMSO.

Social Services Committee (1987c) *Problems Associated with AIDS*. Third Report from the Social Services Committee, Session 1986–87, Volume III Minutes of Evidence (8 April–13 May 1987) and Memoranda, HC 182–III. London: HMSO.

Sontag, Susan (1989) *AIDS and its Metaphors*. Harmondsworth: Penguin.

Street, John (1988) 'British government policy on AIDS: learning not to die of ignorance', *Parliamentary Affairs*, 41(4): 490–507.

Street, John (1993) 'A fall in interest? British AIDS policy', in Berridge. V and Strong, P. (eds) *AIDS and Contemporary History*. Cambridge: Cambridge University Press.

Terrence Higgins Trust (1987) 'Memorandum submitted by the Terrence Higgins Trust', in Social Services Committee, *Problems Associated with AIDS*, Third Report from the Social Services Committee, Session 1986–87, Volume II Minutes of Evidence (4 February–25 March 1987), HC 182–II. London: HMSO. pp. 101–3.

Townsend, Peter, Davidson, Nick and Whitehead, Margaret (1988) 'Introduction to inequalities in health', in *Inequalities in Health: The Black Report; The Health Divide*. Harmondsworth: Penguin.

Treichler, Paula (1987) 'AIDS, homophobia and biomedical discourse: an epidemic of signification', *Cultural Studies*, 3: 263–305.

Treichler, Paula (1989) 'AIDS and HIV infection in the Third World: a First World chronicle', in Kruger, B. and Mariani, P. (eds) *Discussions in Contemporary Culture: Remaking History*. Seattle: Bay Press. pp. 31–86.

Treichler, Paula (1992) 'Seduced and terrorized: AIDS on network television', in Klusacek, Alan and Morrison, Ken (eds) *A Leap in the Dark: AIDS, Art and Contemporary Cultures*. Montreal: Véhicule Press.

Treichler, Paula (1993) 'AIDS narratives on television', in Murphy, Timothy and Poirier,

Suzanne (eds) *Writing AIDS: Gay Literature, Language and Analysis*. New York: Columbia University Press.

Tulloch, John (1989) 'Australian television and the representation of AIDS', *Australian Journal of Communication*, 16: 101–24.

Tulloch, John (1992) 'Using TV in HIV/AIDS education: production and audience cultures', *Media Information Australia*, August: 10–27.

UNESCO (1980) *Many Voices, One World. Report of the International Commission for the Study of Communication Problems*. Paris: UNESCO.

Van der Gaag, Nikki and Nash, Cathy (1987) *Images of Africa: The UK Report*. Oxford: Oxfam.

Walsh, Lynne (1996) 'Health warnings', *Index on Censorship*, 2: 176–7, 179.

Watney, Simon (1987a) 'The subject of AIDS', *Copyright*, 1(1).

Watney, Simon (1987b) *Policing Desire: Pornography, AIDS and the Media*. London: Comedia.

Watney, Simon (1988a) 'AIDS, moral panic theory and homophobia', in Aggleton, P. and Homans, H. (eds) *Social Aspects of AIDS*. Lewes, E. Sussex: Falmer. pp. 52–4.

Watney, Simon (1988b) 'Visual AIDS – advertising ignorance', in Aggleton, P. and Homans, H. (eds) *Social Aspects of AIDS*. Lewes, E. Sussex: Falmer. pp. 117–82.

Watney, Simon (1988c) 'Missionary positions: AIDS, "Africa" and race', *Differences: A Feminist Journal of Cultural Studies*, 1(1): 83–101.

Watney, Simon (1989) 'The subject of AIDS', in Aggleton, P., Hart, G. and Davies, P. (eds) *AIDS: Social Representations, Social Practices*. London: Falmer Press. pp. 64–73.

Watney, Simon (1990) 'Safer sex as community practice', in Aggleton, P., Davies, P. and Hart, G. (eds) *AIDS: Individual, Cultural and Policy Dimensions*. London: Falmer Press. pp. 19–34.

Watney, Simon (1991) 'AIDS: the second decade: "risk", research and modernity', in Aggleton, P., Hart, G. and Davies, P. (eds) *AIDS: Responses, Interventions and Care*. London: Falmer Press. pp. 1–18.

Watney, Simon (1992) 'Short term companions: AIDS as popular entertainment', in Klusacek, Alan and Morrison, Ken (eds) *A Leap in the Dark: AIDS, Art and Contemporary Cultures*. Montreal: Véhicule Press.

Watney, Simon (1993) 'Hard won credibility', *Gay Times*, October: 22–3.

Watney, Simon (1994) *Practices of Freedom: Selected Writings on HIV/AIDS*. London: Rivers Oram Press.

Weeks, Jeffrey (1985) *Sexuality and its Discontents: Meanings, Myths and Modern Sexualities*. London: Routledge.

Weeks, Jeffrey (1988) 'Love in a cold climate', in Aggleton, P. and Homans, H. (eds) *Social Aspects of AIDS*. Lewes, E. Sussex: Falmer Press.

Weeks, Jeffrey (1989a) 'AIDS: the intellectual agenda', in Aggleton, P., Hart, G. and Davies, P. (eds) *AIDS: Social Representations, Social Practices*. London: Falmer Press. pp. 1–20.

Weeks, Jeffrey (1989b) *Sex, Politics and Society: The Regulation of Sexuality since 1800*, 2nd edn. London: Longman.

Weeks, Jeffrey (1993) 'AIDS and the regulation of sexuality', in Berridge, V. and Strong, P. (eds) *AIDS and Contemporary History*. Cambridge: Cambridge University Press.

Wellings, Kaye (1988) 'Perceptions of risk – media treatments of AIDS', in Aggleton, Peter and Homans, Hilary (eds) *Social Aspects of AIDS*. London: Falmer Press. pp. 83–105.

Wellings, K. and McVey, D. (1990) 'Evaluations of the HEA AIDS press campaign December 1988 to March 1989', *Health Education Journal* (49)3: 108–16.

Whitehead, Margaret (1988) *The Health Divide*, in Townsend, P., Davison, N. and Whitehead, M. *Inequalities in Health* with *The Black Report*. Harmondsworth: Penguin.

Whitehead, Margaret (1989) *Swimming Upstream: Trends and Prospects in Education for Health*. London: King's Fund Institute.

Wight, Daniel (1993) 'Constraint or cognition? Factors affecting young men's practice of safer heterosexual sex', in Aggleton, P., Davies, P. and Hart, G. (eds) *AIDS: Facing the Second Decade*. London: Falmer Press. pp. 41–60.

Wight, Daniel (1994) 'Assimilating safer sex: young heterosexual men's understandings of "safer sex"', in Aggleton, P., Davies, P. and Hart, G. (eds) *AIDS: Foundations for the Future*. London: Falmer Press. pp. 97–109.

Wilton, Tamsin (1994) 'Feminism and the erotics of health promotion', in Doyal, Lesley, Naidoo, Jennie and Wilton, Tamsin (eds) *AIDS: Setting a Feminist Agenda*. London: Taylor and Francis. pp. 80–94.

Wilton, Tamsin and Aggleton, Peter (1991) 'Condoms, coercion, control: heterosexuality and the limits to HIV/AIDS education', in Aggleton, P., Hart, G. and Davies, P. (eds) *AIDS: Responses, Interventions and Care*. London: Falmer Press. pp. 149–56.

Woffinden, Bob (1988) 'Campaigns that die of ignorance', *The Listener*, 3 March.

Woods, Chris (1989) 'The moral majority behind the throne', *Capital Gay*, 24 November.

Index